HOLLYWOOD NATION

HOLLYWOOD NATION

Left Coast Lies, Old Media Spin, and the

New Media Revolution

JAMES HIRSEN

WITH NEWSMAX.COM

THREE RIVERS PRESS

NEW YORK

Library of Congress Cataloging-in-Publication Data

Hirsen, James L.
Hollywood nation: left coast lies, old media spin, and the new media revolution / Jim Hirsen.
—Includes bibliographical references and index.
1. Mass Media—Objectivity—United States. I. Title
P96.O242U64   2005
302.23'0973dc22   2005012563

ISBN-10: 1-4000-8193-9
ISBN-13: 978-1-4000-8193-6

Printed in the United States of America

Design by Debbie Glasserman

10 9 8 7 6 5 4 3 2 1

First Paperback Edition

TO THE BEACONS OF LIGHT
WHO HAVE GUIDED MY LIFE

CONTENTS

1. Hollywood Nation   1
Stroll with Joel

2. Stars of Page and Screen   25
Just Dhue It

3. Sexing Things Up   56
Holly Court

4. Info Mania   82
O'Reilly Factors In

5. The Game Changes   121
Crier Confab

6. Enter Stage Left   142
Noonan Time

7. Tinseltown Tampering   158
Morris Musings

8. Media Mindbend   187
Miller Speak

9. Mel Mutiny   206
Dayna Extra

10. Land of the Free   233

Afterword   241

Notes   255

Acknowledgments   263

Index   265

HOLLYWOOD NATION

1

HOLLYWOOD NATION

Who *cares what celebrities think?*

I was often asked that question after I wrote my previous book, *Tales from the Left Coast,* which chronicled Hollywood's political activity. During a discussion on MSNBC's *Scarborough Country,* for example, UCLA film professor Richard Walter maintained that celebrities are influential in "the movies that they make, not the press conferences that they hold." He said, "Nobody cares a lot about what Jessica Lange thinks politically or intellectually. Do you? Do I? Why should it matter? They don't."

Professor Walter was sounding a familiar refrain, but a somewhat delusional one, as I've discovered in my years of covering the ins and outs of Hollywood. At the very least it's an attempt to duck a substantive debate. When you hear someone remark, *Who cares what entertainers say?,* you can pretty much bet that person is trying to avoid a serious look at the kinds of messages that are coming to us from the entertainment community.

This kind of disregard creates a problem, though, because like it or not, celebrities *do* matter. They influence all of us, often in powerful ways.

USA Today addressed this issue in an article entitled "When Stars Speak, Do We Listen?" At a time when actors like Martin Sheen, Anjelica Huston, and James Cromwell were leading high-profile protests against the war in Iraq, the newspaper commissioned a survey to determine whether celebrities "really have any influence" over the public, and over politicians and policy. At first glance, the poll seemed to lend some support to Professor Walter's position that America doesn't listen to actors on political issues: 87 percent of those surveyed responded that no celebrity could cause them to change their position on the war. Only about a third "felt celebrities were 'somewhat' effective in influencing the views of the president and other elected officials."[1]

Polls like this have a built-in defect, though. Paul Waldman, coauthor of the book *The Press Effect: Politicians, Journalists, and the Stories That Shape the Political World,* told *USA Today* that people are hesitant to admit they are influenced by anybody, much less a celebrity. Most folks, Waldman noted, "like to believe 'I made up my mind myself.' "[2]

The news media are certainly affording stars plenty of opportunities to voice their opinions on the issues of the day. Why? Because, as Waldman pointed out, the simple fact is that some "starstruck" news organizations are "more likely to agree to an interview with Jessica Lange on the topic of Iraq than some guy from the Council on Foreign Relations."[3] The more visibility these celebrities have, the more likely they are to hijack the debate.

Think about it: if the public weren't influenced by famous names and faces, then celebrities wouldn't be getting paid big bucks to hawk products and services, and celebrity endorsements wouldn't be so actively pursued by activist groups, charitable organizations, and politicians.

Actually, the public is listening to celebrity spouters more intently than ever. In fact, when we talk about the entertainment community's extensive influence, we're not just referring to famous actors who jabber on issues. Sure, Sean Penn, Martin Sheen, Michael Moore, Susan Sarandon, Tim Robbins, Barbra Streisand, Alec Baldwin, and all the other celebs who hop to the podium to lecture the country on their political views are a big part of the story. But they're by no means the whole story. In *Tales from the Left Coast* I focused on those celebs and their politicking, but as I examined the situation further I realized how much more there is to the psyche-swaying picture.

For starters, Professor Walter was partly right when he said that actors are most influential in "the movies that they make." Inadvertently, he was acknowledging something that lots of left-leaners try to deny: Movies, TV shows, music, and other entertainment products don't merely amuse us or divert us from reality; often they convey messages about political, social, and cultural issues. And since Tinseltown remains such a liberal bastion, as we witnessed during the last presidential election with the Dem fund-raising machine, those messages usually come with a distinct lefty twist.

Hollywood and its companion products are massaging many of our behaviors, attitudes, and ideas, but Left Coasters tend to admit that only when it suits their PC purposes. As film critic Michael Medved points out, studio heads like to boast that they do good by, say, showing a character in an action movie snap on a seat belt before a high-speed chase, or including "safe sex" scenes that prominently feature condoms. But those kinds of shots might account for a few seconds in a two-hour movie. Don't audiences also receive messages about behavior from other parts of the film—like the violent chase and shootout that follow the buckle-up, or the graphic sex scene that inevitably accompanies the condom wrapper? No way, say Hollywood's defenders.[4]

Tinseltowners often fall back on the shopworn pretext "It's *only* a movie." But aside from the logical inconsistency of that position, folks instinctively know that films and TV shows do matter when it comes to shaping opinions, values, and behavior. And they matter a bundle. In fact, entertainment just happens to be one of the weakest portals of entry for us humans.

Hollywood influence is becoming particularly significant now that, as a people, we seem to be placing a higher and higher value on our entertainment needs and wishes. We Americans have quite a bit of leisure time on our hands. And we want to fill that time with gobs of entertainment. Whether it's eating at a restaurant, shopping at a mall, throwing darts in a bar, or driving in a car, we crave diversion, excitement, and just plain old fun. Our obsession with amusement has created a world in which, as Joel Siegel of ABC's *Good Morning America* tells me, "entertainment is unavoidable."[5]

Here we're talking about what's usually called pure entertainment. In recent years, though, something else has emerged that has even more clout over the way we see the world. It used to be that people got their news from their daily local *Times* or nightly network broadcast. But increasingly folks are getting their scoops and forming their opinions the entertainment way.

If you look closely you'll notice that Hollywood has spilled over into the news business. Not content with merely playing roles, Tinseltowners now intrude on journalism's turf. Through things like documentaries, docudramas, and agenda-driven movies, Hollywood can stretch the truth and bend the mind. Most conspicuously, filmmaker Michael Moore and others have redefined the documentary, corrupting the genre by presenting misleading information and outright falsehoods as fact. In *Roger & Me, Bowling for Columbine,* and *Fahrenheit 9/11,* Moore presented staged events as real and fiction as fact. And he carefully left out details that might inconvenience his arguments. Despite his apparent lack of concern for the truth, in one boo-ridden instance Moore was actually given an Academy Award for Best Documentary.

Film studios and TV networks are now releasing docudramas, which can be even more slanted and distorted because they blatantly meld fantasy with reality. Another Oscar winner, director

Oliver Stone, has built his career around films that purport to represent historical events but are closer to *Shrek* in their accuracy. Stone's film about John F. Kennedy's assassination prompted a *Newsweek* cover story headlined "The Twisted Truth of *JFK:* Why Oliver Stone's New Movie Can't Be Trusted." Stone offered a similarly skewed take on Richard Nixon. Cable TV host and news commentator Monica Crowley, whose first job out of college was working for the former president, tells me that "Oliver Stone had the script for the movie *Nixon* done and ready to go. He waited until Nixon died to put it into production, because he knew that Nixon would have sued him. The portrayal of Nixon was completely off the mark, not that I expected anything less—or different, I should say—from Oliver Stone. Oliver Stone's approach to history is to take his own theories, as wild and inaccurate as they may be, and fold them into actual historical facts."[6]

Still, films can pack such a powerful punch that many people take the tall tales seriously. That's why Hollywood honchos have the influential means that they do to shape the message. If they so desire, they can put a particular spin on a topic and get people to pay mega-attention to the argument. In essence, they can circumvent the news media—and the journalistic standards that require some degree of faithfulness to the historical record—and still trumpet their political messages. Because of this, such "entertainment products" can knead and knuckle people's beliefs and do things that the *Dewdrop Dispatch* or the Peoria nightly news broadcast could never pull off.

At the same time, the news business itself is undergoing a Tinseltown makeover. To function as a free society, we need information delivered to us in an accurate, unadulterated, and uncensored manner. But these days our needs and wants seem to be at odds a bit, because we're looking to receive our news and analyses in fun, bite-sized morsels. The truth is that bare-bones facts can be so—I believe the word is—*boring.* So papers dress up communiqués with eye-pleasing charts, headlines, photos, colors, and the like. Television uses brightly lighted sets, telegenic anchors, attention-grabbing sound effects, and arresting sound bites to give pizzazz to otherwise lackluster dispatches. And news organizations produce special reports and documentaries that aim to do more than just inform us; they try to make our imaginations take flight, tickle our funny bones, or scare the pants off us in a Saturday-matinee kind of way.

Ever so slowly things have gone through an adjustment. Now News is Big Entertainment. And Entertainment is Big News.

Anyone who has perused the East or Left Coast Times, toggled through the evening alphabet broadcasts, tuned in to a cable news show only to find his or her favorite sitcom star, or switched back and forth between a beloved action hero's flick and his gubernatorial press conference knows exactly what I'm talking about. These days high-profile personalities from L.A. to Broadway appear regularly on TV and film to give their news and views. Politicians do the late-night circuit. And journalists and anchors find their own celebrity stars shooting north.

When Anderson Cooper moves from a reality show, *The Mole,* to grab an anchor spot on CNN; when Meredith Vieira transitions from *20/20* to *The View* to a syndicated version of the game show *Who Wants to Be a Millionaire;* when network news shows devote time to "reporting" about prime-time program happenings and featuring reality-show castoffs, we can pretty much see that the borderlines between news and entertainment have been zapped.

Former *Nightline* host Ted Koppel has noticed what's occurring. While speaking at the Hollywood Radio and Television Society's newsmaker luncheon at the Beverly Hilton Hotel, the ABC News anchor griped about news personalities being placed in non-news settings. "When we began taking our journalism more lightly, people began taking us less seriously," Koppel complained. "I have no problem whatsoever with entertainers and comedians pretending to be journalists; my problem is with journalists pretending to be entertainers."[7]

Koppel was speaking only about the damage being done to the profession of journalism. But the fact is, this intense blending of information and entertainment fare is having a real impact on all of us. As things have progressed, we're finding it harder and harder to distinguish between fact and fiction, truth and insincerity, and virtue and vice.

When we used to talk about Hollywood, we were referring to a specific SoCal locale. But Tinseltown's influence has seeped beyond its borders and now affects our whole society.

TINSELTOWN TRENDSETTERS

How can the entertainment community have so much influence over us? One big factor is our ongoing love affair with the famous, which seems to supply us with a kind of emotional power drink. Celebrities, and everything that surrounds them, provide a tonic for our psyches, a sort of glam Gatorade, if you will. We drink the sparkly elixir, and before the final drop hits the tongue we're already craving more.

James Houran, a clinical psychologist who has researched the subject of celebrity obsession in America, remarks that each of us has a little Larry King inside: "There is a celebrity stalker in all of us."[8] Houran conducted a survey of six hundred people and determined that one person in three is a moderate to advanced celebrity worshiper. By my calculations, that means a little more than 33 percent of folks are deifying celebs, another 45 percent are the deified celebs, and 21 percent are still hoping to someday be deified.

The dazzle addiction isn't new. But for most of human history, fame was usually visited on an individual as a result of an actual *accomplishment*. For centuries, warriors, conquerors, kings, and the like were revered.

Things have changed, though, in a supersized way. In the Information Age, when we've got hundreds of TV channels to choose from, countless websites available to us, and magazines devoted to any topic we can imagine, we're constantly introduced to new faces and new stories. It's as if we've got an ever-expanding roster of celebs who are pretty much famous simply for being famous. Fresh stars are popping up like ragweed in a hayfield.

It's not just that technology exposes us to all kinds of people we might never have encountered decades ago. In the modern age, we have lots of spare time, a concept that our ancestors could never have imagined. As psychologist Joyce Brothers tells me, "We have the time and the effort and willingness to pay attention to things that aren't a matter of food and shelter and other needs." When those needs are taken care of, she says, "we start to look for other sources of interest or satisfaction or belonging or relating to others."

Dr. Brothers believes that we are attracted to celebrities because we are acting out instinctive patterns. "In order to survive centuries ago," she tells me, "human beings had to be able to tell pretty fast whether somebody was a friend or a foe. And the more times you saw somebody, the more chances that person was a friend." So today, since we're exposed to celebs so frequently, they become familiar, part of the tribe. Dr. Brothers cites a popular syndicated television show as an example: "When you see the same face again and again and again—these six people—they are familiar. So we assume they are *Friends*."9

Professor Geoffrey Beattie of Britain's University of Manchester theorizes that stories involving stars are our contemporary version of fairy tales. Beattie believes that because we attach such importance to lives of the famous, our brains are programmed to recall details of the celebs' experiences more than our own. The mere mention of their names conjures up the stories of their lives.10

Familiarity helps explain why, whether we admit it or not, as a society we pay so much attention to what the famous are doing, saying, wearing, and so on. But of course, celebs have a certain glamour about them that, short of an extensive makeup, wardrobe, and surgery overhaul, most of us will never have, and that's what makes them trendsetters.

It's long been the case that the entertainment biz has provided the measuring stick by which we determine who, and what, is attractive or fashionable. As Joel Siegel puts it, "None of this is new. It's been going on forever." Siegel cites the famous example of how "undershirt companies went bankrupt" in the 1930s after Clark Gable appeared sans T-shirt in the Oscar-winning film *It Happened One Night*. Gable was the leading star of the day, a major sex symbol, and so, Siegel says, men took the cue from him and "stopped wearing undershirts."

John F. Kennedy was that rare politician who had a glamorous air about him. As Siegel remembers, Kennedy broke with tradition by not wearing a hat at his inauguration. Hats were part of the standard look for men in those days—even at "ball games, they wore a hat," Siegel notes. But as soon as people saw the fedora-absent inaugural footage, formal head attire went out of fashion.

Siegel also recalls the influence of Marilyn Monroe's most famous scene from *The Seven Year Itch,* the "scene where the subway blows her dress up." He tells me that at the time "women in Japan stopped wearing underwear to get that Marilyn Monroe look."[11]

Today we see the same sort of thing. Brad Pitt might be seen on the big screen without a shirt and the look is adopted by Joe Boxers everywhere. Meanwhile, Angelina Jolie might appear on the little screen looking as if she, too, is missing an undergarment and, voilà, an eye-popping female fashion is born.

Our obsession with celebrities troubles a lot of folks. Many parents express real concern about how their children respond to stars who don't appear to be appropriate role models. The wife of Maryland governor Robert Ehrlich spoke out a few years back about the example being set by pop icon Britney Spears, the former Mouseketeer whose stage act has included ripping her clothes off, tossing a snake around her neck, and slithering in syncopated rhythm. Speaking at a domestic violence conference, Kendel Ehrlich said that it is important for women to get as much education as possible to avoid becoming dependent on anyone else. Then she said, "It is incredibly important to get that message to young women. You know, really, if I had an opportunity to shoot Britney Spears, I think I would."

Mrs. Ehrlich obviously got a little too fired up. But as ill-chosen as her words were, many parents undoubtedly agree with her general argument that we need to pay attention to the images the popular culture is sending to our children. To understand why Britney would inspire such vitriol, we might take a look at what Madame Tussauds museum in London did with a recent exhibit. The museum claimed that it was tired of people saying that its wax models of the famous weren't lifelike enough. So it decided to make Britney's waxwork model breathe. The sculptors at the museum created a likeness of Spears in a pole-dancing pose with her back arched. To add realism, they installed a breathing mechanism so that, in the end, the waxwork model of the pop princess would have a mobile chest. London's *Sun* newspaper reported that a source said, "For the first time we are installing balloons in her chest so it heaves in and out."

I hear Madame Tussauds is planning to do a Bill Clinton figure. It's going to use balloons in a different way, though. You push a button and Bubba's head swells another notch.

Parents know that kids look up to stars like Spears, and especially that our children believe such celebs set standards of beauty. Kids aren't the only ones trying to live up to the Hollywood ideal, though. A lot of us try to achieve the standards set by the stars we glorify. We get the message that if we want to be "in," we've got to get our image to coincide with the person on the screen, magazine, daytime soap, or evening news.

Unfortunately, there's a huge gap between that ideal standard and the reality that smacks most of us in the face, gut, and rear when we look in the mirror. The gap has always been there: The glamorous depictions of Hollywood stars of the Golden Age weren't any more representative of real folks than Joan Rivers is of today's seventy-somethings. But it does seem as though the distance between the ideal and the real just keeps getting bigger.

Even big Hollywood stars sometimes get frustrated over the disparities between expectations and reality. Speaking about the fact that, physically, things have sort of shifted for her over the years, Whoopi Goldberg joked, "My ass is bigger. That was a shock. I was like, 'Whose ass is that and why is it attached to my body?' I was being stalked by my own ass, and my ass said to me, 'You know what? I'm here to stay. I'm not gonna get any smaller, and I don't care how far you run or how hard you work out. You are gonna have a big ass.' And my **** [breasts] said, 'You know what? We fell. We fell, you didn't even know it. So why are you worried about it now? It's not like you're gonna get us knocked off, 'cause who's gonna believe that your **** suddenly went from here to here. Nobody.' "[12]

Still, Hollywood keeps pushing perfection. The emphasis on youth, looks, and fame now extends far beyond Tinseltown to reach Main Street U.S.A. Supposedly anyone can achieve the right look simply by buying the formula being peddled. That formula can be anything from cosmetics to clothing to perfume to diet— and even, increasingly, to plastic surgery. People from just about every walk of life are getting liposucked, tummy-tucked, im- planted, rearranged, sculpted down, and tightened up. More than 8.7 million people underwent cosmetic procedures in 2003, up 33 percent from the year before, and in 2004 9.2 million folks sur- gically altered their bods, up another 5 percent; this according to the American Society of Plastic Surgeons.

We even have a special breed of reality show that documents people's transformations as they go from bland to grand. There's MTV's *I Want a Famous Face,* where individuals go for the cele- brity look-alike gold. There's ABC's *Extreme Makeover,* in which participants are handled by an "Extreme Team" of plastic sur- geons, cosmetic dentists, makeup artists, hairstylists, personal train- ers, dermatologists, and more. And there's Fox's *The Swan,* where women compete in a massive surgery contest and ultimately go up against one another in a beauty pageant. It seems that the more makeover shows there are, the more surgeons' phones ring off the hook.

Actress Bette Midler commented that these nip-and-tuck reality programs "assume that you are going to be overjoyed and a happy person if you look okay. You'll look okay for a while, but eventually gravity will take its toll, once again. And you'll have to go back under the knife again! So it is best if you make some sort of peace [with yourself] at some point."

Midler made a broader point about the current culture, noting that "there are so many things happening in the media that are hard to absorb." No doubt she spoke for a lot of us when she said, "To have seen all of the changes in society that are so severe in such a short time, it really takes your breath away."[13]

Well, except for the Britney Spears wax figure at Madame Tussauds. Only a power failure can take *her* breath away.

A NEWS BREED OF STARS

We should have seen it coming. As the celebrity appetite grew and the circle of fame widened, it was only a matter of time before newsrooms would get the Hollywood bug. The journalist as celebrity has definitely arrived. Otherwise Brian Williams wouldn't be the perfect shade of bronze, and Greta Van Susteren wouldn't have Bette Davis eyes.

Nowadays, top journalists are just as famous as the headliners they cover. Before Tom Brokaw and Dan Rather stepped away from their anchor desks, they and their ABC counterpart, Peter Jennings, formed a trio of news superstars, who were afforded some of the same perks that Hollywood celebs enjoy: fame, wealth, and buy ten, get one free Botox punch cards.

ABC's Barbara Walters has made celebrity interviews her trademark, and she's become so famous in her own right that it seems when watching we're simply bystanders to a conversation between two Tinseltowners. Walters defends the importance of serious journalism: "News used to be considered a public trust. It was and perhaps still is what gives the networks [their] dignity and integrity. It deserved respect, and so, I think, do we."[14] Perhaps she's thinking that she deserves respect for her interviews with the shotgun-wielding Menendez brothers and the thong-snapping

Monica Lewinsky. Or maybe for her work on the morning chat fest *The View*, in which she and four other women engage in sometimes mindless discussion of current events. Or for this comment she made after interviewing actor Jude Law: "He's awfully cute. I might have done him."[15] For much of her career Walters has straddled that line between hard news and lighter fare. In fact, when she switched over to ABC in the 1970s, half of her compensation came from the news department for cohosting the *ABC Evening News* and the other half from the entertainment department for her one-hour prime-time specials.

Walters's ABC colleague Diane Sawyer similarly has earned fame and fortune while floating effortlessly from tabloid to hard news and back again. She started out her TV career as a local weather girl, and after she joined CBS News she worked on everything from the *CBS Morning News* to the *Early Morning News* to the groundbreaking newsmagazine show *60 Minutes*. Now at ABC, she not only does prime-time specials—often competing with Walters to land a big celebrity interview—but also cohosts the network's morning show, *Good Morning America*.

Sawyer has literally gone Hollywood—spouse-wise. As Fox News's Laurie Dhue pointed out when I interviewed her, "Diane Sawyer is married to one of the most famous movie directors ever," Mike Nichols. Dhue speculates that Sawyer might have received added fame "because of whom she married and vice versa."[16]

Yeah, kind of like Camilla Parker Bowles.

Sawyer's morning-show rival, NBC's Katie Couric, has become one of the biggest stars around. Couric has also been involved with a Hollywood power player, having an on-again, off-again relationship with the famous television producer Tom Werner. Like Barbara Walters, she insists on being taken seriously as a journalist; she once reminded Larry King that her official title at the *Today* show is "coanchor," *not* "hostess." She has played the role of journalist, interviewing world leaders, national political figures, and writers. But her career also shows how fuzzy the boundary between news and entertainment has become. As we'll see in more detail in Chapter 3, she once took off her journalist hat as part of an NBC ratings-boosting effort and yukked it up on late-night television when she filled in for Jay Leno on the *Tonight Show* for an entire week.

Things like that make it hard to take the mainstream claim of journalistic integrity seriously. So does a decision to give a prestigious anchor position to a person with, to put it mildly, a questionable background. That's exactly what ABC News did when it handed over the reins of the Sunday-morning show *This Week* to former Clinton aide George Stephanopoulos. I suppose it mattered more to ABC that Stephanopoulos had a smidgen of Clinton stardust stuck to his shoulders like dandruff. Somehow his partisan political background didn't raise problems for the ABC honchos; Diane Sawyer even complimented him on *Good Morning America,* by saying, with a straight face no less, "You've been completely nonpartisan in covering the news."[17]

With so many actual journalists blurring the lines between news and entertainment, it shouldn't be a shock that Hollywood is going newsy. It's not just docudramas and other movies, either. Now shows whose first goal is to entertain are trying their hand at news coverage of a sort. The most famous example is the Comedy Central cable network's *The Daily Show,* which bills itself as a "fake news" program. The thing is, though, host Jon Stewart has landed interviews that real journalists would give their Renaissance Weekends for—including one with 2004 presidential candidate John Kerry, at a time when the Dem was avoiding the networks like a trip to Supercuts. And lots of young people regard *The Daily Show* as their source of actual news, not "fake news."

So who's to tell what's real news and what's pure entertainment anymore?

LEFT TURNS

The cross-pollination between news and entertainment raises a lot of important questions, which we'll explore in detail in this book.

It has particular relevance to a topic that has been fiercely debated in recent years—the subject of media bias.

For all the attention that has been focused on this topic—and as we'll see, commentators on both sides of the aisle have been hurling accusations of bias at the media—the debate has strangely been focused on the news media alone. With the entertainment community attempting to give society a liberal wedgie, we need to take a closer look at the messages that Hollywood is emitting.

When you're talking about Tinseltown, the key players typically wallow in the same worldview as their shadow figures in the mainstream press. And a lot of the members in both camps share the same feelings about faith, family, freedom, and France.

Yes, it's true, in each sector you'll find the occasional renegade thinker. In Hollywood, we've seen Mel Gibson, Arnold Schwarzenegger, Dennis Miller, and Tom Selleck go their own cognitive way. And in the news biz we've seen individuals like Lou Dobbs, John Stossel, and Bill O'Reilly buck the trend, although such folks usually end up having a neon Post-it stuck on their duffs that reads "conservative commentator," "extreme right-winger," or "costume adviser to Prince Harry." This is in contrast to the scads of good liberal guys and gals who sport PC lapel pins but are just called journalists.

What do you suppose Hollywood actors, directors, and producers talk about when they mingle with TV news anchors, directors, and producers at a chichi party? Well, you can pretty much bet the conversation doesn't include a discussion of how the U.S. can shake loose from the UN, how we can get Fidel Castro to switch out of his despot duds, or when Congress is going to get with a zero-based budgeting plan.

You are, however, pretty much guaranteed to hear party guests singing the political praises of Ted Kennedy, Andy Rooney, and George Clooney.

If you ever do happen to find yourself at one of these elite gatherings, I recommend that you avoid expressing any opinions that might be in sync with a Toby Keith song or a Thomas Sowell column or the following calamities may occur:

- People nearby will grab for their oxygen bongs.
- A guy in a Che Guevara cap will sneeze on your goat cheese appetizer.
- Guests will draw straws to see who's stuck driving you to Pahrump.
- Your voter's registration card, NRA membership card, and pocket Constitution will be lifted from your wallet and used as beverage coasters.
- Someone will text-message the DNC headquarters, and a crew of MoveOn volunteers will rush to the scene, slap you on a gurney, and whisk you off to a Greenpeace convention.

If you truly wish to avoid such potentially traumatizing incidents, it's probably better if you keep your conservative, libertarian, or independent mouth shut.

That's definitely what those with a Left Coast mindset would prefer conservatives do—keep their lips zipped. The Hollywood-Manhattan tag team would like to hang on to the control it's enjoyed for years. With the advent of talk radio, cable news, and the Internet, which has eaten away at the liberal dominance of the news media, the elites can't bear to think about the same thing happening in Tinseltown.

NOW ENTERING HOLLYWOOD NATION

So, like it or not, Hollywood's a powerhouse. And the mainstream press is still the elephant in the room, or should I say donkey. When people try to dismiss the cultural juice that celebrities generate or deny that the news bigwigs are playing with our minds like a lump of Spago pizza dough, they're simply ignoring reality.

Clint Eastwood's *Million Dollar Baby,* taken in conjunction with the Terry Schiavo story, is a good example of what I'm talking about. During the same time period when Clint Eastwood snagged four Oscars for his euthanasia-promoting flick (including the biggies, Best Picture and Best Director) and a real-life battle between a husband, his in-laws, and the courts, played out on stations and newsstands across the country, the alphabet news channels and mainstream press were reporting the results of some stacked polls that suggested most people thought assisted suicide was just swell. Would it really be a big surprise to discover that, following the mind-rolf, public opinion actually *was* nudged in a certain direction?

Dave Chappelle is the Comedy Central cable star-turned-runaway comic. Like many of today's comedians, he has some vulgar material. But he has also come out with a few observations on the culture that are worth a listen.

Chappelle was doing a show at Sacramento's Memorial Auditorium when his own celebrity status interfered with his performance flow. As the audience kept shouting out a phrase associated with a character from his TV program, interrupting his act, he told the crowd, "The show is ruining my life." He griped about how it had made him a "star" and how as a consequence his fans no longer treated him as an individual. "This [stand-up] is the most important thing I do, and because I'm on TV, you make it hard for me to do it," Chappelle said. He added, "People can't distinguish between what's real and fake. This ain't a TV show. You're not watching Comedy Central. I'm real up here talking."

People can't distinguish between what's real and fake? It's happening more and more.

I've been living in the whole media microcosm myself for a while. I've spent a lot of years of my life covering the ins and outs of Hollywood and the ups and downs of the news biz. Funny how the two worlds have moved closer and closer together.

When I began writing this book, I set out to see if I could determine what effect the Tinseltown touch was having on us as a people and on society at large. I ended up interfacing with an eclectic group of well-known figures, including actor/director Mel Gibson, comedian Dennis Miller, cable television giant Bill O'Reilly, former White House speechwriter Peggy Noonan, ABC entertainment editor Joel Siegel, former White House adviser Dick Morris, Court TV news anchor Catherine Crier, political analyst and TV writer Lawrence O'Donnell, author Ann Coulter,

Fox News anchor Laurie Dhue, family therapist and talk radio host Laura Schlessinger, psychologist Joyce Brothers, actress Morgan Brittany, *Extra* host Dayna Devon, *Celebrity Justice* host Holly Herbert, cable TV host and news commentator Monica Crowley, talk radio phenom Michael Savage, talk radio and TV icon George Putnam, former *National Enquirer* president Iain Calder, and University of Southern California professor Kelton Rhoads.

As I look out across the country now, I find myself with a sense of enhanced vision. I see a place where sometimes down is up. Often small is big. And more frequently than I ever imagined, false is said to be true. It's an alien landscape with a familiar setting. And high atop a prominent hill is a sign that reads "Hollywood Nation."

Stroll with Joel

Joel Siegel is truly a Renaissance man. He's worked as a radio news-caster, book reviewer for the *Los Angeles Times,* feature reporter for WCBS-TV, radio host on WCBS Radio, freelance writer, advertising agency copywriter/producer, and even as a joke writer for the late Sena-tor Robert Kennedy.

He managed to pick up five New York Emmys as the entertainment critic for WABC-TV along the way.

Siegel has been the entertainment editor and film critic at ABC's *Good Morning America* for more than two decades.

Siegel and I met at an L.A. restaurant to discuss everything from movie reviews to what makes the news.[1] As you'd suspect, he's a fasci-nating guy.

HIRSEN: Film critics are looking at more films than anyone else. Maybe more than anyone should. It seems to me that for some film critics, they begin to get jaded in this sense: that the classic plotlines, the ones that would be in Greek tragedies and Shakespeare, the ones that involve heroes and villains and good and evil, begin to get hackneyed, and they're look-ing for filmmakers who are going to pick plotlines that are "edgy."

SIEGEL: That's very interesting.

HIRSEN: They [the plotlines] are sometimes devoid of a moral universe. But the critics may love them. I see this kind of di-
chotomy happening all the time. What do you think about
it as a theory?

SIEGEL: As a theory, I think it's absolutely true. I know these guys because we go to the movies together. I don't understand how
you can be a film critic and hate the movies. There are a number of these people who do what I do who hate movies.

Quentin Tarantino is really interesting. I loved *Pulp Fiction*. I
hated *Kill Bill 1,* really hated it, because it was what you suggested. It was devoid of any kind of moral structure. What
was he trying to tell me? I mean, you watch a hundred and
forty people getting murdered and blood spurting, and are
we supposed to think it was a good idea? Or a bad idea? Are
we supposed to be repelled by it? Or are we supposed to em-
brace it? He didn't put it in any context whatsoever. In my review of the film I said that—I give grades to movies—and I
said I'm going to have to give this an Incomplete.

HIRSEN: So he shocked the audience.

SIEGEL: Who knows, but he made the movie he wanted to make. And
I wrote the review I wanted to write.

HIRSEN: When a film wallows in ugliness, can that be an artistic
statement?

SIEGEL: I have a good education. I went to UCLA, and at UCLA, in a
class in literature, I learned something called the "fallacy of
imitative form." And the fallacy of imitative form is, If you
want to write a poem about how boring the world is, you
don't write a boring poem. And if you want to make a movie
about how ugly the world is, you don't make an ugly movie.

HIRSEN: Since reviewers sometimes praise ugliness, do you think there
are those who have developed a twisted view of cinema?

SIEGEL: I think one of the things that has happened, that happens to
critics—I think you're right. Some of it probably is [that they
are] jaded. Some of it, they want to see something new.
Sometimes you get into a situation where you've seen so

many, so much of the same thing, that it's cyclical. By the end of summer, we've seen so many movies filled with special effects that in late August if anything opens up with a hint of intelligence we . . .

HIRSEN: Sort of jump on it?

SIEGEL: Exactly. We bend over backwards to promote it. We give it a better review than we would have had we seen it in June. And that's true.

HIRSEN: The documentary as journalism, do you have a take on that?

SIEGEL: A documentary should be journalism, and more often than not, they're not. I did not like *Bowling for Columbine.* I didn't like it at all. I thought it was filled with cheap shots. On the record I'll say this—I thought Michael Moore did something that I didn't see how anybody could do: it made me feel sorry for Charlton Heston.

And, you know, I know Dick Clark. I've known Dick Clark for a long time. The first New Year's Eve I was on television in New York, my job was to cover New Year's Eve for the eleven o'clock Channel 2 News. I was up on the top of a movie marquee in Times Square and on the other side of the movie marquee was Dick Clark. I'm this newcomer. I'd never been there before. I don't know anything. I'm from a local station. He's doing his network show; he's all around the world. He couldn't have been nicer. I know people who know him and who've worked with him. He really is a wonderful guy. And Michael Moore blindsides him. It just isn't right. I was not a fan of *Bowling for Columbine.* I just didn't like it. To me, that's not journalism. Journalism is the art and the craft of going out and seeking a truth. And what Michael Moore did in *Bowling for Columbine* is going out and reinforcing his prejudices. And that's not journalism.

HIRSEN: There's a lot of talk about the fact that more and more media are under more and more control of conglomerates. What are your thoughts on that?

SIEGEL: I know from personal experience that it hasn't affected me or what I do at all. Not for a second. The fact that I review

Disney movies, and I give Disney movies scathing, negative reviews or flowery, positive reviews; I've never heard a word from anybody out in the hierarchy or anyone I've worked for about whether I had reviewed a movie positively or negatively or whether I should review a movie positively or negatively.

HIRSEN: You don't get a memo from Eisner?

SIEGEL: No, no, no, nothing. They're too smart. I think another truth is when they make a bad movie they know they've made a bad movie. I think this is true for Disney and Warner Brothers and Paramount and everybody else who makes movies. Not a word. Nothing. Only twice, and I've been doing this for almost twenty-five years, has there been any pressure on me. One was from—I had a chance to interview Clint Eastwood when he had a movie coming out. Clint Eastwood didn't talk to anybody and he was going to allow himself to be interviewed by me only if I gave the movie a rave review.

HIRSEN: Oh, really?

SIEGEL: Yeah, and I didn't. And I didn't talk to him but I gave the movie a positive review. But it wasn't a rave review and we lost the interview. The executive producer of *Good Morning America* said, "No problem."

[The second was] when I first started, I was on CBS and William Paley had this idea he wanted to clean up New York. This was in the early seventies, and New York was in bad shape. He wanted to do—simultaneously with WCBS Radio and CBS-FM Radio and WCBS Television—the three outlets together doing a Clean Up New York campaign. I was going to be the television guy doing feature stories on the things to do. They couldn't do it. The lawyers wouldn't let them do it, because the three stations had to be independent.

HIRSEN: You've been around the entertainment business and you've watched people. People go very quickly sometimes from waiting on tables to waiting on limos. That's L.A. What emerges—not just the wealth, but the fame—brings with it the entourage, the trappings of fame. It seems as though celebrities can become isolated, disconnected from the world.

SIEGEL: Here's a true story about that. Often it's not the celebrity's fault. I did a panel at this last Tribeca Film Festival where I interviewed Garry Marshall. Marshall's a great filmmaker, and he's made some wonderful films. The focus of the panel was about Garry Marshall and his pretty women, because he directed *Pretty Woman.* He's made stars of great actresses. Julia Roberts was not part of this thing because the people from the Tribeca Film Festival couldn't get to Julia Roberts. They kept getting no's from people around Julia Roberts, and they knew if somebody had been able to get to Julia Roberts, she would have said, "Sure, of course. This man made me a star. I love him." Actresses tend to love their directors, because that kind of relationship does develop, especially when the films are successful and good things happen to both sides. But they couldn't get to her. And that happens. That happens a lot.

HIRSEN: Then someone who is in a celebrity position has to resist, because they're surrounded by people who live off their enterprise. In other words, they have people who are employees that tend to be yes people.

SIEGEL: It depends, I think. It seems with celebrities, the really huge types, I think that's probably true. Although you find huge stars who are very accessible and just really nice, decent, great people.

HIRSEN: I'm saying it's terribly important when somebody achieves a level of fame to have people that can be honest, so that they won't always say, "Julia, that's a great idea" no matter what it is.

SIEGEL: That's right. That's right. Oh, there's a great line. We're sitting here. We're about a half a mile from the Fox Studios. Darryl Zanuck had one of the great lines of all times. At some meeting he hollered, "Don't say 'yes' until I'm finished talking."

HIRSEN: [Laughs] Shows like *Good Morning America* have journalists, and people who are conveying information, who have become celebrities in their own right. Say, for example, Diane Sawyer, Katie Couric, and . . .

SIEGEL: Barbara Walters.

HIRSEN: Yes. And they have the trappings. Does that sometimes affect the way they . . .

SIEGEL: You know, I honestly don't think so, because I think if it had affected the way they practiced their craft that they wouldn't have been that successful. I know Katie personally, because we share colon cancer; I had it and her husband had it. So I've worked with Barbara, I've worked with Diane, and they don't have entourages. It's not like dealing with a Hollywood star. They're very accessible, they work all the time, they get the interviews because they're on the phone, and they're on the phone personally.

HIRSEN: Do they have to make an effort to sort of stay in touch . . . ?

SIEGEL: Oh, yeah.

HIRSEN: . . . with real people . . . ?

SIEGEL: Oh, yes.

HIRSEN: . . . with real America . . . ?

SIEGEL: Yeah, absolutely.

HIRSEN: . . . because otherwise . . .

SIEGEL: Otherwise it's gone. Absolutely. Yes it is. They do. I know about Barbara and Diane; they do that. They do know real people, they spend time with them, and they like real people. You're a human being before you're anything [Laughs]. You're a human being before you're a cop. You're a human being before you're a firefighter. You're a human being before you're a reporter. Your first priority is to be a human being.

HIRSEN: Do you think that there's, in terms of hard news versus soft news, a pressure on? Have you noticed a change in *Good Morning America* over the years or is it pretty consistent?

SIEGEL: No, no, things have changed. I think things have changed because of what the audience wants.

2

STARS OF PAGE AND SCREEN

In his life, Andy Warhol garnered a lot of credits to his name. But the late artist and filmmaker is perhaps most often noted for a provocative prediction he made. He said, "Every person will be world-famous for fifteen minutes." It seems that he saw fame as a manifestation of a growing consumerism in our culture. In our insatiable quest to distract and amuse ourselves, Warhol foresaw a need for a never-ending supply of fresh celebrity faces. He had a unique understanding of our celebrity fixation, a passion on the part of the public that was evident to him in his era and continues to grow to this day.

Warhol is also credited with coining the term *superstar*. Filmmaker Chuck Workman, in fact, chose that word as the title for his Warhol documentary. In *Superstar,* writer and humorist Fran Lebowitz observes, "Andy Warhol made fame more famous."

Making fame more famous: that's really a great way to define what it means to be a superstar in our society today. A superstar's name and likeness often acquires a secondary meaning, and his or her personal accomplishments, life story, and public appearances take on an inflated presence. Just look at someone like Madonna, a master at media manipulation who has consistently kept herself in the public eye for more than two decades.

Of course, celebrities are nothing new. Hollywood, for example, has always understood the concept of fame and how it can be exploited. But what happens when those reaching superstar status are no longer just entertainers?

This is not just an academic question. In recent years the blurring of news and entertainment has produced a new breed of stars, or even superstars: journalists and newscasters.

Former news bigs Dan Rather and Tom Brokaw and current anchor Peter Jennings are all considered to be journalists. And although at times Katie Couric, Barbara Walters, and Diane Sawyer take on host duties, they all switch hats and jump into journalist roles when called on to do so, or when news constipation strikes. But just like Hollywood celebrities, they are stars as well. And they have all of the same kind of influence that fame affords. So when the individual who is supposed to be transmitting the facts becomes a Warhol superstar in his or her own right, what are the consequences?

In their book *The Press Effect: Politicians, Journalists, and the Stories That Shape the Political World,* Kathleen Hall Jamieson and Paul Waldman include a chapter titled "The Press as Shaper of Events." They cite Douglas Cater, who assigned the phrase "fourth branch of government" to the press, for his notion that reporters possess a "substantial degree of independent political power." Cater argues that a journalist "can choose from among the myriad events that seethe beneath the surface of government, which [of those events] to describe, which to ignore. He [the journalist] can illuminate policy. . . . He can prematurely expose policy and, as with an undeveloped film, cause its destruction. At his worst, operating with arbitrary and faulty standards, he can be an agent of disorder and confusion. At his best, he can exert a creative influence on Washington politics."[1]

Basically, Cater is saying that journalists, in regard to government, can do a world of good or a load of damage. Any way you slice it, their position provides them enormous power to sway.

Timothy Cook goes even further than Cater in his book *Governing with the News.* He suggests that the news media are an unelected part of the state, writing that "the American news media today are not merely part of politics; they are part of government."[2]

According to Jamieson and Waldman, media figures are no longer mere observers and transmitters of truth. The authors unequivocally state that "with the choices they make in carrying out the enormously difficult task to which they have been assigned, journalists help determine the course of events."[3]

When looking at journalists from this perspective, we can see how, if they have the added quality of being a Hollywood-type celebrity, it only increases their political, societal, and cultural clout.

Sometimes they exert influence through the words they use, the personas they project, or the behaviors they display. But at other times these things aren't packing the proverbial punch. Rather, influence is coming into play in the *way* things are being communicated.

THE BODY OF THE MESSAGE

Even when our words aren't truthful, our bodies are. Although communication experts differ in regard to the exact figure, most peg the percentage of communication that takes place outside of the words themselves at anywhere from 50 to 90 percent, depending on the individuals involved.

Businesses, trial lawyers, and media organizations often hire experts in the field of body language to obtain advice and gain insight about customers, clients, and/or opposition. In my work as a trial attorney, I used the services of such professionals when selecting juries, preparing to put on cases, and so on. It was here that I really learned about the power and scope of the nonverbal. I was told that a juror's perception of my presentation and arguments would be chiefly within this realm. This meant that my posture, voice, tone, and inability to control my smirk would have a greater communication impact than the actual words I used.

Nonverbal communication expert Jan Hargrave looked at the now famous testimony of former president Bill Clinton on his relationship with former White House intern Monica Lewinsky. Her comments in the *Houston Business Journal* suggest that, in his case, body language ended up betraying a fib. Clinton "touched his nose about once every four minutes," which was the "giveaway," according to Hargrave.

Studies done by UCLA psychology professor Albert Mehrabian drive home the nonverbal point. Mehrabian found that 55 percent of our communication is visual while 38 percent of what is being perceived comes from the audio incidentals (tone, cadence, pitch, diction, and so forth). When you do the math, that means only 7 percent of the message being received is the result of the actual words being said.[4]

The nonverbal communication component becomes especially significant when the material being communicated is being transmitted via a television host, broadcaster, expert, or actor on the little, big, or giant screen. And it doesn't really matter whether the individual who is doing the communicating is really a journalist or is just pretending to be one. What matters is whether he or she is *perceived* to be a conveyor of facts. If so, the person becomes what I call a "de facto journalist."

This comes into play when we look at television advertising. When actor Robert Young moved from his TV role as Marcus Welby, M.D., to his equally famous commercials, he used the line "I'm not a doctor, but I play one on TV." It matters, too, when someone wants to sell an idea. *West Wing* star Martin Sheen has pitched everything from his favorite presidential candidate to his foreign policy advice with a subtext of "I'm not the president, but I play one on TV."

By virtue of their breadth of exposure, the settings in which we encounter them, and their ability to fake a Midwest accent, we have a sense of familiarity with those we invite into our homes to give us the scoop. Their faces say, "You know me."

A raised eyebrow, a shift of facial expression, a subtle change in the tone of voice, if done by a news broadcaster or anchor, can communicate more than words could ever say. Nonverbal cues are sometimes given unconsciously. That's a pretty compelling concept. With studies showing that journalists are capable of "cultural bias," as Tim Russert has admitted, what impact does it have when Russert and buds communicate bias the nonverbal way?

Former NBC news anchor Tom Brokaw has rejected the notion of the existence of a mainstream media bias. He told C-SPAN's Brian Lamb, "The idea that we would set out, consciously or unconsciously, to put some kind of ideological framework over what we're doing is nonsense."[5] As I read those words, I asked myself, How can anyone be *sure* whether he or she has *not* done something when that something could have been done *unconsciously*? I can't figure that one out, unless Tom had been getting some assistance from the Amazing Kreskin.

In October 1996, PBS aired a *Frontline* program called "Why Americans Hate the Press." The promo for the show asked the question "Would you be surprised to learn that reporters are held in the same low regard as undertakers and insurance salesmen . . . and only slightly higher than politicians?"

One of the primary reasons that was given for the low professional rating is that the public is dissatisfied with journalists who are being treated like celebrities and reporters who are being presented as stars. The program observed that the perceptions and expectations that we have for journalists and stars differ. We look for stars to be good-looking, charismatic, and geared toward performing. But we look for something else in our journalists. We expect them to spot the important stories for us, deliver the material we require, and satisfy our need to know what's going on around us.

With the news and celebrity melding process that's taking place, though, there seems to be some public frustration and maybe even a touch of aggravation.

AMUSED OR CONFUSED?

Diana Dempsey, a former Fox anchor and NBC foreign correspondent, thinks that "TV news is going more and more in the entertainment direction." Dempsey doesn't care for the trend. She says she believes it "cheapens the TV news business. It takes the journalism out of TV journalism, leaving only the TV aspect, which is all about ratings."[6] She is also of the opinion that station management and news directors are unable to see the detrimental aspects of turning journalists into celebrities.

Jay Witherbee, a news director for ATV, a Canadian television network, explains that he needs publicity to get ratings and he needs stars to generate publicity. "There is no such thing as bad publicity," Witherbee says. "I feel badly when the coverage is mean-spirited, but if it helps attract viewers, then it's not all bad."

Even local media personalities can find themselves being treated like Hollywood celebs. Witherbee notes that there is an effort made to "try to capitalize on their popularity."[7]

Canadian sociologist Peter Butler has a Joe Somebody take. He says, "Getting the news from a celebrity is far more entertaining than watching Joe Nobody."[8]

On the other side of the fame-seeking coin is C-SPAN. C-SPAN's *Washington Journal* is an example of a program where the powers that be actually appear to go to extremes to *avoid* turning anyone into a star. Conventional news readers aren't used. Instead C-SPAN employees who make it through an in-house audition fill the host slot. To prevent any single individual from becoming the "face" of the program, hosts on the show are rotated. They choose the topics and book the guests, but none can claim to be a full-time anchor. The approach is to have hosts read newspaper articles out loud while guests comment on a particular item and callers from across America chime in with their two cents. It could be that the network has more freedom to operate in this manner because it doesn't have the concerns that a typical local or national news department on a standard network does—

meaning that since it gets its money from the cable industry, it can be as boring as it wants to be.

Like it or not, anchors rising to the level of stardom are becoming as common today as Ray-Bans on Melrose. On occasion we even see a local famed figure crossing over into the pop culture.

TV ANCHORS AND REAL-LIFE LEGENDS

The Mary Tyler Moore Show premiered on CBS in September 1970, and the headlining character turned the world on with her smile for seven years. While this show about fictional television station WJM became one of TV's classic sitcoms, not many people realize that one of its central characters was based on a couple of real-life news personalities.

The character of local celebrity anchorman Ted Baxter, played by Ted Knight, was in fact a comedic amalgam of two Los Angeles news superstars—George Putnam and Jerry Dunphy. Putnam is a legendary broadcaster who pioneered political commentary and audience input in newscasts. He has covered every presidency since Herbert Hoover's and was reading the news for NBC as early as 1939. His L.A. competitor, Dunphy, was also a widely recognized TV news anchor for forty years. He interviewed four presidents and survived a gunshot wound, two heart attacks, and triple bypass surgery. He passed away at the age of eighty. Together, with their looks, style, and affable presence, Putnam and Dunphy provided the inspiration for the Baxter character.

The two anchors had an uncanny resemblance to each other. And, of course, to Ted Baxter. Both became nationally known newsmen, but what's even more interesting is that they crossed over into pop-culture stardom, appearing in television and feature films. Putnam was in a number of films, one of the first being *Fourteen Hours,* which launched Grace Kelly's pre-royal career. Dunphy, meanwhile, appeared in movies like *Beverly Hills Cop III* and *Hard to Kill.*

Now in his nineties, Putnam is still broadcasting away and has appeared in a dozen films, the most recent being the 1996 block-buster *Independence Day*. I had a chance to speak with Putnam about his career and about moving back and forth between the worlds of news and entertainment.

Twelve feature films go a long way toward making the face of a news anchor recognizable. When I ask him how he first entered the film business, he replies, "I was, perhaps, much more Mr. Show Biz than [other journalists]. I was fairly attractive, fairly young, and the Hollywood scene adopted me." But he never forgot his broadcasting roots. Putnam would always portray either a journalist or a reporter, and he explains, "I always demanded that I use my own name." Even when Arnold Schwarzenegger asked him to "use some other name," he said no.

Putnam worked with many of the greats like Robert Mitchum and Grace Kelly, folks who were considered to be icons in the Golden Age of Hollywood. I ask Putnam, "How would you compare the celebrities in Tinseltown today with the stars of yesterday?" His answer comes swiftly. "Couldn't carry their pencils," Putnam declares.

"What is the difference?" I probe. "Oh! Stardom was stardom," he explains. "They weren't washing and putting their laundry out on the back line. They lived as stars. It was, of course, the studios. The studios made and built and maintained stars. They told you who to be seen with, who to eat with, who to dine with, which car to drive. They ran your life."

As part of that process of controlling their stars, the studios muzzled actors. When I ask if it's true that celebrities back then weren't as politically outspoken as they are today, Putnam agrees. "It was unheard of for a star," he says. "Can you imagine a Clark Gable taking a stand on politics?"

On the Left Coast today, such restraint is a faint relic of the past. Just ask Martin Sheen or Susan Sarandon or Michael Moore or Tim Robbins or Sean Penn or any of the other outspoken lefties who populate Tinseltown. And while they might not appear as glamorous as some of their predecessors did, they still have an extraordinary amount of fame, which gives them an incredible ability to insert themselves into the national discourse.

TRUTH DEFECTORS

In true sitcom formula, *The Mary Tyler Moore Show*'s Ted Baxter ended up being a parody of a celebrity news anchor. But George Putnam, a model for Baxter, never descended to such depths. The reason is that he always put his obligations as a newsman first. When I ask him what makes a great journalist, he offers the essentials: "Insatiable curiosity. Objectivity, of course. Perseverance. And then, most of all, integrity."

Guess former CBS newsman Dan Rather could have used a chat with George.

In fact, plenty of today's journalists could benefit from Putnam's advice. It seems that the temptations of celebrity are becoming more alluring than the desire to reveal the truth and disseminate critical information to the public.

This is precisely the problem that author Gay Talese, who coined the phrase "New Journalism," has with the news business today. Talese told one interviewer, "The reason that I never liked the term 'New Journalism' was that I think it marked the beginning of journalists wanting to be celebrities and often of journalists thinking of themselves as celebrities."[9]

When fame enters the journalistic picture, so can the Hollywood-style trappings. For example, as fame increases, the attention, perks, and entourages can grow right along with it. In these kinds of circumstances, it's easy for a celebrity journalist to lose touch with the real world.

In certain instances, the desire for fame can supersede the obligation to truth. Some journalists have actually made stuff up only to become celebrities in the process. It's as if fame and infamy momentarily trade places.

Jayson Blair was a writer for the *New York Times*. In scores of pieces, Blair either mixed fact with fiction or pawned off the ideas of others as his own. In a bizarre subplot, he was able to move up the journalistic ladder, despite the fact that a senior editor had warned that something wasn't quite right about the young reporter. It appears as though the *Times* might have been unable to see clearly because of a diversity blindfold it had obligingly strapped on.

Blair's downfall came when he was caught falsifying an interview with Private Jessica Lynch's dad. (Private Lynch was the soldier who was captured in Iraq and later rescued by American soldiers.) By the time the Blair dust had settled, managing editor Gerald Boyd and executive editor Howell Raines had been persuaded to end their careers with the *New York Times*.

Blair himself was fired. But following his dismissal he promptly scored a publishing deal and wrote a book entitled *Burning Down My Masters' House*. In it, he ended up dealing from a deck that was filled with not-so-subtle race cards and making the television talk-circuit rounds to promote the product.

LOOKING THROUGH *SHATTERED GLASS*

Before Jayson Blair let the world know the level to which the *New York Times* had sunk, there was Stephen Glass. Glass was the reporter who rocked another icon of the mainstream press, the *New Republic*. And just like Blair, he violated the number-one commandment of the news industry: "Thou shalt not make things up."

Glass's journalistic transgression of passing off fiction as fact was the basis of the film *Shattered Glass*. The movie demonstrated how the lust for fame can be a corrupting influence within the journalism profession. Glass was able to get more than twenty articles published in one of the world's most respected newsmagazines using trumped-up sources, phony locations, and/or nonexistent events.

In the film, the character of Glass is artfully played by Hayden Christensen. Christensen transforms himself into an affable sociopath who seduces friends and coworkers with feigned insecurity. As the ethically challenged Glass commits a series of magazine misdeeds, he's careful to include his tagline, "Are you mad at me?," for maximum diversion. Ultimately, however, his fabrications are exposed, and no more diversions can save the overly imaginative journalist.

What does the infamous Glass himself think of the film? He assessed it in this way: "It was extremely painful and difficult to watch. There were large chunks of it, or at least significant chunks of it, that I looked at the ground, I didn't look at the screen. . . . That being said, it's a good movie."

As it turns out, the whole story is more than a cautionary tale for would-be reporters. It's a prime illustration of the importance of the alternative media, which have become the paramount check to the establishment media that sometimes play tug-of-war with the truth. The person who uncovered Glass's deceptions didn't work for the esteemed *New Republic* or elsewhere in the mainstream media. Rather, the reporter, Adam Penenberg, wrote for the online publication Forbes Digital Tool. In the film, when the actor who plays Penenberg, Steve Zahn, discovers the extent of Glass's fabrication, he appears stunned and disturbed, but ultimately a bit gleeful at the coup he has scored for the New Media.

Penenberg was the first of a new breed of Internet heroes who exposed the mainstream's print and broadcast chicanery. Guess the moral of the story is, for the sake of the truth, Man your modems and keep up the dig.

One thing's for sure: journalism schools, including the one I teach at, will no doubt use the Stephen Glass story as an object lesson.

But has Glass himself actually learned his lesson? Are there repercussions these days for professional ethics violations or personal moral failings? Not exactly. Glass has been given the big-time opportunity to write, embellish, and possibly fabricate again. He released an autobiographical novel based on his experiences called *The Fabulist,* was hired by *Rolling Stone* to pen an article on Canadian drug legislation, is writing a second novel, and has applied to the New York Bar to become an attorney.

FACTS AND FICTION

The Blair and Glass cases, sensational as they seem, are not isolated incidents. *USA Today* had its own case of the journalist blues thanks to a fellow named Jack Kelley. Apparently, a team of reporters investigated for seven weeks and found that Kelley had fabricated stories, lifted quotes or other material from competing publications, lied in speeches he gave for the newspaper, and even conspired to mislead those investigating his work.

USA Today issued a report that began with this prologue: "Any appraisal of how Jack Kelley got away with years of fraudulent news reporting at *USA Today,* despite numerous, well-grounded warnings that he was fabricating stories, exaggerating facts and plagiarizing other publications, must begin with this question: Why did newsroom managers at every level of the paper ignore, rebuff and reject years of multiple serious and valid complaints about Kelley's work?"[10]

Kelley ended up resigning from *USA Today* in January 2004, after acknowledging that he conspired with a translator to mislead editors who were overseeing an inquiry into his work. The *USA Today* report put forward the idea that Kelley's name rose to a celebrity level that was more essential than his work as a journalist. As of this writing, it's unclear whether Kelley will capitalize on the media attention to score a book deal or some other profitable gig.

The Blair and Glass cases seem to indicate that charges of plagiarism and fabrication could actually boost the celebrity profile of this flexible breed of journalists. Martin Grove, a columnist for the *Hollywood Reporter,* makes this case. "People have an awareness of these colorful characters whose careers in journalism are suddenly front-page news themselves," Grove says. "It makes the character of the journalist something the audience is interested in. What it suggests to Hollywood storytellers is that journalists lead exciting lives." He adds wryly, "We do know that's not the case."[11]

As journalists, reporters, and writers get more and more visibility on the tube, they also sometimes gain the Hollywood-actor kind of fame. It used to be that news guys and gals were more of the humble gumshoe type, with pencils perched on ears, cameras slung around necks, and spiral notebooks in hands, trying to get the facts on the big story before the competition did.

A reporter by the name of Bob Woodward would have a lot to do with changing all of that. Today he is the assistant managing editor at the *Washington Post*. But decades ago, Woodward, along with Carl Bernstein, helped to break the Watergate scandal, which ultimately brought about the resignation of President Richard Nixon. Woodward could be called the prototype of the print-world celebrity.

His star quotient was greatly enhanced by an Oscar-winning flick, *All the President's Men*. The film did a lot to glamorize reporting. The grand mystery of the movie, and of the Watergate saga, was Woodward's use of a source he called "Deep Throat," anonymous until May 31, 2005.

Of course, it didn't hurt his babe appeal to have the movie role of Woodward played by the Sundance Kid.

ANCHORS AWAY

For the big-time celebrity newsmen, there can be a downside to all that fame.

In August 2004 the Commission on Presidential Debates (CPD), in breaking from the practice of using a single moderator for all the debates, announced that three different moderators— Jim Lehrer of PBS, Bob Schieffer of CBS, and Charles Gibson of ABC—would be assigned to referee one debate each. Curiously, the CPD rejected the idea of using network anchor people. "Janet H. Brown, a spokeswoman for the commission, said it had avoided using anchors as moderators since 1988 for fear that they would overshadow the events," the *New York Times* reported. Brown explained that "it's important for the moderators to focus attention on the candidates."[12]

Evidently, the plan didn't sit too well with NBC News's uninvited Tom Brokaw. Brokaw has had considerable experience in moderating political debates, and said so in a letter to Brown. "Not once did candidates, campaigns or press critics suggest I was more concerned with my role than with the role of the candidates," he wrote.

Brokaw also stated that Brown's observation "leaves the undeniable impression that you believe if we were moderators, we'd be preening, egocentric performers. I deeply resent that implication."

Maybe Brown got Brokaw mixed up with the NBC symbol.

Whatever the case, the CPD's decision showed that to some people, the journalists themselves have come to overshadow the stories they are supposed to cover. And a lot of Americans seem to be fed up with that. In fact, more and more of us are turning to other sources to get our news. With so many journalists becoming stars, I guess it was only natural that we'd turn straight to entertainers themselves to find out what to think about the world around us.

WISECRACKING THE NEWS

We have witnessed a big shift in recent years. Today we have TV stars bringing us the news, and in large part the headlining stuff seems to be coming to us in the form of late-night television. Many people now choose to get their current affairs updates and political dispatches not from a Peter Jennings or a Brian Williams but from a Jay Leno, a David Letterman, or a Jon Stewart instead.

Political messages are popping up all over the late-night comedy/talk shows. For starters, the hosts of the diversionary programs are being viewed as comic Cronkites, whose punch lines become headlines for their vast audiences. The young in particular are using the entertainment fare to receive information and form opinions. A Pew Research survey taken before the 2000 presidential election found that almost half of those between the ages of eighteen and twenty-nine and more than a quarter of all adults gained their info about the campaign from late-night comedy shows. Another Pew survey in 2004 determined that one in five young people regularly get campaign news from late-night comedy shows like *Saturday Night Live* and *The Daily Show with Jon Stewart*.[13]

No surprise, then, that big-time politicos can't wait to appear on late-night shows. Sometimes this can cause a stir, as it prompts questions about the political overtones of the comics' shows. Jay Leno, for example, angered some on the Left when he publicly supported his friend Arnold Schwarzenegger's campaign for governor of California. Back on August 6, 2003, Leno even allowed Schwarzenegger the *Tonight Show* platform to make his surprise announcement that he would be a candidate in the recall election against Democrat incumbent Gray Davis.

Hollywood libs could have forgiven Leno for his Schwarzenegger support, seeing that the Terminator brings in big ratings numbers. But when Schwarzenegger won the election, Leno showed up at Arnold's victory bash. If lefties in California were initially shocked that Arnold had won, they became downright despondent when they saw Leno introduce the governor-elect. Jay quipped that the whole thing was "a testament of just how important one appearance on the *Tonight Show* can be."

Shortly thereafter, libs on the Internet began to track the frequency of Leno's Bush-bashing jokes. Apparently, Leno toned down his bashing of the president after 9/11, and he had a little fun at the expense of the French, too. Maybe Leno softened a bit because he had a deeper understanding of some of the issues of the war on terror, since his wife, Mavis, has worked tirelessly to help female victims of the Taliban. Whether or not it's related to his support of Arnold or his diminished Bush hits, Leno was charged with being a right-wing wacko by the *Washington Post,* the *New York Times,* and the *LA Weekly.*

The same Internet tracking showed that Leno's main competitor, David Letterman, did not show the same restraint when it came to President Bush. Others noticed as well. *LA Weekly*'s Nikki Finke had this to say about the late-night hosts: "Leno may be the ratings winner. Stewart is the critics' darling. But, day in and day out, Letterman is the hands-down leader when it comes to unabashed Bush bashing."[14] Finke praised Letterman for having the "brass balls" to make fun of the president.

Letterman even took on the White House directly when he got in the middle of a big news story involving the president.

It all started with a typical Monday-night Letterman show, when he showed some footage of a bored boy situated behind the president as he gave a campaign speech. The lad's name was Tyler Crotty, son of a prominent Republican from Orange County, Florida, and major Bush fundraiser, Richard Crotty. The press nicknamed Tyler "Yawning Boy" because of his wide-mouthed inhalations.

Inspired by Dave's bit, CNN programmers ran the footage on *CNN Live Today*. But then CNN anchor Daryn Kagan jumped in with this update to viewers: "We're being told by the White House that the kid, as funny as he was, was edited into that video, which would explain why the people around him weren't really reacting." Later that same day, another anchor, Kyra Phillips, showed the footage once again on another CNN program called *Live From . . .* , saying, "We're told that the kid was there at that event, but not necessarily standing behind the president."

The fact of the matter is, the White House never complained about the footage. And the Letterman video was real; the boy really was behind the president during the speech. CNN admitted its error and retracted the report. It placed a call to Letterman's New York headquarters, but apparently not in time for Dave to get the word before that night's show began taping.

Letterman got a bit testy on the air. After showing the clip of Kagan telling viewers that the White House said the tape was fake, Letterman responded by saying, "That is an out and out 100 percent absolute lie. The kid absolutely was there, and he absolutely was doing everything we pictured via the videotape." He laid into CNN for failing to contact *The Late Show with David Letterman* to confirm the story. And twice he referred to the Bush White House as liars.

Later, Letterman's people got word from CNN. "According to this," Letterman announced during the taping, "CNN has just phoned and . . . the anchorwoman misspoke. They never got a comment from the White House. It was a CNN mistake." Then he lightened things with the quip "Now I've called the White House liars, and you know what that means—they're going to start looking into my taxes!"

Thursday of that week CNN apologized on the air to Letterman. Kagan, the anchor who first reported that the White House had labeled the tape a fraud, offered the first statement of contrition, saying, "The White House, it turns out, I guess never did call us about the tape. . . . And we've been looking through our tapes and apparently we now see no evidence that it was faked. So Dave, we apologize for the error. I hope that makes things good with us. If you need me to come up and do a stupid human trick or a stupid pet trick, I have that, too. But hopefully we're just okay. We apologize."

That night, Letterman said it was a "landmark day, because for the first time in twenty-five years of network television broadcasting, the first time ever since I've been doing this, someone has apologized to me."

White House assistant press secretary Reed Dickens told the *Washington Post,* "We think it's all in good nature, very good-humored."[15] But Letterman remained skeptical. He told his audience, "This whole thing just smells. Doesn't it smell a little bit? I mean, it just seems all just a little too tidy, just a little too neat. And now, the guy, the kid in Florida—and his old man—was really upset in the beginning. . . . Well, now everybody down there loves it. Everybody couldn't be happier; everybody thought it was hilarious. So you see, it's just a little too tidy. Stuff like this never ends happily, certainly not happily for me. I was waiting for the lawsuit, I was waiting to be arrested, I was waiting to be beaten to a pulp, and now, oh . . . we couldn't be happier."

LENO DUCKS LABEL

During the 2004 presidential cycle, reports went out that the Bush White House had been chatting with the *Tonight Show* about a possible presidential appearance. When you think about it, a guest spot with Arnold's good buddy would probably have been preferable to one with the seemingly anti-Bush Letterman.

But then, according to the *New York Daily News,* it looked as though the White House was having some concerns about a Leno visit because of an interview the comedian gave with *LA Weekly.* Nikki Finke, the same journalist who praised David Letterman for having the "brass balls" to take on the president, wrote a series of articles criticizing Leno for apparently kowtowing to the Right. Leno reportedly telephoned Finke to correct the record.

In the Finke interview, Leno said, "I'm not conservative. I've never voted that way in my life." Evidently, he really worried what a Dubya win would do to the makeup of the Supreme Court. And he believed "the wool was pulled over our eyes" with the Iraq War. And he thought the White House began using terrorism "as a crutch" after 9/11. And he felt that during the campaign, John Kerry ought to "make Bush look as stupid as possible." And he opined that "the media is in the pocket of the government, and they don't do their job," so "you have people like Michael Moore who do it for them."

Not exactly the sentiments of someone with Republican affinities. Leno's people nevertheless continued to pursue a Bush or Cheney appearance. Not surprisingly, neither the president nor the vice president appeared on the show before the election.

For me, once again the whole episode illustrates just how far people in Hollywood will go to shake that conservative label.

DAILY NEWS

Arnold Schwarzenegger isn't the only pol to turn to a late-night comedy show to try to boost his candidacy. In 2003, for example, Senator John Edwards unveiled his plans to run for president on

The Daily Show with Jon Stewart. And in another late-night TV comedy scene, then–Dem presidential candidate Reverend Al Sharpton hosted NBC's *Saturday Night Live* and impressed viewers with a mean James Brown routine.

More and more it seems that political strategists and politicians see comedy shows as part and parcel of a political campaign. GOP consultant Mike Murphy thinks things have evolved in this direction in part because it's easier to face a comedy-show host than it is to "sit in the hot seat with Tim Russert."[16]

Increasingly, *The Daily Show with Jon Stewart* is taking the lead in political influence. The program was originally created by Madeleine Smithberg and Lizz Winstead in the mid-1990s for Comedy Central. Back then it was simply called *The Daily Show.*

Its first host was Craig Kilborn, who went on to snag his own late-night spot on CBS. There were rumors that he didn't get along with the show's decision makers, but for whatever reason Kilborn left when he got the CBS gig and was replaced by Jon Stewart in 1999. The show would never be the same. Neither would the news, which Stewart spoofs to the nines.

Jon Stewart proudly calls *The Daily Show* a "fake news" program, but clearly viewers—and politicians—now take the show's message very seriously. Stewart himself, like some other politically minded comedians, seems to have morphed into the role of pundit and opinion maker. This new status became clear in the fall of 2004, when Stewart made the rounds to promote his best-selling book *America,* a parody of a civics textbook.

Stewart made a splash when he went on the now-defunct CNN debate show *Crossfire.* Rather than promote his book, he forcefully condemned *Crossfire* and the news media in general. Stewart told cohosts Tucker Carlson and Paul Begala that their show was not only "bad," it was actually "hurting America." Shows like *Crossfire,* he said, were "helping the politicians and the corporations" and leaving out "the people." He even declared, "I'm here to confront you, because we need help from the media and they're hurting us," and said what *Crossfire* did was "not honest" but was in fact "partisan hackery."

The appearance made national news; reportedly the footage of the *Crossfire* appearance was downloaded on the Internet more than a million times. Suddenly Stewart had sparked a national debate about the proper role of the news media in a free society. It was heady stuff for a guy who had worked as a puppeteer and then paid his dues on the stand-up comedy circuit. Stewart had appeared on HBO's *Young Comedians Special* and the *Late Show with David Letterman* before scoring the host gig for a program on Comedy Central called *Short Attention Span Theater.* He moved to MTV, where he hosted a short-lived show called *You Wrote It— You Watch It.* Later MTV gave him his own program, *The Jon Stewart Show,* which Paramount would expand and syndicate nationally. It ran from fall 1994 through spring 1995. He used the opportunity to perfect the zany style he'd later take to hilarious heights on *The Daily Show.* But neither that nor the Hollywood films he appeared in seemed the standard preparation for the role of "fake news anchor" and sometime pundit he later assumed.

Still, when Stewart took over the helm of *The Daily Show,* it became a ratings hit. By the time the 2004 presidential campaign heated up, evidently more young people than ever were turning to Jon Stewart for hard news info. Stewart's show drew more male viewers aged eighteen to thirty-four than any of the network evening news shows during the period encompassing the Iowa caucus, the New Hampshire primary, and the State of the Union address. When told of the phenomenon, Stewart reacted with his usual burlesque style, saying, "A lot of them are probably high."[17]

But real news figures have leaped at the chance to reach that demographic. Those who have appeared on *The Daily Show with Jon Stewart* include former secretary of state Madeleine Albright, former vice president Al Gore, Senators John McCain and Joseph Lieberman, former congressman and presidential candidate Dick Gephardt, perpetual candidate for prez and activist Ralph Nader, former senator and Viagra pitchman Bob Dole, former first lady and current senator Hillary Clinton, former secretary of state Henry Kissinger, former antiterrorist adviser and author

Richard Clarke, former senator Bob Kerrey, and 2004 Democratic presidential nominee John Kerry.

The appearances of the last two, Kerrey and Kerry, reveal a lot about how hard it is to tell whether *The Daily Show* is pure entertainment or real news or some mixture of both. And the fuzzy boundaries raise some troubling questions about whether we're getting the straight scoop or being taken for a loop.

BOB KERREY'S UNFUNNY MISSTEP

In the midst of the 9/11 Commission hearings, who did one of the commission members turn to for advice? Well, in the case of Bob Kerrey, just before a historic session with the president and vice president of the United States, the former senator looked to Jon Stewart for some direction.

Kerrey was apparently following in the footsteps of several other commissioners who made TV appearances in April 2004. During a visit to *The Daily Show*, Kerrey asked Stewart if there was a question he wanted him to ask President George W. Bush or Vice President Dick Cheney. Stewart joshed, "Yes, I got one. What the 'blank' is wrong with you people?"

Kerrey came back at Stewart with, "Yes, we'll do it." He added that "he, Bush, is bringing his buddy [Cheney], that's exactly right, for safety."

By the way, Kerrey is the grandstander who couldn't keep Condoleezza Rice's name straight during questioning but felt the need to rebuke the then–national security adviser for forgetting specific details of conversations held three years prior.

House Majority Whip Roy Blunt issued a statement criticizing Kerrey for his poor judgment. It read, "Just two days before the 9/11 Commission is scheduled to question the President of the United States about intelligence failures that precipitated the loss of more than 3000 Americans, Senator Bob Kerrey asked a comedian for pointers. . . . This is not a laughing matter. The 9/11 Commission has been charged with investigating exactly why

September 11, 2001, happened. Kerrey's comedy show routine certainly makes me wonder whether he is interested in finding the truth about intelligence failures or staging a comeback tour."

Did someone really need to tell the former senator that meeting with the president and vice president of the United States about intelligence failures that precipitated the massive loss of lives was not the stuff of comedy?

JOHN KERRY DODGES THE NEWS MEDIA

In 2004 millions of Gen-Xers and Yers were deciding how to select the next president of the United States. Dem candidate John Kerry scheduled a national TV interview during the election period, to respond to charges by a group called Swift Boat Veterans for Truth. The more than 250 decorated veterans had questioned the candidate's version of his military record and disputed his account of his actions during the Vietnam War, which had earned him multiple medals in four months' time.

Major network news shows on CBS, NBC, and ABC were ready and willing to roll out the red carpet out for Kerry. But he took a pass and opted instead to appear on—what else?—*The Daily Show.* This was an unprecedented event for Stewart's program. He had had on a past prez (Bill Clinton), a VP candidate (Joe Lieberman), and a bevy of Dem primary candidates. But never before had the show featured a presidential nominee on its comedy couch.

Kerry had appeared on a late-night TV show earlier in his campaign, when he rumbled onto the set of Jay Leno's *Tonight Show* atop a Harley-Davidson motorcycle. The *Washington Post* noted that he was upstaged, though, by canine puppet Triumph the Insult Comic Dog, who summed up Kerry's effort to become the leader of the free world with this description: "The poop I left in the dressing room has more heat coming off it than his campaign."[18]

The Kerry campaign explained to the *Post* why the candidate agreed to do the comedy show while passing up the conventional news venues. "Jon Stewart understands perfectly all the important issues facing this country right now," a Kerry spokeswoman said.[19] There was talk of reaching out to younger voters and discussion of "another presidential candidate" who had appeared on Arsenio Hall's program, played a saxophone, and won the election.[20]

With his tongue firmly in his cheek, *Daily Show* executive producer Ben Karlin said that the program would "focus exclusively on events of 30 years or more ago . . . and not on anything relevant to anything beyond 1964."[21] Karlin planned to conduct a "meaningful conversation absent of incredulity, because [the interview] is not going to go anywhere if you just say, 'What the [expletive] is going on?' "[22]

Stewart ended up asking some of his patently droll questions like this one: "I watch a lot of the cable news shows, so I understand that you were never in Vietnam?" Kerry answered with, "That's what I understand, too, but I'm trying to find out what happened."

When Kerry went into a canned statement about the economy, jobs, the environment, America's role in the world, and on and on, Stewart interrupted with a serious question. "I'm sorry," the host blurted out. "Were you or were you not in Cambodia?" Kerry looked uncomfortable. For a while the guest and host stared each other down until Stewart moved onto some of the other items that opponents were saying.

"Are you the number-one most liberal senator in the Senate?" Stewart inquired, joking that some claimed the candidate was "more liberal than Karl Marx." "No," Kerry replied.

"Are you or have you ever flip-flopped?" Stewart solicited. "I've flip-flopped, flap-flipped," Kerry answered.

Stewart asked, "Is it true that every time I use ketchup, your wife gets a nickel?"

"Would that it were," the condiment king prattled.

COMIC AS PUNDIT

All in all, Stewart seems to get pleasure out of needling the journalists he's outdrawing. Comedy Central held a town hall meeting in Manchester, New Hampshire, as part of the cable network's *Indecision 2004* campaign coverage. As moderator, Stewart got a chance to diss a gaggle of big-name TV news personalities. After asking questions like "What's the difference between embedding and, say, following someone around?," Stewart walked over to the *Weekly Standard*'s Bill Kristol and *Time* magazine columnist Joe Klein, separated their chairs in the manner of a high school teacher, and teasingly said, "Stop it. If you guys don't stop it, someone is going to ask you to do a show."

At the commencement of the Democratic National Convention, Stewart invited reporters to a morning session. He tweaked the journalists by saying, "I'm concerned about the incredible number of people who say they get the news from you guys." He went on to criticize the media for "being stage-managed," and he described the nation's capital as a place of "absolute self-delusion and arrogance."

Howard Kurtz, media critic for the *Washington Post* and CNN, tried to interrupt, but Stewart thwarted the attempt with "Your network is silly."[23]

At another event during the Democratic convention, *Nightline*'s Ted Koppel got into an out-of-the-ordinary discussion with the *Daily Show* host. As Koppel began to interview Stewart, the comic-anchor began to sound a bit like Bill O'Reilly. He lamented the pseudo-objectivity of news media figures today and hit on some of the same points he made during his infamous *Crossfire* appearance.

Stewart used a hypothetical, pretending to be a news anchor who was moderating a debate on health care and insurance. He then ended up taking on all of the roles and giving the following performance:

"I have with me Donna Brazile and Bay Buchanan. Let's go. Donna. 'I think the Democrats really have it right here. I think that this is a pain for the insurance companies and the drug companies and this is wrong for America.' Bay. 'Oh no, what it is . . . ' And then she throws out her figures from the Heritage Foundation, and she throws out her figures from the Brookings Institute, and the anchor—who should be the arbiter of the truth—says, 'Thank you both very much, that was very interesting.' No it wasn't! That was Coke and Pepsi talking about beverage truth. And that game has, I think, caused people to think, 'I'm not watching this.' "

Koppel pointed out that on Stewart's own show he "can use humor to say 'BS, that's a crock,' " but added that he himself "can't do that."

Stewart disagreed, "No, but you can say 'that's BS.' You don't need humor to do that because you have what I wish I had, which is credibility and gravitas. This is interesting stuff, and it's all part of the discussion and I think it's a good discussion to have, but I think it's important to take a more critical look. You know, don't you think?"

Koppel replied with one word—"No." Then he stated, "I've had enough of you. You're finished." He smiled and ended the discussion.

It was then that it occurred to me, even if we don't always get the best information from him, it's great to have a guy on TV that elicits a chuckle. He's such a kidder, that Ted Koppel.

"A COMEDIAN IN A DIFFERENT FORMAT"

Another longtime wisecracker who veers more toward the news end of the business is Dennis Miller, who used to host his own show on CNBC. Like Stewart, Miller analyzed the hot issues of the day with a hefty dose of comedy. Also like Stewart, he's taken an unorthodox path to having his own news-centric themes, having gotten his break on *Saturday Night Live* and been very successful as a stand-up comedian.

Miller had a lot of options available to him when CNBC came calling, yet he chose to do a daily talk show at that time. When I interviewed him, I asked him whether he had any journalistic ambitions with the show. He said he didn't. Rather, he said he was simply "going to be a comedian in a different format."

Still, much like Letterman, Leno, and Stewart, Miller had on an impressive array of guests that conventional news shows would have coveted, including former president George H. W. Bush, Arnold Schwarzenegger, and Al Sharpton.

It just goes to show how the rules continue to be rewritten, kind of like the swimsuit regs at the Miss Universe pageant.

ENTER THE ZONE

The news media have been dubbed The Fourth Estate because of their profound influence on government policy and their traditional role of providing an outside check and balance to governmental power. But with today's culture being so enamored with public figures from the world of entertainment, the industry that brings us film, television, and music is now head butting our beliefs, trends, and generational ethos. It's what I refer to as "The Fifth Estate," and it emanates from the geographic state of mind known as Hollywood.

What occurs when news personalities become stars and Hollywood celebrities become info sources is a melding of the Fourth and Fifth Estates. Imagination and shadow mingle with reality and substance, and we find ourselves entering the media Twilight Zone.

Just Dhue It

Laurie Dhue tells me that she paid her "dhues" in an unusual way. "I started out rolling the TelePrompTer for Catherine Crier, which most people don't know," she reveals. She made her way up the CNN ladder. In her words, "I started out entry level and worked my way up to an assistant producer. Then I became a booker. I was writing all the interviews for the anchors and convincing people to appear on CNN." Her first anchor position was at CNN, where she did weekend programs like *CNN Saturday, CNN Sunday, World View,* and *The World Today.*

She began her tenure at MSNBC in 1999 as anchor of *Newsfront.* She hosted MSNBC's *Special Edition* and served as a substitute news anchor for the weekend edition of NBC's *Today* show.

Dhue signed on to the Fox News Channel in 2000 and is currently a news update anchor and host of weekend specials.

She has a remarkably high-profile cyberstatus. A Google search of her name at present yields over 3,200 web pages. Fans have created numerous discussion groups devoted to her. Some have thousands of members.

Dhue's experience with three major cable news networks makes her a journalist who's truly representative of the cable news era. "I was cable when cable wasn't cool," she quips, giving credit for the phrase to Ted Turner and country singer Barbara Mandrell.

I had the opportunity to talk with Dhue about her journalism experiences and the current state of the media.[1]

HIRSEN: What about this whole notion of bias? Do you think there really is such a thing as objectivity in reporting?

DHUE: There's objectivity on all of the networks. Some of the correspondents on CNN, NBC, ABC, CBS are more unbiased than others. I would say all of our straight news people at Fox are fair and balanced. That's our motto. The people who are straight reporters and anchors—who are not paid to give their opinions like Sean Hannity or Bill O'Reilly or Alan Colmes are paid to take one side or the other—I think are extremely fair. Yes, there is bias in journalism. I just happen to think there is not nearly as much of it at Fox as there is on the other networks.

HIRSEN: You're a very expressive person. Are you ever concerned that inadvertently an opinion will emerge through your gestures or facial expressions?

DHUE: That's a great question. I think I had to be more careful about that when I was first starting out. My first TV experience was on CNN. I had been a producer and a booker behind the scenes so I actually never had to do a small market thing. I was immediately an anchor on CNN. I think that I used to betray my feelings more than I do now. With experience obviously comes knowledge that you might need to back off from an expression that you're making.

On the other hand, if I'm sad about something, I'm not afraid to show it on air, just through what I'm doing with my mouth or what I'm doing with my eyebrows. Or if I'm excited or happy about a story, I'm not afraid to raise my eyebrows and put a smile on my face, because I think that's what the audience wants to see. The audience does not want to look at a robot. Those days are over. You know, I am often described as one of the pretty blond women on Fox. Yes, we all have personalities and that's something that Roger Ailes has not only appreciated but encouraged—to show some personality, darn it.

HIRSEN: You did the coverage of the Reagan funeral. That had to be emotional.

DHUE: Oh, my Lord! I've got to tell you. I was on [the air] the day after Reagan died. Greg Jarrett and I cohosted the two o'clock hour less than twenty-four hours after he died. I'm sure we all had long faces. It was very solemn. It was a very sad but also a very dignified time, and I think we all tried to convey that. But I know when I was doing some of the interviews with people who knew him or had worked with him, I am sure that I had a long face, and that's okay.

HIRSEN: Walter Cronkite cried over the death of John F. Kennedy—

DHUE: Oh, my God, Mike Wallace wept on *Larry King Live*. He couldn't even talk. Do you know how humanizing that is? And even as a fellow journalist and someone who has long respected Mike Wallace, it gave me the chills and it put tears in my eyes to see Mike Wallace crying.

HIRSEN: Is it different when you are acting as a moderator?

DHUE: When I'm moderating a political discussion, when I'm moderating a debate, I have to say that I try very hard not to nod my head in agreement or smile or frown if I agree or disagree. Sometimes it pops out, but I think we're all very careful to try not to do that unless, of course, you're Sean Hannity or Alan Colmes and you're being paid to do that.

HIRSEN: The whole advent of cable and twenty-four-hour cable news was such a change for journalism. Linda Ellerbee did a special on the subject called *Feeding the Beast*.

DHUE: Yes, yes, right.

HIRSEN: It seems to me that there is a tendency for news to compete with cable and cable to compete with tabloid. What is your take on how cable news has changed journalism—or has it?

DHUE: Sure. Sure it has. Cable itself has evolved so much since 1980, when everybody laughed at Ted Turner when he said, "I'm going to launch myself a twenty-four-hour news network."

Nobody's laughing now, and nobody laughed a few years later, and nobody was laughing after the Gulf War of 1991, which put CNN on the map. I'll tell you one thing that I was thinking about earlier. Something that Ted Turner once famously said to folks at CNN. He always said from the beginning, "News is the star; the anchors are not." And the exception was Larry King, who never has claimed, nor will he ever claim, to be a journalist. Larry King is in his own league. And he has said, "I'm not a journalist. I'm a talk show host."

HIRSEN: So Larry King is in the same category as Sean Hannity or Bill O'Reilly, in the sense that people understand his show is different from a news program?

DHUE: The anchors were never the stars on CNN. Fast-forward a few years and you've got big names on CNN. Some of those people became big names—Wolf Blitzer, because of his many years on CNN and his style. Bernie Shaw became well known because of CNN. Others were hired later, like Paula Zahn and Connie Chung. A lot of the names that are big today became big because of cable, like Shepard Smith, who is becoming a huge phenomenon. Nobody knew who he was a few years ago either. Katie Couric, Matt Lauer, and Diane Sawyer, they're all huge celebrities in their own right.

HIRSEN: The notion of a star, an entourage, a hefty salary—these are things that we associate with Hollywood. Do you think that these types of things are having an effect on the way that individuals cover the news?

DHUE: Is there an effect of celebrity and fame? Perhaps. Certainly it's an ego boost. I myself have quite a following. It is an ego boost, but I can only speak for anchors at Fox News Channel and for myself. I know it doesn't affect my ability to be a good journalist. And I don't think it affects anyone else's ability to be fair and balanced at all. Perhaps it garners us more viewers. Now perhaps there are more people watching because, "Oh, that's Shepard Smith. Oh, yeah, he's the guy I read about in *People* magazine. I want to see what he's all about." But no one walks around Fox and says, "Look how famous I am." Now, I can't speak for the other people at the other networks, because I've been gone for five years from CNN, so I don't know if people walk about like peacocks there.

HIRSEN: We're talking about fame. You yourself have a following. You have a following on the Internet.

DHUE: I know, I know.

HIRSEN: You have a glamorous image. There was a movie remake recently called *The Stepford Wives*.

DHUE: Yes.

HIRSEN: I've never heard anybody use this term, but is there a sort of "Stepford anchor" out there?

DHUE: Sure.

HIRSEN: In other words, people may point to Roger Ailes and wonder if he seeks out the glamorous image—the glamorous woman, in particular, although there is an equivalent in terms of a glamorous man. Do you feel a pressure or anything like that?

DHUE: I'll tell you what. Roger Ailes is a red-blooded American man and so are most of the executives who are running these networks. I'm not afraid to say that. Roger Ailes? Sure he likes attractive people, and he likes for us to look good. But looking good and being smart and being a good journalist, they're not mutually exclusive.

3

SEXING THINGS UP

The whole news star phenom is bringing other Tinseltown values into the info-dispensing setting, one of the most notable being—SEX.

As glitter would dictate in this Hollywood Nation, the emphasis on the buff and the beautiful is no longer limited to commercial, movie, and soap opera stars. Everyone seems to be getting younger, fitter, and ever more appealing to the eye—not just actors and models, but also politicians and, as it turns out, journalists.

Consider news anchors. In the past, anchors were typically fatherly-type figures. I guess the idea was that the public would feel most comfortable getting important information from a Ward Cleaver kind of character. For instance, in Cleaver-esque style, Walter Cronkite went from a well-liked parent to a much-admired grandparent personality during his time with the *CBS Evening News,* so much so that he gained the title of "the most trusted man in America." He even beat out the formidable NBC duo of Chet Huntley and David Brinkley.

The current crop of anchors is more of what we might call "Alpha male" in appearance and sound. Yeah, they've gone the Tom Cruise route. Funny thing is, though, for the up-and-comers especially, the leading-man male thing is working, and the star quality of the guys is definitely on the rise.

SEXIEST ANCHORMAN

The sex appeal of anchormen was thrust to the forefront in July 2004, when *Playgirl* magazine asked its readers to answer that all-important journalistic question "Which Anchor Would You Most Like to See in *Playgirl*?"

The magazine offered eighteen guys to choose from, including hunky eighty-five-year-old *60 Minutes* commentator Andy Rooney. Other contenders for hot dude anchor were the big-three network news honchos: CBS's Dan Rather, NBC's Tom Brokaw, and ABC's Peter Jennings. Rounding out the macho men of the microphone were Charlie Gibson, Matt Lauer, Harry Smith, Brian Williams, Bill Hemmer, Lester Holt, Anderson Cooper, Geraldo Rivera, Brit Hume, Shepard Smith, Ed Bradley, Wolf Blitzer, Keith Olbermann, and Sean Hannity.

The winner was to be announced in September 2004 and profiled in the magazine's October issue, and *Playgirl* pledged to make a contribution to a charity of the winner's choice. The most titillating offer was this one: the victor could pose nude for the magazine.

When I read about that proposal, I realized the *Playgirl* contest could give a whole different meaning to the term "news layout."

In the midst of the sexy search, *Playgirl* editor in chief Michele Zipp leaked early results to the *Washington Post*. Fox News's Hannity was in the lead at the time, with 2,000 votes, but Zipp was careful to add that CNN's Anderson Cooper and MSNBC's Keith Olbermann were "very close behind him" and that the results were "changing every hour."

Olbermann apparently made a push to overtake his competitors. The host of *Countdown* reportedly linked his own website to *Playgirl* magazine's and seemed to lobby vigorously for the win. It paid off: Despite the stiff competition, Olbermann won the Internet election, smug mug and all.

After the vote, there was a rumor that a recount was being planned. Guess some readers in Florida mistakenly cast their ballots for Pat Buchanan.

Olbermann opted not to pose in the buff, but he did get a fair amount of media attention for being named sexiest anchor. The whole episode just goes to show that when it comes to our newsmen, we're not necessarily looking for the most trusted sources anymore.

PAGING DR. BRIAN WILLIAMS

Even if anchors aren't choosing to pose nude, their looks have no doubt become an important part of the package. Just look at Brian Williams, the man who replaced Tom Brokaw at the NBC anchor's desk. Sure, Williams worked his way up the ladder in his more than two decades in the news business. But you have to admit the guy does look like he was sent straight from central casting.

Like many of his fellow newsmen, the NBC anchor is being treated more and more like a celebrity. A case in point came in 2004, when *TV Guide* covered a story about him the same way it might put out a piece on Paris Hilton. The *Guide* reveled in the soap opera–like quality of the scene.

Flying on the Delta shuttle from New York to Washington, D.C., Williams heard the flight attendant's voice come over the PA system, asking whether there was "a doctor on board." Although he has two honorary doctorates, Williams is not a medical doctor. In fact, he hasn't even played one on TV. Luckily, though, he is a former emergency medical technician and volunteer firefighter.

Williams ended up using his paramedical expertise to help a sixty-four-year-old passenger who was having difficulty breathing.

The newsman checked the man's blood pressure, gave him aspirin and water, and remained with him until the plane could return to LaGuardia, where a crew of paramedics was waiting.

When the ailing passenger recognized Williams, he quipped to *TV Guide,* "This is a hell of a way to get viewers." Which made me think: If the NBC execs thought it would boost the ratings, they'd probably dress Williams up in scrubs and stick him on *E.R.*

GLAM POWER

In case your cable box has been stuck on EWTN and you haven't noticed, images of the female body are everywhere. The feminine form is being used to market everything from gourmet meals to a new set of wheels. But now, it seems, some news divisions are using the feminine form to lure viewers.

Female journalists have come a long way in the past few decades, making inroads into what was once an almost entirely male-dominated industry. From the morning and daytime news programs, to the news magazine shows, to the network specials, and beyond, women have taken their chairs, desks, sofas, podiums, and stages. Things haven't necessarily been easy, though. And even some of the most accomplished women in the news industry have had to endure undue scrutiny of their appearance.

The premium placed on looks can actually cut two ways. Undoubtedly, some journalists—female and male—have received plum positions based more on their looks than on their journalistic talents, and that can undermine the quality of the news coverage that the public receives. At the same time, though, experienced and talented journalists who also happen to be attractive can have their credentials unfairly questioned.

Some television news divisions have been frank about their interest in hiring attractive people to draw in viewers. In 2004, for example, a local station in Fort Worth, Texas, created quite a stir by hiring a group of glamorous anchors. KTVT, also known as CBS 11, hired Suzanne Sena for its weekend programming, Maria Arita to do its evening slots, and Shannon Hori to coanchor its early-morning newscast. News director Tom Doerr gave his take on the station's personnel innovation. "There is some truth to the fact that viewers like attractive people," Doerr explained. "They can be fabulous-looking people, but if they're not intelligent, if they're not omniscient, if they're not acting as an interpreter of events and putting them into some context or perspective, they're not gonna be successful."[1] Evidently, the strategy worked for the station, as CBS 11's ratings began going up.

Arita, who had almost twenty years of television experience before landing the anchor position, explained how good looks had proved to be a mixed blessing. "Believe it or not, the beauty thing has not served me well at all," she told a reporter. She said that when she used to go to speak with people at CBS or ABC "to get their opinions on how to get to the next level, their answers were always, 'Well, you're much too attractive. I don't see it happening unless you start at the bottom rung.' And I'd already paid my dues for ten to twelve years at that point."[2]

Arita argued that CBS 11 was being "unfairly" singled out for hiring attractive women. "In the past," she pointed out, "people were usually very close-minded about that: 'How could you possibly be beautiful and smart at the same time?' . . . I think that [at CBS 11], if you are beautiful, that's a wonderful thing. But if the work doesn't tell the story about you, you're out."[3]

Could it be that Arita was experiencing "reverse lookism"? If so, she wouldn't be alone.

Like Arita, a talented, hardworking anchor named Alicia Booth learned that it's possible to be considered *too* attractive. Things were going along splendidly for Booth as an anchor at WCNC-TV in Charlotte, North Carolina. Then in a local weekly alternative newspaper she was voted the "sexiest woman in Charlotte." When her new status was made public, instead of beaming with pride over their attractive news personality, the powers that be at WCNC yanked Booth away from the anchor desk and demoted her to reporter.

Unfortunately for the TV station, this was all captured in a five-part PBS series called *Local News: One Station Fights the Odds.* This behind-the-scenes look at WCNC's newsroom revealed that the decision to reduce Booth's rank was based on focus-group research indicating that Booth was too attractive for the station's female viewers.

Perhaps it's not surprising, then, that some women in the news business—including Maria Arita—have tried to change their image in order to be taken more seriously. Arita, for instance, once threw away her makeup and donned eyeglasses. A famous example of a female journalist who did the same was Ashleigh Banfield. A one-time rock singer, Banfield decided to do a switch of persona and underwent an extreme makeover of the librarian kind, dyeing her blond tresses brown and putting on spectacles. She ended up landing a job on MSNBC and ultimately became a point person for the war on terror.

Banfield emerged as an emblem of MSNBC's effort to lure Gen-X viewers. The cable network apparently thought it had found the answer to its ratings doldrums. But then Banfield courted controversy when she criticized news departments—including her own—for their coverage of the Iraq War. Compounding the problem were rampant rumors of the reporter's diva-like demands. NBC reportedly gave Banfield the boot, so she went looking elsewhere for network and cable possibilities.

Though she was no longer working in prime time, Banfield's star power didn't disappear entirely. In fact, when she married Bloomberg Financial exec Howard Gould (the great-grandson of nineteenth-century railroad magnate Jay Gould) in the summer of 2004, the wedding received coverage in the widely read celebrity glossy *People* magazine. Sure enough, *People* asked her why she didn't wear her "trademark glasses" during the ceremony. "I was trying to look more feminine," Banfield responded, "and I didn't have any reading to do."

TAKING A POSITION

While being good-looking can sometimes complicate matters for people in the news biz, some journalists have shrewdly played on their looks to attract attention and advance their careers. Here we see another example of how, in our Hollywood Nation, the line between news and entertainment is being erased.

Consider Sharon Tay, the morning news anchor on the Los Angeles WB affiliate KTLA. In 2002, Tay and her news team collected an Emmy Award for the Best Regularly Scheduled Daily News. She had previously scored an Emmy for her work cohosting a KTLA community affairs program called *Making It: Minority Success Stories.* Those journalistic accomplishments, impressive as they are, didn't attract nearly the attention that Tay's outside activities did in 2004.

You see, Tay isn't just an anchor. She is also a pinup in a men's magazine.

Her home base is, after all, Los Angeles, the capital of glitz and glam, and she is blessed with movie star looks. Still, the sight of a morning news anchor posing seductively for the camera was enough to send journalism professors reaching for a cold compress.

Tay posed for *Razor,* a magazine in the same mold as the ones banned by Wal-Mart in 2003 (*Maxim, Stuff,* and *FHM*). In other words, she posed for a publication loaded with pictures of women wearing outfits that use very little in the way of fabric. She did an assortment of pics, one of which was an above-the-waist nude shot with only a couple of vital points protected. Tay has a website, too, which has photo clips and beauty tips to boot. But foldouts and e-spreads aside, Tay says she has no interest in modeling. "I'm way too short!" she insists.[4]

Funny, but the readers of *Razor* weren't all that concerned about Tay's height. It seems they had other measurements in mind.

Puffed-up profs and dogged detractors criticized Tay for her decision, saying that flaunting physical attributes obscured the border between show biz and news. For example, Martha Lauzen, a professor at San Diego State University who specializes in the treatment of women in the media, said that "anchors become celebrities, and celebrities become news. But appearing in men's magazines influences how viewers may perceive them. It can cause confusion, and a news organization has to take responsibility for that."[5] Another critic, Ron Fineman, who authors a website that critiques TV journalists, argued, "If a journalist is a serious news anchor, a certain public image should be maintained, and 'sex kitten' shouldn't be one of them." Tay also endured criticism from Professor Judith Marlane of California State University, Northridge, who served as head of news and affairs at WWOR-TV in New York and has written two books on the role of women in television news. Commenting on Tay's photos, Marlane said, "The blurring between news and entertainment has become so blatant in terms of the entertainment side of the equation that there really is no longer a blur." Marlane complained that female news anchors who pose for men's magazines demean the journalism profession and have "set women back, undermining all the years of advancement that have been made."[6]

KTLA Prime News anchor Hal Fishman, a well-known veteran and fixture in Los Angeles television news, spoke out in Tay's defense. In an on-air commentary, Fishman remarked, "A professor said what these women have done has demeaned the whole profession. I disagree. I think women have come so far in TV news that they are not judged by the blouse they wear."

A choice of blouse, though, may help propel a career. In spring 2005 MSNBC launched two new shows, *MSNBC at the Movies* and *MSNBC Entertainment Hot List*. The network proudly announced the host of both shows would be "Emmy Award–winning journalist Sharon Tay."

Tay has had some role models on the Left Coast who have also perplexed the media profs by using their feminine wiles to further their starry news horizons.

Jillian Barberie is the cohost of *Good Day L.A.* on KTTV and the sometimes host of the national version of the same show, *Good Day Live*. She discusses news and entertainment on the show with her two cohosts, Steve Edwards and Dorothy Lucey.

Hailing from Canada, she's parlayed her poster girl image into a thriving career. She's garnered lots of attention from the male population by doing football game–related weather reports on *Fox NFL Sunday*. For the show, she dubbed herself the "weather broad." She also uses her website to present herself as a glamorous Hollywood star, something she's fast becoming. She has been a cover girl for *FHM* magazine and has appeared on sitcoms like *Quintuplets* and *Good Morning, Miami,* and in films like *Cursed.*

Barberie's career highlights what Professor Marlane called the "blatant" emphasis on entertainment in today's news business. Barberie is listed on KTTV's website as part of the Fox 11 "News Team," but her TV persona is more of a personality as opposed to an anchor. She doesn't hold herself out to be a journalist, so maybe she ought not be held to the anchor standard, whatever that currently happens to be.

Another news story with sizzle involves L.A.'s local UPN affiliate, KCOP. In 1999, the station hired a female news anchor by the name of Lauren Sanchez for its late-evening newscast. Sanchez, whose first job in the media was as a news assistant for the network, came back to KCOP from the Fox Sports Network, where she had worked as an anchor for *Fox Sports Tonight* and on a sports series called *Going Deep.* She had also spent a period of time as a reporter at a local station in Phoenix, ABC's KTVK-TV, and on the entertainment show *Extra.*

Despite the fact that she has a solid background in journalism, Sanchez apparently likes to shake things up with her choice of apparel. She wears short skirts and micro tops to match. Her news delivery is unusual, too, with its brisk rhythm and contemporary dance music accompaniment. KCOP promotes the show as "news with attitude."

Evidently Sanchez showed some attitude outside of the news program as well. An extensive pictorial of her appeared in *Open Your Eyes (OYE),* a publication whose cover describes it as the "magazine for the modern Latino man." Although there was no nudity involved, Sanchez did appear in some OYE-popping outfits.

The piece on her was titled "News Flash!" with a subtitle that read, "If they had an award for America's hottest news anchor, we're confident Lauren Sanchez would win it." It seems that the *OYE* writer was more than just mildly enthusiastic as he shared these Sanchez thoughts: "Newscasters just aren't supposed to be this hot. At least that's what pops into my head every time I see Lauren Sanchez reporting on L.A.'s UPN 13 News. It's downright distracting. How's a man supposed to pay attention to what's going on in the world when the news anchor looks like she belongs on the Big Screen or—better yet—the Victoria's Secret catalog. But make no mistake about it: Lauren is more than just a pretty face."

Yeah, she's a pretty nice ratings-grabber.

ANCHORS GONE WILD

You may be wondering, with all the broadcast sensuality that's going on, are there any boundaries? Well, some limits of sorts were reached in a highly publicized case involving one journalist's extracurricular activities.

The drama begins with two contrasting scenes. The first one involves a journalist at the federal courthouse reporting on the 2002 ten-count corruption trial of former congressman James A. Traficant. The second one has a young woman competing with other women in a wet-T-shirt contest, where along with the others she strips naked and dances onstage. The twist comes in when it's realized that the character who appears in both scenes is one and the same.

This is the story of Catherine Bosley, a successful news anchor who ultimately resigned from her position at a CBS affiliate in Youngstown, Ohio. Bosley's story, as well as her anatomy, became public when photos of her *au naturel* night on the town were posted on the Internet.

Now, you might think that a female journalist shedding garments for prize-winning cash would be the stuff of a TV producer's ratings sweeps fantasy. Well, it was—just not for Bosley's station. The story went national in January 2004, when the photos went up on the web and Bosley stepped down after admitting she had entered the wet-T-shirt contest while on vacation with her husband in Florida. ABC's *Good Morning America* covered the story, with Diane Sawyer interviewing the Youngstown anchor about the controversy. *Fox News Watch* also devoted a segment to the Bosley story, as did ABC's *The View*.

For Youngstown's WKBN, the story only caused problems. Gary Coursen had been handed this controversy only a week after being promoted to the position of the station's news director. After Bosley handed in her resignation, Coursen posted the following on the WKBN website: "Catherine is a seasoned veteran who consciously chose to engage in behavior that she knew was inconsistent with the responsibilities of her chosen profession." He also indicated that "returning Catherine to the air would cast the department in a seedy, tabloid light."

Still, Coursen got "overwhelming negative feedback" from viewers about the decision to let Bosley go. "WKBN has done nothing. We did not dance nude, nor did we fire Catherine, yet we have somehow come out the bad guys," the news director wrote.

Jon Deniro, a Youngstown trucker, was so exasperated that he set up a website called Boycott WKBN. He pleaded with visitors to the site "to correct the injustice done to Catherine Bosley" by "writing letters, emails, or even telephoning WKBN TV 27, CBS headquarters, various other news media, and the sponsors and advertisers who do business with WKBN." In Deniro's view, Bosley's resignation "is in no way due to her job performance, it is based solely on her actions while she was on vacation 1,400 miles away from the TV newsroom. She did nothing illegal, nothing unethical, nothing that would offend the majority of people in our society, nothing that would cast doubts about her honesty, credibility, or integrity as a news reporter—and let's keep in mind that she was not in any way representing her employer WKBN at the time."

While most professional critics disagreed with Deniro, at least one media critic thought the hand-wringing about the wet-T-shirt contest was misguided. Media scholar Neal Gabler agreed that Bosley had "exercised poor judgment," but he thought the critics were missing the larger point. "You know once upon a time, anchormen and anchorwomen were hired for their journalistic credibility, for their journalistic talents," Gabler said. "But let's face it. In local news, anchorwomen and anchormen are hired because they are personable, because they are attractive, and because they know how to read a TelePrompTer. I don't see how appearing in a contest like this, wet-T-shirt or not, in any way compromises your personability, your ability to read a TelePrompTer, or your attractiveness. In fact, in this case, it may confirm it."

Gabler expressed the view that credibility, for many in journalism, is a figment of the imagination. "What she compromised here was the illusion of credibility. She wasn't a journalist. She didn't have some long, long history of reporting stories. It was the illusion of credibility she undermined. And I think you've got to kind of expose the hypocrisy of the station."[7]

Bosley brought a lawsuit against the many websites that had posted her name and naked image. She alleged that she had not given anyone permission to use her picture, much less to post it on the web. This resulted in a game of judicial Ping-Pong. On March 8, 2004, Judge James Gwin of the U.S. District Court in Cleveland, Ohio, granted a temporary restraining order blocking at least twenty Internet sites from continuing to display the pics of Bosley in the buff. On March 25, the Sixth U.S. Circuit Court of Appeals said that Gwin's order raised serious constitutional issues because it was a restraint on free speech. On March 31, Judge Gwin struck back, granting a preliminary injunction ordering the websites to once again remove the Bosley pics. On April 21, a three-judge panel of the United States Court of Appeals for the Sixth Circuit slapped Judge Gwin again by putting a hold on his order.

Unfortunately for Bosley, the damage had already been done. The name "Catherine Bosley" turned out to be the most searched name on the Internet for the week ending January 24, 2004, according to the Lycos.com newswire. Believe it or not, the e-search for Bosley's name even surpassed that of Paris Hilton.

FROM PERKY TO SULTRY

While Neal Gabler pointed out a reality of local television that many critics are loath to acknowledge, the fact is that appearance matters a heck of a lot in the world of national news as well. Take, for example, NBC's Katie Couric. You might say that Couric has undergone a media evolution of the mega-Hollywood kind. Her image metamorphosis is a textbook illustration of the growing emphasis that's being placed on clothing, fashion, appearance, and the like for TV journalists across the land.

If you search your memory bank, you'll probably recall the Katie who first captured America's early-morning heart. She was the fresh TV face who sported a pixie hairstyle, wore understated outfits, and had "perky" written all over her.

In February 1997 on CNN's *Larry King Live,* King kicked off an interview with Couric by asking her about her title on the *Today* show. "What are you officially? Coanchor?" he inquired. Couric made her reference preference known by saying, "Yes, coanchor. Not hostess."

Then King brought up something that made the coanchor bristle. He asked whether she liked the "perky" image. She responded, " 'Perky' is a word that tends to be a little bit demeaning, because I think it seems to indicate a certain vapidity that I don't feel like I possess." The term was, she said, "a subtle putdown." After all, she remarked, "I don't think you very often see a man being called perky."

Now flash-forward to the present. *Today*'s Katie is very different from yesterday's. She's grown her hair out, gotten a whole lot blonder, tightened her clothes, donned stiletto heels, and simulated the tan of Malibu Barbie.

During her career she's interviewed world leaders, political figures, presidents, first ladies, pop icons, and movie stars. But it seems the coanchor's defining moment, at least visually, took place in 2003 on a soundstage in Burbank, California.

In a May ratings sweeps idea that could have been called "host swap," the *Tonight Show*'s Jay Leno traded places for a day with the

Today show's Couric. In his new morning gig, Leno kept his jokes subdued and unblued. He interviewed then–secretary of state Colin Powell and former mayor Rudy Giuliani. One of his deeply probing questions went to Secretary Powell. He asked, "How hard is it to be a diplomat in the Middle East right now?"

Katie took to the evening time slot. She was apparently determined to shed her "perky" image. What she ended up doing was trading it in for a sexy one. The powers that be convinced her to have the front panel of the *Tonight Show* desk removed so that her glamorous gams and six-inch heels would be fully exposed. The girl-next-door was AWOL. In her place was a blond starlet in a short, black, snug-fitting, plunged-necked slip of a dress. Couric bowled the audience over during her opening monologue when she pointed directly at her cleavage and coolly said, "For all you people from L.A. who have never seen them before, these are actually real!" When she interviewed actor Mike Myers, he had three words to describe her outfit. "Look at you," Myers stated as he ogled in *Man Show*–like fashion. He added, "You are all . . ." Then he purred. Couric also interviewed *American Idol* judge Simon Cowell, where she put on a wig and played *Idol* judge Paula Abdul in a spoof of the highly rated show.

The new Katie instantly became the darling of the press and the talk of the town. And she earned herself a brand-new adjective. It appeared in headlines like "A Hot Time 'Tonight': Sexy Katie Sizzles—Ratings Up."[8] It turned up in the reviews of her performance that said things like "Early-bird sweetheart Katie Couric turned on her sex appeal during a rare night-time appearance."[9] It surfaced in papers that reported things like "Couric, meanwhile, showed off her sexy side."[10]

Nobody was calling her "perky" anymore. But come to think of it, they weren't calling her "anchor" either. Conversations about Couric's late-night appearance were reportedly centered on "her sexy, va-va-voom black dress that had guests talking about her attributes other than reporting."[11] As it turned out, those womanly attributes helped bring in 42 percent more viewers than Leno normally would.

In her book *Spin Sisters,* former *Ladies' Home Journal* editor Myrna Blyth attributed some Hollywood-style habits to Couric, including paying $550 for haircuts (Hey, that's even more than Bill Clinton paid for the one on the tarmac) and using the services of a personal trainer whose fees were rumored to be $7,500 a week. Blyth also wrote that "Katie loves to play up the fact that she's a typical frazzled working mom" but that this "typical" working mother pulled down a massive salary and probably lived in "a typical $3 million East Side Manhattan apartment." She wrote that "whenever possible, Katie shrewdly plays up her unique combination of being just like all the Soccer Moms out there and not being a bit like them."[12]

What? Don't all Soccer Moms these days wear Stuart Weitzman sneakers and Cambio jeans?

ZIPPING THINGS UP

It was an anchor swap of sorts. Paula Zahn was hired away from the Fox News Channel by CNN, while Greta Van Susteren left CNN for Fox. The publicity over each of the shows was blazing.

In Zahn's case, it came in the form of a lively visual and audio promo. CNN launched an ad campaign for its revamped A.M. news program, *American Morning.* Did the network tout Zahn's more than two decades of experience in the field? Not exactly. The ad, which ran about ten times on the cable news channel the weekend before the show debuted, featured an announcer asking the following question: "Where can you find a morning news anchor who's provocative, supersmart, oh yeah, and just a little sexy," at which point the music paused and the announcer crooned, "CNN. Yeah, CNN."

The words "smart," "provocative," and "sexy" were flashed on the screen, along with some shots of Zahn's profile and lips. The background music came to an abrupt halt and what replaced it was the unmistakable sound of a zipper.

The ad was pulled after its one-weekend run.

The executive who purportedly okayed the Zahn ad was Jamie

Kellner, who had launched both the Fox and WB networks and now had been tapped to reinvigorate CNN. His Hollywood influence had been noted when he had hired Andrea Thompson to be a news anchor for *Headline News.* She's the actress who had exposed on *NYPD Blue* whatever body parts the FCC then allowed. When nude photos of Thompson showed up on the Internet, Kellner's decision became even more controversial.

With regard to the Zahn ad, CNN chairman and CEO Walter Isaacson said in a statement, "It was a major blunder by our promo department." He added that "the ad was never seen or approved by anyone outside the promo department. I was outraged, and so was Paula Zahn, who has spent more than twenty years proving her credibility day in and day out on the air."

Zahn herself said in a statement, "I had no knowledge of the promo until it aired; when I saw it I was offended."

I spoke with Fox News anchor Laurie Dhue about the zipper commercial. Dhue, who has also worked at CNN and MSNBC, found it somewhat difficult to accept Zahn's statement. She believes that the normal protocol of a cable news organization would necessitate Zahn's approval of the ad. "You'd have to sign off on that," Dhue explained. "I know how Fox works. If they were going to run a promo like that I would think they'd say, 'Hey, you know what, Laurie? We're going to do a zipper sound.' And I'd probably say, 'Sure. That's funny, that's great. Do it.' "[13] Dhue acknowledged that the ad might have been in poor taste. But she also remarked, "I just thought it was interesting the way they [CNN] backpedaled less than twenty-four hours later."[14]

In the other half of the anchor swap, the attention focused on Greta Van Susteren and also involved her looks. Van Susteren went public with the story of how she'd had a little work done between the time she left CNN and the debut of her new Fox show. She told the *Washington Post* that she had the "indentations" removed from under her eyes.

But photos hinted that a much more dramatic makeover may have taken place. Experts were chatting about a plethora of look-altering procedural possibilities. Van Susteren's promo videos

looked very different from the CNN image that folks remembered. She had been converted from a tough-talking, take-no-
prisoners former defense lawyer into a bona fide info-babe. The
eye indentation removal seemed to have transformed her hair, skin
tone, teeth—just about every square inch of her face.

The publicity generated from Van Susteren's new image paid
off, establishing the audience for her budding Fox program.
Maybe CNN should have kept the zipper around a bit longer.

The interesting thing is, though, that Hollywood makeovers
used to be whispered about in posh Beverly Hills bistros. Now
they were basically being bragged about.

It has become somewhat unnerving. I keep thinking about that
old *Twilight Zone* episode where everyone looked identical. Are
we really all going to end up someday with the same body and
face? Because it sure seems that the men and women who are having the mounting peels, sucks, shots, and tucks are looking eerily
twinlike.

When you start to talk to folks, especially those whose looks
play a pivotal role in their work—that is, media and Hollywood
personalities—the issue gets to be a little sticky. But I understand
the phenomenon within the industry. It's just something that now
more than ever goes with the territory.

Dayna Devon, the host of *Extra,* is familiar with the plastic
surgery trend. Her husband is one of the surgeons on the reality
show *Extreme Makeover.* Devon has noticed how the folks in Idaho
and Omaha are having makeovers of their own. She sees a connection with celebrity obsession and the Xerox copying that's occurring in places all over the country.

Celebrity illusion seems to have laid the groundwork for today's
obsession with looks. "It's funny, because, going back to my teenage years and looking at those covers of magazines, I didn't know
at the time that they were airbrushed," Devon tells me.[15]

In photos, imperfections can be and usually are eliminated.
Devon describes what happens at a glamour shoot, explaining that
hours are spent in hair and makeup and every wrinkle is removed.

"I used to spend a lot of time really trying to look like those magazine covers," Devon admits. "Then I had a more realistic expectation after a lot of that [information] became more public."[16]

Devon notes that there's starting to be "a little bit of a backlash." She gives an example to illustrate what she means. "If you've noticed some of the tabloids lately . . . you've seen the cellulite on the front covers, and they show these huge, full-page pictures of all these celebrities getting in and out of cars, bending over at the beach, whatever." She sees how celebrity cellulite is being outed, so to speak, and thinks that "the pendulum is swinging the other direction. It's more, not how beautiful and how great they are, but that they're just like you."[17]

STAR SEARCH

Hollywood's worship of perfection in general, and its dismissive approach toward actresses of the chronologically unacceptable kind specifically, was the subject of a unique documentary put together by actress Rosanna Arquette. In *Searching for Debra Winger,* Arquette interviews a few dozen actresses and one film critic on the subject of age as it relates to women in the industry.

The movie's title was inspired by Winger's unusual exit from the Hollywood scene. In *Searching,* Winger recounts how the producer Don Simpson approached her on the set of the film *An Officer and a Gentleman* and did something that would ultimately, years later, inspire her to walk away from Tinseltown. She says, "You know, rest his soul, Don Simpson, who was then at Paramount, came to my door the second day of— You know, I was young. I'm trying to think how old I was. I think I was twenty-four, twenty-three—and knocked on my door and gave me a little manila envelope, which usually means drugs. And I looked at it and he said, 'Umm, you know, we watched the dailies—little bloated.' And it was a water retention pill."[18]

Winger looks on that incident as a turning point in her life. She continued, "I mean I look back on that now. I can't say, 'cause it's too dirty, what I said in response, but I think that in that moment you can be made or broken, really. And for some reason. I mean I wasn't made in that moment. I didn't rise up and say, 'Oh, now I know.' You know, I didn't become a feminist out of that, which maybe I should have, and I also didn't get broken. I had to struggle a lot but I knew it was wrong. I knew that it wasn't about my face, or it wasn't about somebody like that running my life."[19]

It took Winger several years to muster the strength to let go of her career. At the age of just thirty-nine, Winger gave it all up.

Although Winger looks like she could mount a big-screen comeback anytime she wishes, plenty of actresses today say that there are obstacles to getting work when forty is looming. The other actresses featured in Arquette's film seemed eager to let out their grievances on that subject. For example, Frances McDormand tells about a conversation she had with friend and fellow Oscar winner Holly Hunter that centered on whether or not to go under the knife. She says, "There's a really important reason why one must not succumb to the idea of plastic surgery in our profession. Because in ten years' time, stories are going to need to be told about—I'm forty-four—they're going to need to be told about fifty-four-year-old women, and there's not going to be any women that look like they're fifty-four [Laughs]. So I said, 'Listen, Holly, if you can hold on, darlin', we're going to corner the market—we'll all corner the market. When they need a nice fifty-four-year-old-looking woman, we'll be there."[20]

Similarly, Tracey Ullman says, "[It's] really disturbing to me to see women of thirty-six [years of age] in this country being so frightened of getting old. And using this Botox and [goes into character] 'Honey, I've got collagen. I gotta put ice on my lip. Honey, I have—you know you'd never know. My surgeon's an artist.' It breaks my heart. I think there's more dignity in aging in France, in England and Europe, where I'm from. I think you see many more women having better careers in their fifties and sixties. And here, I mean Gene Hackman, Al Pacino, Sean Connery—name three women of that age that are still working."[21]

Whoopi Goldberg has an in-your-face take on the subject. In *Searching,* she says that the "reality is that most people look like me. . . . I'm cute, but ****, honey, you know, this is

Hollywood—this is a different world. And what is considered to be—and we see it, because all these women cut their bodies up. They cut their faces up. It's creepy. And they are sort of reproducing [Laughs] like an amoeba."[22]

The pressure on women to look forever young and beautiful has now spread beyond Hollywood to the world of television journalism. At a youngish age, *Celebrity Justice* anchor Holly Herbert tells me that she already feels the pressure. "It's been thrown in our faces, and it is true," she explains. "I hear it all the time: 'Oh, you know, you've only got so many years left,' and that does scare me. In my head, I'm twenty years old, but I know time is ticking." Herbert wonders, "Who is going to take over for these women? I mean are they going to have twenty-something women become the next Barbara Walters?"[23]

Laurie Dhue, who has seen the Arquette film, tells me that female anchors have "shelf lives," but she believes that "the shelf lives of women journalists are a lot longer than they used to be. She points to Barbara Walters, who is "still very much in the game." She mentions other prominent women in the news business, such as Diane Sawyer, who "I think is nearing sixty years old, and Meredith Vieira, Lesley Stahl, and on and on and on. . . . I think that the staying power for women and men is a lot longer because our society is getting older. You're going to have more baby boomers around so why not have the people in the news reflect that?"[24]

While Dhue offers a more optimistic perspective than some other critics do, she acknowledges that women do feel pressure to turn to plastic surgery and other techniques to perpetuate youth. She comments, "I think women in general are having more plastic surgery than they used to. So if television news anchors are a microcosm of that, then sure. I think we will be seeing women, as they get older, perhaps having some procedures. I don't think everyone will."[25]

In fact, Dhue believes plastic surgery is more widespread than people think. She says, "There are plenty of people on CNN, on MSNBC, on Fox who have had work done. Not just Greta. And if it makes you look better, that's great. I do not have a problem with it. There may come a day in my life where I choose to have a procedure, and if I do I will probably keep it to myself. But I don't have a problem with it whatsoever. It doesn't make you any less of a journalist or any less of a person."[26]

The whole "sexing things up" phenomenon may not make one any less of a journalist, but it does seem to be changing the face of those who transmit information via visual images.

And it's definitely had a rosy effect on the lip gloss industry.

Holly Court

Holly Herbert is an eleven-year television news veteran, who has anchored and reported in Los Angeles, Miami, and San Diego, among other markets.

Herbert reported from the field on the 9/11 terrorist attacks, the 2000 Florida presidential recount, the 1997 Heaven's Gate cult mass suicide, and the 1994 Northridge earthquake. She was also on the scene daily in Miami for the duration of the Elián González saga.

Herbert has been the host of the nationally syndicated TV show *Celebrity Justice* since its debut in September 2002.

I talked with Herbert about truth, justice, and the celebrity way.[1]

HIRSEN: It seems that your timing to become anchor on *Celebrity Justice* couldn't have been better. I can't remember a time when there have been as many celebrity court antics as there are now.

HERBERT: I'm not really sure. To me there have always been celebrity cases out there. It's just over the past several years more and more outlets are covering stories like these. Think about it. There are cable news channels, Court TV . . . so I think they [the stories] have been out there, but news is changing. The celebrity cases, people are hearing about them more and more. That's *Celebrity Justice.* We are designed to cover these cases.

HIRSEN: You mentioned that the stories have been brought onto cable and onto other news shows. Do you see a difference in the way your show is covering them and the way you used to cover them as part of a regular newscast?

HERBERT: I've been doing news over the past ten years. I do think that celebrities have increasingly become more of a day-to-day story in the newscast. Maybe fifteen years ago, you'd be talking about a board meeting that you were going to cover. Well, people aren't going to be interested in that anymore. Now especially in Los Angeles [celebrities are] leading the local newscast many times.

As far as the difference from my work as an anchor reporter and doing *Celebrity Justice,* I cover every story the same way—gathering facts, getting the interviews, putting the story together, and telling both sides. So there's really no difference as far as how I put together, and how I deal with the celebrity case, versus a noncelebrity case. But there is absolutely a certain level of frenzy in the air when you are covering a story that involves a celebrity. I was down there for Winona Ryder [shoplifting case] and at the time I was actually working for KABC, the local news station, and . . . I was on my cell phone, we had several camera crews, one at each door. . . . It's all done in secrecy, bringing the celebrity in and whatnot, and you're just running all over the place trying to get a picture, because if you don't get it, chances are another station is going to.

HIRSEN: I wonder about your take on the legal system. They've done polls with the public, and some of the polls say that the stars can't get a fair shake, particularly in the black community—the reaction to O.J. Simpson and to Kobe Bryant. But on the other hand, there's the notion that somehow it's a two-tiered system; that because celebrities are generally wealthy, they can hire the best lawyers and they can "work the system." Do you have any thoughts on these two views?

HERBERT: I have to tell you, it's a question that everybody asks me and I can never answer with a simple yes or no. It's always a case-by-case basis. It's open to interpretation. A lot of it, I think, depends on your predisposition, on whether you like that celebrity or not. As far as my experience and some of the people that I have talked to, I do think that prosecutors tend to be more careful in dealing with a celebrity case, because all eyes are on them. A lot more people are watching. There are a lot more who are following the case, not only professionally but personally as well, watching their every move. And so I think there's a lot at stake for the prosecution. . . . I think that when it's a high-profile celebrity case, a lot of people automatically just assume that the celebrity is being treated differently.

HIRSEN: Do you think we are obsessed with fame and celebrity and entertainment?

HERBERT: Celebrity-obsessed—it's a very interesting term. I think people are fascinated by them because here they are. They have all this money. They live these fairy-tale lives. We love to know what's going on, hungry for the latest information. Then you get a celebrity who gets into trouble or who is dealing with some type of legal issue, and that's even more interesting on many levels. I mean it just adds. It's kind of like it's your life, but bigger. As far as some of the legal issues that they are going through . . . I think a lot of people can identify maybe more with the celebrity. They are human.

HIRSEN: Television is a visual medium and image is such a big part of it. This was brought to the surface, I think, particularly in the story of Greta Van Susteren, who was public about her make-over as she moved from CNN to Fox. I think today men and women alike feel a pressure and are image-conscious, especially in the television industry. I wondered about your thoughts on that.

HERBERT: Well, I have a lot of thoughts on what you said. It's a well-known fact that men, older men, have [more] longevity in the business than women do. You see a lot more older men in television than you do women. I wish it wasn't like that. I hope to God that it changes. Absolutely there is a pressure on many levels to look good. My focus personally is I'm a journalist. . . . My first concern is making sure that my story is correct.

Don't get me wrong. I mean I want to look good. I try my best. . . . People, I think, are interested in the eye candy part of it as well. I still personally hope that my journalism, and paying my dues, and my education, and learning my craft and all, mean something.

HIRSEN: You know this from covering *Celebrity Justice* that the celebrities in Hollywood have an entourage that sometimes shields them from the outside world, and they can lose contact. For a reporter/journalist to have the trappings of celebrity, does that conflict with the craft of getting to the facts or keeping in touch with the community?

HERBERT: I think that times are changing and you are seeing now more on-air people who have no experience whatsoever except for they either look good or they know somebody. And I think there are a lot of unqualified people out there. But they are entertaining and they look good. So it's a battle because there are, I guess, news outlets that need those kinds of people or want those kinds of people instead of the true journalists.

HIRSEN: There's so much talk about bias. What do you think about journalists and objectivity?

HERBERT: That's your job—to be objective.

HIRSEN: Nobody criticized people who cried while reporting that JFK was shot. Walter Cronkite shed a tear. But there was some criticism over the coverage of 9/11—for example, how Reuters said the word "terrorists" should not be used. You're involved in very emotional subjects with people who are, in some cases, beloved and others hated. So how do you deal with that, how do you deal with your own humanity?

HERBERT: You know, I think it's very hard because you are taught to be objective, fair, balanced. I've got to have the other side. And people notice that. All I can say is, as far as being objective, you do the best that you can. But, you know, journalists are people, too. And I can remember countless times where I have had to go and knock on someone's door who had just lost a child in a tragic accident. And it's just impossible to keep yourself together.

HIRSEN: So, Holly, like on your show, if there ought to be a law, what law would you—

HERBERT: Oh, boy. I love that because I am asked that question all the time and you know what? I never have an answer. There ought to be a law that—I guess that you're paying your dues, and working hard, and using your experience, and it pays off in the end when you get older. How about that?

4

INFO MANIA

News legend Edward R. Murrow once said that there is no such thing as true objectivity in handling the news. In his view, the job of a reporter is "to know one's own prejudices and try to do the best you can to be fair."[1] Not a bad approach to take in the news biz, or in life.

As Murrow suggested, objectivity and fairness inhabit the realm of the ideal. We innately know that they can never be completely or consistently attained. After all, reporters are human beings. (At least that's what we teach in journalism school.) And that means they can't really have pure mental, emotional, and spiritual independence from the subject matter they're dealing with. No doubt they'll have opinions on government, religion, politics, the environment, war and peace, social issues—you name it. They are likely to be registered with a political party and may even give campaign contributions or involve themselves in grassroots organizations. They will hail from a specific geographic area and have economic, cultural, and community components soldered on their internal circuitry. They will be of a specific race, ethnicity, and gender that will have contributed to the shaping of their world-view and societal outlook.

They think about being accepted by their peers, too. Instead of letting ethics steer them, they are often driven by "a desire to be 'in the club' with other journalists," as family therapist and talk radio host Laura Schlessinger puts it.[2]

Communication professionals make decisions about what is newsworthy, noteworthy, and unworthy. The question then arises, Worthy according to what standard? Is it that which is most important to corporate owners? Is it that which will draw the most readers, listeners, or viewers? Is it that which is most compelling? The answer is Yes, Yes, Yes, and then some. Whatever the means of measurement, one thing is for certain: It is impossible to select the content itself without first peering through a lens that is shaded by a personal perspective.

All that said, we should still expect journalists to *strive* to achieve objectivity—or as Murrow put it, to recognize personal bias and do one's best to be fair. But many big-time news figures simply refuse to acknowledge any prejudices. Peter Jennings of ABC described colleagues as being "largely in the center without particular axes to grind, without ideologies which are represented in our daily coverage—at least certainly not on purpose."[3] NBC's now-retired Tom Brokaw was especially adamant about the topic: "The idea that we would set out, consciously or unconsciously, to put some kind of ideological framework over what we're doing is nonsense," he affirmed.[4] And CBS's Dan Rather weighed in on the subject by saying, "I've worked around reporters all my life. Most reporters, when you get to know them, would fall in the general category of kind of commonsense moderates."[5]

But like a mosquito sitting atop the Leaning Tower of Pisa, the typical metropolitan media figure may simply be unaware of his or her tilted view of the world. For many in the news business, their ideological slant goes unrecognized (by them, anyway) but nevertheless profoundly shapes how they present information to the public.

WHO'S GOT THE BIAS?

A fairly substantial percentage of people are unhappy with the current news situation. Polls taken about the press indicate that the public is not particularly pleased with the job that the news notables are doing. The percentage of people who think the press is properly performing that all-essential duty of safeguarding our representative democracy fell from 55 percent in 1985 to 45 percent in 1999.[6]

It seems, too, that the public is developing a cynicism about the news media. A survey published in 2004 found that a majority of Americans (53 percent) agree with the statement "I often don't trust what news organizations are saying." And while 43 percent disagree with the statement, only 9 percent completely disagree with it.[7] The lack of confidence in news organizations appears to cross political party lines. Approximately six in ten Republicans (58 percent) say they often do not trust what news organizations report, and almost half of Democrats feel the same way about what they're hearing from the media pros. Regrettably, almost half of the public (48 percent) are of the opinion that "people who decide what to put on TV news or in the newspapers are out of touch with people like me."[8]

Radio talk show host and *New York Times* best-selling author Michael Savage remembers being a kid and seeing Walter Cronkite's face on his flickering Philco television set. "He was the voice of America. I trusted him," he admits. "Now I see that Walter Cronkite, Dan Rather, and Peter Jennings are not the trusted father figures I grew up believing them to be. To me, back then, they were Mount Rushmore. They were the truth-sayers. The best in their field." Savage laments, "Today I have found out the granite that I thought they were made of was really nothing but feldspar. Never in my lifetime have I witnessed such a breakdown in journalistic integrity."[9]

For a few decades, most complaints about bias in the mainstream media came from the right side of the political spectrum. But it wasn't until recent years that the argument really gained traction and inspired serious debate in this country. Leading the way were conservative tomes on the subject of media bias, most notably Bernard Goldberg's *Bias: A CBS Insider Exposes How the Media Distort the News* and *Arrogance: Rescuing America from the Media Elite,* William McGowan's *Coloring the News: How Crusading for Diversity Has Corrupted American Journalism,* and Ann Coulter's *Slander: Liberal Lies About the American Right.* These and other commentators documented example after example of how liberal ideology distorts much of the information we receive from the news media.

Such arguments prompted some high-profile liberal leaners to abandon the sort of defense that Peter Jennings, Tom Brokaw, and Dan Rather have attempted. They no longer say that journalists are moderates who have no pronounced ideologies. Instead they've adopted a new line of argument: that the media slant to the *right.*

I know that upon reading this statement, throngs of you are having laughing fits. But hysteria and incredulity aside, this is the view that many journalists, authors, and Hollywood celebs have adopted, and this questionable concept is being disseminated in some sneaky ways.

To begin, the conservative arguments spurred left-leaning authors to churn out books as fast as Barbra Streisand can blog a Bush bash. So now we've got Greg Palast's *The Best Democracy Money Can Buy,* Joe Conason's *Big Lies: The Right-Wing Propaganda Machine and How It Distorts the Truth,* Al Franken's *Lies and the Lying Liars Who Tell Them: A Fair and Balanced Look at the Right,* David Brock's *The Republican Noise Machine: Right-Wing Media and How It Corrupts Democracy,* and Eric Alterman's *What Liberal Media?: The Truth About Bias and the News,* just to name a few.

As you will see, the subject of media bias is just something that seems to make fingers point in every direction.

AN INSIDER TALKS

In 1996, Bernard Goldberg wrote a story for the *Wall Street Journal* that had a lot of folks in the mainstream media shaking in their industry boots. In his article, Goldberg shared his views on the lack of objectivity that existed in network news. What caused the wave of journalistic jitters was not just the revelation itself, but also who it was doing the talking. You see, Goldberg worked at CBS News. He'd been there since 1972. Much to the disappointment of those who wanted to attack him, it turned out that Goldberg had been a supporter of George McGovern. He had voted against Ronald Reagan. He was pro-choice and pro–gay rights. No way was he a card-carrying member of the "vast right-wing conspiracy." Yet here he was hanging some unwashed linen out on the clothesline.

In the two books he subsequently wrote, *Bias* and *Arrogance,* Goldberg argues that members of the media are cut off from the majority of Americans. Anchors, reporters, news writers, and their fellow travelers reinforce one another's views, and they simply take for granted that most people share their perspective. In other words, Manhattan-based media mavens presuppose that their underlying views on the major issues of the day are the correct ones.

Goldberg writes that most journalists are "people who see themselves as incredibly decent, even noble. They're the good guys trying to make the world a better place. That's why many of them went into journalism in the first place—to make the world a better place. Bias is something the bad guys are guilty of. So rather than look honestly at themselves and their profession, they hang on for dear life to the ludicrous position, *to the completely absurd notion,* that they, among all human beings, are unique—that only they have the ability to set aside their personal feelings and their beliefs and report the news free of any biases."[10]

He cites the huge and growing stack of data substantiating

his view. Goldberg writes that "the uncomfortable truth—uncomfortable for ideologues on the Left, anyway—is that there now exists 'a huge body of literature—including at least 100 books and research monographs—documenting a widespread left-wing bias in the news,' according to Ted Smith III of Virginia Commonwealth University, who has done extensive research into the subject. And much of the evidence comes *not* from conservatives with axes to grind but straight from the journalists themselves, who in survey after survey have identified themselves as liberal on all the big, important social issues of our time."[11]

Before the release of his first book, Goldberg received plaudits for his reporting. For example, *Washington Post* TV critic Tom Shales called him "one of the brainiest network news correspondents." Goldberg also received six Emmy Awards and was the lead reporter on a program that won a Peabody Award. But after *Bias* came out, critics somehow argued that he had written the book because he was a rotten journalist and wanted to get back at his former supervisors.

And they say that the backbiting in *Hollywood* is bad.

DISTORTIONS, DIGS, AND DOUBLE STANDARDS

One argument that Goldberg likes to make—and that many critics have taken issue with—is that journalists almost invariably identify conservatives as such but often don't give labels to liberals. While appearing on CNN's *Reliable Sources* on March 23, 2002, for example, Goldberg summed up the biased branding by saying, "The only time the news media utter the words 'left wing' is when they are talking about an airplane." And in *Bias* he writes that during the Clinton impeachment trial in 1999, ABC's Peter Jennings "made sure his audience knew which senators were *conservative*—but uttered not a word about which ones were *liberal*."[12]

Are these unsubstantiated claims made by a disgruntled journalist, as some critics suggest? Uh, not really. Consider the in-depth study produced by two Stanford University scholars, David Brady and Jonathan Ma, in 2003. Brady and Ma examined articles published in the *New York Times* and the *Washington Post* between 1990 and 2002 and discovered that Goldberg's basic premise was correct. They concluded that the labeling problem—that is, identifying those on the Right as conservative but leaving off the label of those on the Left—was "endemic." For example, the study found that over the course of six congressional sessions, the *Times* and the *Post* labeled conservative senators up to five times as often as they did liberal senators.

And even when the liberal label was applied, reporters often presented liberals in a more favorable light than conservatives. For example, during the 102nd Congress, various *New York Times* stories described Senator Tom Harkin as "a kindred liberal Democrat from Iowa," "a liberal intellectual," a "respected mid-western liberal," and "a good old-fashioned liberal." And Senator Ted Kennedy of Massachusetts was called a "liberal icon," "a liberal spokesman," and "the party's old-school liberal." Senator Barbara Boxer of California was praised as a "reliably outspoken liberal."

What about the guys on the Right? Well, the *Times*'s descriptions of them were a lot more colorful and a lot less kind. Senator Jesse Helms was labeled as "the most unyielding conservative," "the unyielding conservative Republican," "the contentious conservative," "the Republican arch-conservative," and "perhaps the most tenacious and quarrelsome conservative in the Senate." Reporters made it a point to wallop Senator Malcolm Wallop of Wyoming with the words "very conservative." And Senator Don Nickles of Oklahoma was dinged with the distinction of being "one of the most conservative elected officials in America." Senator John Kyl of Arizona was given the appellation "a Republican hard-liner." Senator Phil Gramm was said to have "touched on many red-meat conservative topics" and was categorized as "the highly partisan conservative Texan." Senator Sam Brownback of Kansas was called "a hardcore conservative" and a "hard-line conservative and one of Newt Gingrich's foot soldiers." Senator Larry Craig of Idaho was dubbed "an arch-conservative."

The *Washington Post* followed the same pattern as the *Times*. The paper lauded Senator Paul Sarbanes of Maryland as "one of the more liberal senators but [with] a record of working with Republicans." Senator Harkin was bathed in bipartisan light as being an example of "a prairie populist with a generally liberal record, although he's made a few detours to more conservative positions demanded by his Iowa constituents." The *Post* said this about Senator Carol Moseley Braun of Illinois, who later ran for president to the left of Howard Dean: "Though a liberal at heart, she is more pragmatic than ideological." And about Senator Ted Kennedy, the *Post* gushed that he was "a hero to liberals and a major irritant to conservatives" and that he had "an old-style liberal appeal to conscience."

So what did the *Washington Post* have to say about the senators on the Right? Well, it apparently had some tilted titles it felt compelled to dispense. The paper described Senator James Inhofe of Oklahoma as "a hard-line GOP conservative." And Senator Helms was nothing less than "a cantankerous, deeply conservative chairman" and "a crusty senator from North Carolina."

It's clear that Helms was nothing like the cheerful, happy-go-leaky Patrick Leahy.

COULTER COMBAT

Ann Coulter has also contributed to the case against the liberal media with her best-selling book *Slander: Liberal Lies About the American Right*. She agrees that the news media have peculiar labeling habits. In *Slander* she writes that "adjectives like 'moderate' and 'far right wing' are a crucial part of the journalistic rewards system for politicians. It is how pompously boring newspapers and magazines hurl epithets at politicians they don't like and suck up to the ones they do." And she notes that when a label is softened, like when the term "moderate" is placed in front of the word "Republican," it "is simply how the blabocracy flatters Republicans who vote with the Democrats."[13]

Commenting on the political leanings of members of the media, Coulter observes that "the media elites covering national politics would be indistinguishable from the Democratic Party

except the Democratic Party isn't liberal enough. A higher percentage of the Washington press corps voted for Clinton in 1992
than did this demographic category: 'Registered Democrats.' "[14]

And she hits libs on the Upper West Side of Manhattan with a
hypocrisy hammer, noting that "most of the time, liberals do not
imagine the world is real. Their contribution to political debate is
worthless, since even they do not believe things they say. The
more shocking and iconoclastic they are, the more fashion points
they accrue. Liberal Manhattanites believe in redistribution of
their own wealth and ceaseless police brutality like they believe in
Martians."[15]

When I kibitzed with Coulter, I explored these and other topics related to media bias.

First I asked, "Do you believe there has ever been neutrality
in journalism?" She answered with an unequivocal "No." She
remarked that "the *New York Times* has introduced an odious
practice. Faux neutrality is support of sedition."[16]

I then asked whether she thinks that the network morning
shows such as *Today* and *Good Morning America* are affecting the news. She returned to the wording of her book, character-
izing Katie Couric as "the affable Eva Braun of morning
television," and added, "I suppose they affect the news by not reporting it."

Coulter's cynicism seemed to be thrown into full throttle when
I asked her whether the profession of journalism has lost its ethical
foundation. "Point one," Coulter said, "since when is journalism a
'profession'?" She continued wheeling down the questioning road
with "What counts as a journalist? Do TV weathermen count?
Do TV sport broadcasters count?" She then gave America's sweetheart one more flick, asking, "Does Katie Couric count?"

Even if journalism is not really a "profession," Coulter believes
its standards are comparable to the world's oldest one. She re-
torted, "Asking when journalism lost its ethical foundation is like
asking when Communism lost its sense of humor. When did
prostitution lose its moral footing?"

PC PAINTBRUSH

In his book *Coloring the News,* William McGowan takes a closer look at one particular component of media bias: the news media's apparent obsession with diversity. McGowan shows how the news industry seems to be going out of its way to make sure that both journalists and their news coverage are PC-approved.

"Almost every major news organization," he writes, "has mounted a 'pluralism plan' with aggressive hiring and promotion goals, and created a special 'diversity steering committee' to oversee it." McGowan also points out that "special fellowship programs" have been established to achieve the proper multicultural status in America's newsrooms. And he notes that "at an increasing number of news organizations, the pay and promotion opportunities of senior editors are linked to the number of minority journalists they hire, retain and promote."[17]

(Interestingly, here too we see news organizations succumbing to the same pressures that Hollywood is. Throughout its long and remarkably successful run, the sitcom *Friends* received criticism from special interest groups because almost all the show's characters were white. Evidently, the cast didn't look enough like America, it didn't have people of color, it didn't have any Arab students on temporary visas, it didn't have a transgender glee club . . . .you know the drill. All the nagging at the producers finally paid off in 2003, as *Friends* added a black female paleontologist to the cast. Producers had reportedly put out a call specifically for a woman who was black, Hispanic, Asian, Middle Eastern, and/or Native American.)

The diversity shenanigans are not just confined to the personnel department. In the actual news coverage, facts that might be contrary to certain prodiversity views are disregarded. Special assignments and columns are reserved for coverage of minority issues. McGowan argues that news organizations do all this to encourage "what the news industry refers to as 'separate and distinct minority points of view.' "[18]

The American Society of Newspaper Editors has even created a job category with the dubious title of Diversity Director. News organizations have developed style guides to ensure that they show proper PC sensitivity toward matters of race, ethnicity, and sexual preference. In addition, newspapers have revised their photo policies and are using images that have the approved diversity look. And of course, like every other PC employer, the information media conduct seminars to teach the fine points of diversity hiring, diversity management, and diversity Simon Says.

With all this stress on diversity, we have to wonder if the emphasis is also swallowing up objectivity in news coverage. The issue of immigration provides a good example for analysis purposes. McGowan states that journalists approach the subject of immigration using "a highly romantic, sentimental and historically distorted script which assumes immigration to be an unqualified blessing and minimizes its costs." The significance of assimilation is summarily brushed aside by what he calls "journalistic avoidance or tepid cultural relativism."[19]

The diversity decree is also altering coverage of stories involving black people. According to McGowan, fear of offending the African-American community has led news organizations to soft-pedal, or even ignore, crimes committed by black people, especially when they might indicate anti-Semitism or racism on the part of blacks. He cites, for example, the inaccurate reporting on the anti-Semitic violence in Brooklyn's Crown Heights in 1991, as well as the violence in a Harlem department store in 1995. Moreover, he argues that the news media routinely—and often incorrectly—describe police officers as racist oppressors of minority citizens, as they were in the 1999 Amadou Diallo shooting in New York.

With all the sensitivity training and tolerance talk, it's highly unlikely that certain subjects like illegal immigration or affirmative action can even be discussed, let alone receive fair coverage that highlights different sides of the debate. And guess which side of the debate gets left out?

TALL MEDIA TALES

With the success of books like McGowan's, Coulter's, and Gold-berg's, legitimate critiques of the mainstream news media were fi-nally getting a hearing in the court of public opinion. And as noted, many polls have indicated that Americans are getting fed up with the type of news they're receiving from the media. After being able to ignore allegations of liberal bias for years, big-time journalists finally had to address the charges head-on. Sure, many of them simply denied the accusations—witness the claims of people like Tom Brokaw and Dan Rather—but at least they were being forced to cough up some answers.

And some of them finally came around and granted (grudg-ingly) that there might be something to all these charges of liberal media bias. One night in 2002, Peter Jennings himself apparently felt he couldn't duck the question any longer. When pressed by CNN's Larry King, Jennings said, "Historically in the media, it has been more of a liberal persuasion for many years. It has taken us a long time, too long in my view, to have vigorous conservative voices heard as widely in the media as they now are. And so I think, yes, on occasion there is a liberal instinct in the media which we need to keep our eye on, if you will."

As media watchdog L. Brent Bozell III wrote in his book *Weapons of Mass Distortion: The Coming Meltdown of the Liberal Media,* this was an "astonishing statement." Jennings's remark—even if it didn't come close to acknowledging the full extent of liberal media bias or why such bias is a problem—showed that we were past the time "when the American public was less attuned to the leftward slant in the press."[20]

Once they figured out that strategy would no longer work, lib-erals came up with a new one. They began pushing the theory that the media are being controlled by the Right.

One of the leaders of this new assault is Eric Alterman of the pathologically progressive magazine the *Nation.* I'm a lawyer. I can appreciate advocacy expertise. I have to say if I were forced to hire someone to create an argument that the mainstream media weren't liberal but were actually conservative and that somehow the Right was in control of the messages we receive, and if I needed someone who could put the argument on paper and make the whole thing believable, Eric Alterman would be my guy. He's a scholar and a top-notch writer, and he's witty to boot.

Alterman is one of the most effective advocates of the position that denies that the metropolitan media have a liberal slant and instead asserts that they tilt to the right. His book *What Liberal Media?: The Truth About Bias and the News* promotes the theory.

The fellow has some literary and logic problems, though. I think he may have been indulging in too much late-night *Harry Potter,* because his basic thesis goes against a mountain of data, a stack of scholarly studies, and a gutload of common sense. In my opinion, Alterman's book resembles a fanciful story a lot more than it does a piece of nonfiction. He tells the same basic story that his liberal buddies have been spreading. It's the one that was whispered in the ears of Howard Dean supporters just before the Dem presidential candidate flamed out. It's the same yarn that's been passed on to cybervisitors to the Democratic Underground, MoveOn.org, and various other fringe-left regions. And it is this: that there is some sort of evil conservative cabal, which has been feverishly working to spread the word that the mainstream metropolitan media really slants to the left.

It's a whopper of a tale that Alterman and his like-minded associates evidently believe. The story goes something like this:

> In a dark corner of the nation, a sinister clique of conservatives gathered together. The bevy of bad guys included some wild-eyed religious zealots, several stodgy members of the political right wing, and a bunch of reclusive billionaires. The villainous creatures came up with an ambitious plan. They would conquer the world, philosophically speaking, by grabbing control of the media and switching things over to their point of view.
>
> Their plan was both diabolically ingenious and all-

encompassing in its reach. They would spend huge amounts of money and energy to alter the media. At the same time, they would concoct a myth that the media were actually liberal, and they'd get everyone to accept the hype as truth.

They ended up spending billions of dollars and working a sort of magic. So forceful were they, the bulk of the mainstream media was pressured to move in a conservative direction. Simultaneously, they created an additional medium, an alternative one of their own. The conniving cons ferociously attacked Bill Clinton, forcing him into a whirlpool of scandal. They also did things like swipe an election from Al Gore, strip the Dems of congressional control, and manipulate journalists into becoming embedded with the troops.

They made one little misstep along the way, though. Somehow they inadvertently tipped their hand and the smartest woman on the planet, who later transformed into a Yankee fan and took a seat in the U.S. Senate, was able to identify and inform the world about the "vast right-wing conspiracy."

But it was too late for millions of Americans, who had succumbed to the fiend-flung fabrication and bought the myth of the liberal media hook, line, and sinker.

The End . . . for the moment

CONSPIRACY THEORY

It's quite a tale, but as I mentioned, there are problems with Alterman's pitch.

Over the past quarter-century, numerous studies have shown that journalists are more liberal in their views than the rest of America. And surveys show that reporters, journalists, writers, and others in the mainstream media have voted overwhelmingly for liberal Democrats. Had only the votes of journalists been counted, we'd be saluting George McGovern and Walter Mondale on Presidents' Day.

In addition, studies over the past three decades have indicated that the journalists themselves admit they are more liberal than they are conservative. They are more liberal than their fellow Americans as well. Heck, they're more liberal than Jerry Brown at a Dylan concert.

Even Alterman acknowledges in his book that the vast majority of journalists in the elite media were and are "pro-choice, pro–gun control, pro–separation of church and state, pro-feminism, pro–affirmative action, and supportive of gay rights."[21] He doesn't seem to see these factoids as being all that significant, nor does he make much of the fact that journalists are, in his words, "well-educated urban elites" who "hold socially liberal views."[22]

Like a lot of his bent-headed buddies, Alterman seems to believe that the only people who are truly biased are those of a conservative stripe. And he ignores the information-conveying aspects of film, television, music, and the like, as if the messages launched from such sources don't count.

To shore up the shaky foundation of his case, in *What Liberal Media?*, Alterman cites the names of prominent conservatives who have supposedly slipped up and mistakenly "admitted" that liberal media bias is really a ruse of the Right.

For instance, Alterman cites a statement by Rich Bond from 1992, when he chaired the Republican National Committee. In reference to the bashing of the liberal media, Bond told the *Washington Post,* "There is *some* strategy to it. . . . If you watch any great coach, what they try to do is 'work the refs.' Maybe the ref will cut you a little slack on the next one [emphasis added]."[23] But Alterman fails to note the qualifier that Bond used: the word *some.* Alterman sticks in another statement of Bond's but makes no comment on it—perhaps because it runs contrary to the very premise of *What Liberal Media?:* "I think we know who the media want to win this election—and I don't think it's George [H. W.] Bush."[24]

Alterman also says that Pat Buchanan, the author, commentator, and former presidential candidate, had "cheerfully confessed" that claims of liberal bias were a sham. Buchanan told the *Los Angeles Times,* "We kid about the liberal media, but every Republican on Earth does that."[25] But Buchanan made this statement during his 1996 run for president, at a time when he was most beholden to the media. And he gave the quote less than a month after he had scored his upset victory in New Hampshire against Senate Majority Leader Bob Dole. He was an upstart challenger to an establishment figure, and for that the media seemed to shower him with affection, albeit briefly.

Perhaps more to the point, Buchanan himself has dismissed Alterman's arguments. Writing in his syndicated column in June 2003, Buchanan declared, "As a judge of bias, Alterman is poorly situated. He is so far left he considers network anchors Dan Rather and Peter Jennings to be conservatives. Moreover, he argues from exceptions to prove his rules." Buchanan maintained that contrary to Alterman's claims, the "liberal press" was awfully powerful and included "all three major networks, PBS, NPR and virtually all major U.S. papers—*Boston Globe, New York Times, Philadelphia Inquirer, Baltimore Sun, Washington Post, Atlanta Constitution, Miami Herald, Chicago Tribune, Denver Post, Los Angeles Times.*" He added, "While the *Wall Street Journal* editorial page is neoconservative, *USA Today*—the nation's largest newspaper—is left of center. Not only are the editorial pages of most major papers liberal, the news staffs are overwhelmingly so."[26]

I doubt that's the kind of endorsement Alterman was looking for from one of the few conservatives he cites to support his arguments.

To argue that the media coverage of Ronald Reagan was not biased, Alterman pulls up a quote from James Baker, who served as both White House chief of staff and secretary of the treasury under Reagan. Baker said, "There were days and times and events we might have had some complaints [but] on balance I don't think we had anything to complain about."[27] But Baker was, and still is, a master of diplomacy, and most people know he let others do the complaining for the press missteps of that era.

With much fanfare, Alterman also touts *Weekly Standard* editor Bill Kristol's supposed admission that claims about the liberal media are an invention of the Right. "I admit it," Kristol told the *New Yorker.* "The liberal media were never that powerful, and the whole thing was often used as an excuse by conservatives for conservative failures."[28] But Alterman doesn't seem to realize that Kristol was chastising conservatives for using accusations of liberal bias as cop-outs. Despite what Alterman thinks, Kristol was not denying outright that the mainstream media were liberal.

The funny thing was, though, the very same media that Alterman claimed had swung to the right for the most part went gaga over his book. The *Los Angeles Times* called it "well-documented, even tempered and witty." The *New Yorker* said, "The meticulous care with which [Alterman's] arguments are sourced and footnoted is in commendable contrast to the efforts of some of his more fire-breathing opponents." And the *Orlando Sentinel* asserted that Alterman "lights a candle in the darkness of American punditry."

He lights a candle all right—one that's hollow inside. He presupposes that a single statement given by a conservative betrays some kind of mutual understanding. This is the classic way conspiracy buffs try to prove their premises. Plus he's got a bugaboo about conservative influence in the media that allegedly manifests itself through what he calls the "punditocracy." Alterman describes the professional commentators as working together with the White House to "define the shape and scope of public debate in the elite media."[29] He refers to them as "shock troops." And he lumps individuals like Buchanan, Ann Coulter, and Bob Novak together with people like Kristol, Paul Gigot, and Tony Snow. In his view, they are all outrageous in their "ideological extremism."[30]

Incredibly, though, Alterman denies that George Stephanopoulos, the host of ABC's *This Week,* is still a liberal, even though he served as a loyal aide to Bill Clinton immediately before jumping over to TV. Alterman writes that Stephanopoulos's "desire to be accepted as a journalist" has essentially eliminated him as a voice of the Left.[31]

Alterman and the media critics who emulate him have essentially redefined the meaning of the term *liberal*. It seems that anyone who is left of center, but who disagrees with Alterman's litany of leftist tenets, is classified as having joined the right-wing rivals. The *New Republic,* the *New York Times,* and the *Washington*

Post are not considered to be truly liberal because they may, from time to time, disagree with the *Nation*'s Katrina vanden Heuvel. By doing a semantic juggling act, Alterman reshapes the media to fit whatever suits him. He makes some liberals out to be conservatives and he makes those who are genuinely conservative out to be far-right extremists.

I wonder what Alterman thinks of the admission made by Tim Russert, former aide to Democrat Daniel Patrick Moynihan and moderator of NBC's *Meet the Press.* Offering a more realistic perspective on the bias issue than Alterman does, Russert says, "There's a potential *cultural bias.* And I think it's very real and very important to recognize and to deal with. Because of background and training you come to issues with a preconceived notion or a preordained view on subjects like abortion, gun control, campaign finance. I think many journalists growing up in the sixties and the seventies have to be very careful about attitudes toward government, attitudes toward the military, attitudes toward authority. It doesn't mean there's a rightness or a wrongness. It means you have to constantly check yourself. John Chancellor used to say, 'If your mother says she loves you, check it out.' "[32]

And I also wonder what Alterman thinks of the bias-related admission that *Newsweek* assistant managing editor Evan Thomas made during the 2004 presidential campaign. While discussing John Kerry's presidential bid, Thomas told PBS's *Inside Washington,* "Let's talk a little media bias here. The media, I think, wants Kerry to win. And I think they're going to portray Kerry and Edwards—I'm talking about the establishment media, not Fox—but they're going to portray Kerry and Edwards as being young and dynamic and optimistic and all. There's going to be this glow about them that . . . is going to be worth, collectively, the two of them, that's going to be worth maybe 15 points."[33]

Newsweek's own July 19, 2004, issue lent some credence to Thomas's comments. On the cover of the magazine was a picture of Kerry and Edwards with twin grins and a caption that read "The Sunshine Boys?"

A few months later, Thomas maintained that his comment

about a 15-point bump from the liberal media was a "stupid thing to say." But significantly, he did not back away from his claim that the mainstream media wanted Kerry to win. He thought that advantage could be worth up to 5 points for the Kerry ticket—still a huge amount in a tight presidential race.[34]

It's hard to believe that Alterman can make his argument with a straight face. Even when one takes into account the effects of talk radio shows like Rush Limbaugh's, Sean Hannity's, and Michael Savage's, and of Internet sites like NewsMax.com, the Drudge Report, and WorldNetDaily, it's difficult to make the case that the media scales tip anywhere but overwhelmingly to the left.

A few more things. Politically laden FM and satellite radio talk shows hosted by Howard Stern, Opie and Anthony, Tom Leykis, and others aren't usually given much media-critic attention. But the kind of raunchy talk that's heard on shows like these is typically splattered with liberal themes. In addition to the standard juvenile sex jokes, conversations often expand to include bawdy discourse on family, courtship, morality, homosexuality, and abortion. The patter usually has decidedly liberal overtones, and audiences tend to contain a significant number of loyal Democrat listeners.

Alterman also disregards the success of liberal Internet sites like Alternet.org, Buzzflash.com, DemocraticUnderground.com, DailyHowler.com, FAIR.org, MichaelMoore.com, Salon.com, Slate.com, and MoveOn.org. He claims simply that the sites aren't as partisan and mean as conservative websites. Meanwhile, he tries to push the notion that the Fox News Channel carries more weight than the broadcast media because it supposedly has influence well beyond its size. And he claims that the media faithfully watch cable shows. Must be because of the mesmerizing voice quality and hypnotic eyes of Bill O'Reilly.

Of course, *nobody* in the media reads the *New York Times*. Guess it's just a coincidence that so many TV news stories seem to be lifted straight from the Gray Lady's front pages.

Alterman grumbles about the billions of dollars coming out of the Scaife Foundations, the Bradley Foundation, and the Olin

Foundation, ignoring the far more influential and wealthier liberal-cause-loving ones. He fails to mention, for instance, how over the past century, the Rockefeller, Carnegie, and Ford Foundations have affected the academic and political science arenas, exercised power in the arts and cultural worlds, and expanded their size and scope via think tanks, academic disciplines, and the media.

As Alterman paints his conspiracy picture, he adds more players to the imaginary cabal—American corporations. It seems that in Alterman's mind, corporations are filled with archconservatives who devote time, money, and resources to social issues as some sort of cover or deceptive PR move. The worst kinds of corporations are those that own media outlets. Supposedly, as part of standard operating procedures, they coerce their employees to move to the conservative side of the aisle, or else it's curtains for them. This notion is expressed in one of Alterman's chapter titles: "You're Only as Liberal as the Man Who Owns You."

Well, if corporate bosses dictate their employees' ideology, somebody ought to warn Tucker Carlson.

TUCKERED OUT

The Public Broadcasting Service has lots of problems—low ratings and lack of funds being among them. But when reporters had a chance to talk to PBS president and CEO Pat Mitchell in the summer of 2004, it seems there was only one issue on their minds—Tucker Carlson's new PBS series, *Tucker Carlson: Unfiltered.*

Could it be the press feared that a trend to the right was in the making?

Mitchell was on the defensive. "We are not in the pursuit of that kind of political equivalency," he assured the assembled reporters. "We're not responding to those [political] pressures in any other way than to respond to the original pressure, which is to have all points of view."

The very idea of a nonliberal getting time on the public airwaves had the mainstream press pulling out the long knives. Here's how *Washington Post* television columnist Lisa de Moraes described the PBS chief's announcement that Carlson was getting his own show: "The public broadcasting network gave CNN show host and political analyst Tucker Carlson a PBS program because otherwise the poor dear would only have the one opportunity in his career, which is just unfair. You know, you just can't make up stuff this good."[35]

Did someone light a stink bomb or is that sarcasm I smell?

And the *New Yorker*'s Ken Auletta saw the hiring of Carlson as part of a Republican scheme to take over PBS. In a piece entitled "Big Bird Flies Right," he wrote, "The American right has stopped trying to get rid of PBS. . . . Now it wants a larger voice in shaping the institution." Auletta reported that public broadcasting mogul Bill Moyers had sent him an e-mail that read, "This is the first time in my thirty-two years in public broadcasting that C.P.B. has ordered up programs for ideological instead of journalistic reasons."[36]

Now it seems as though there's a scent of arrogance and accusation in the air.

Suddenly PBS was hiring someone who might actually threaten the Left's long-held dominance over public broadcasting, so apparently liberals had to attribute the move to something other than Carlson's ability. In a lowball journalistic move, reporters spread a nepotism rumor.

The *Miami Herald* reported the following: "That Carlson's father Richard was head of the Corporation for Public Broadcasting from 1992 to 1997 only added fuel to the conspiracy theories."[37]

But when we look at the calendar we find that Tucker's dad was out of the Corporation for Public Broadcasting loop for a full seven years before Tucker got his new gig.

Tucker was understandably offended by the implications regarding his father. He told the *San Francisco Chronicle*, "You just have to trust me when I say it's just one of those—it's like Lee Harvey Oswald a month before the Kennedy assassination was at the Soviet embassy in Mexico City. We know that for a fact. He was seen there. There's a photograph of him leaving the embassy. We know that he was there. What does that have to do with the Kennedy assassination? We have no idea. No link has ever been drawn between the two. It's just an interesting and weird coincidence. And the fact that my father was involved in public broadcasting, to my knowledge as God watches, is a coincidence. Maybe he's part of the same conspiracy along with Wolfowitz, but I don't know about it."[38]

When one hears Carlson's story and sees the media reaction, one gets the sense that the press is downright disgusted that an opposing view would make it to public TV.

Didn't these folks learn anything from Mister Rogers?

MAKING NOISE

Joining Eric Alterman in the attack on "conservative media bias" is David Brock, the self-described former "right-wing hit man" who has advanced his career by becoming a vocal critic of conservatives. He has now authored two books condemning his former conservative compatriots—*Blinded by the Right: The Conscience of an Ex-Conservative* and *The Republican Noise Machine: Right-Wing Media and How It Corrupts Democracy.*

Brock has been building toward this mission. When he came out with *Blinded by the Right* in 2002, his personal story became a hot news item. Here was a former conservative admitting that he had lied in numerous articles that he had published in conservative magazines. The guy was walking and talking proof of the malevolence that supposedly saturates the Right and directs its path. As a reward of sorts for seeing the light, and for being the media antidote to Bernard Goldberg, Brock was treated like a liberal prince.

Frank Rich of the *New York Times* called *Blinded* "a key document." Hendrik Hertzberg of the *New Yorker* referred to it as "an astounding account." Michael Tomasky of the *Nation* said it was "mind-boggling."

Even when acknowledging Brock's departures from the truth, some mainstream commentators ended up defending the author.

For example, in an online discussion, *Washington Post* media reporter Howard Kurtz responded to a reader's criticism of Brock by saying, "There's no question that Brock consciously sought to further his career among conservatives by trashing liberal figures with shaky, sometimes nonexistent evidence—as he himself now admits. This obviously raises questions about whether we can fully believe what Brock says now. But Brock is as hard on himself in *Blinded by the Right* as any critic might be—calling himself not just misguided in his younger days but a knowing participant in a sleaze machine (as he now describes it) who did what he did for fame, money and social climbing."[39]

There were some skeptical voices, though. The left-leaning *Slate* magazine indicated that it was "slightly taken aback at the respectful attention some liberals" were giving Brock's book. *Slate* columnist Timothy Noah noted that "the more Brock insists that he has lied, and lied, and then lied again, the more one begins to suspect Brock of being, well, a liar."[40] In fact, Noah struggled so much with Brock's credibility that he "practically gave himself a migraine trying to figure out which parts of Brock's lurid story were true, and which parts were false."[41]

But those voices of reason weren't all that common among liberals. They were too eager to use him to spread the tale that conservatives really were a sinister group that had taken over the media and the government. And Brock has taken full advantage—not just to draw media attention but also to attract wealthy donors. If, as Howard Kurtz suggested, Brock tried to hobnob his way to the top of the leisure-class ladder when he was a conservative, he's apparently having a much more rewarding experience in his vertical climb now that he's switched worldviews.

To understand how successful Brock has been, you need look no further than Susie Tompkins Buell, the founder of the Esprit clothing line and big-time Democratic donor. Buell went to a Hillary-hugging meeting where she happened to run into Brock. The right-winger-turned-lefty apparently shared his idea for an Internet watchdog site that would monitor the conservative media. Taken with the notion, Buell hosted a fund-raiser for

Brock's project at her Left Coast home, and Brock was eventually able to amass $2 million for what he dubbed Media Matters for America.

Launched in 2004, Media Matters for America describes itself as "a Web-based, not-for-profit progressive research and information center dedicated to comprehensively monitoring, analyzing, and correcting conservative misinformation in the U.S. media." Brock's site crows that "for the first time, Media Matters for America has put in place a system to monitor the media for conservative misinformation."

Because Brock wanted to get the project rolling in a jiffy, Media Matters used a preexisting charity to handle contributions. The organization formed a special relationship with the Tides Foundation,[42] which is a major player in furthering left-wing causes (and which has received millions of dollars from nonprofits controlled by loaded liberal and first lady wannabe Teresa Heinz Kerry).[43]

Interestingly, Brock's watchdog group happened to come into being right around the time that the progressive convert began promoting his latest piece of prose, *The Republican Noise Machine.* In the book, Brock builds off Hillary Clinton's "vast right-wing conspiracy" claim and Eric Alterman's allegations in *What Liberal Media?* He argues that "the most important sectors of the political media" are actually "powerful propaganda organs of the Republican Party." He informs readers that "this development in the media represents a structural change: a structural advantage for the GOP and conservatism, and, I believe, the greatest structural obstacle facing opponents of the right wing. I therefore think it is one of the most important political stories of the era."[44]

Brock also contends that the "gold standard" of the journalism profession has been the virtue of objectivity (which, by the way, is the same virtue that the gold standard of journalists, Edward R. Murrow, said did not really exist). In Brock's view, only the Left retains this trait.

With his ideological shift, Brock seems to have also switched over to a much more simplistic form of thinking, which can be summed up like this: *Liberals rule, conservatives bite.* Apparently, in a Brock-headed world, liberal columnists are evenhanded, while conservatives are closed-minded. He writes about how liberals are so much kinder than conservatives because they "are unmoored to any cohesive political movement and they have no symbiotic relationship with politicians." And he sees liberal books as being sweetness and light, writing that "liberal books are generally more honest, more accurate, and of a much higher quality than are right-wing books."[45]

Makes you wonder if Brock has been to a bookstore in the past few years, or if he would include as honest, accurate, and of high quality such titles as *Big Lies,* by Joe Conason; *The Book on Bush: How George W. (Mis)leads America,* by Eric Alterman; *Thieves in High Places,* by Jim Hightower; *Lies and the Lying Liars Who Tell Them,* by Al Franken; *Dude, Where's My Country?,* by Michael Moore; or *Bushwhacked* and *Shrub,* by Molly Ivins and Lou Dubose.

Brock tells us that liberal magazines and newspapers are so fair and accommodating, they willingly bring conservatives onboard. They seemingly hold their noble nostrils and allow the likes of Andrew Sullivan, Fred Barnes, or the late Michael Kelly to write for their publications. On the other hand, he complains that conservative periodicals are not as gracious in extending the same consideration to libs.

But Brock ignores facts to the contrary, like how NewsMax has former New York mayor Ed Koch and left-of-center political commentator Susan Estrich (whom, incidentally, Brock accuses of now being a Republican defender) in its pundit lineup. And how Christopher Hitchens manages to pop up in conservative magazines all over the place. And how Ellen Ratner regularly makes her liberal way onto various kinds of conservative websites. The list goes on.

In Brock's view, a few decades back, conservative magazines pursued "a common agenda" and "were well-integrated with the Republican Right's political establishment." But "left-liberal publications like *The Nation, The Progressive, Mother Jones,* and *In These*

Times" were somehow at a disadvantage, since they were "ideologically splintered" and remained "genuinely independent of partisan politics."[46]

Excuse me while I pick myself up off the floor. Did he say *Mother Jones*? Maybe he meant to say *Mother Goose.*

Anyway, Brock seems to have overlooked the differences between those who purport to report the facts and those who render opinions. Most of the conservatives he writes about—and many whom his Media Matters website takes to task—would probably identify themselves as commentators or opinion makers, not reporters.

In August 2004 things got even kookier. CNN's *Inside Politics* featured CNN senior political analyst Bill Schneider, who was discussing the remake of the movie *The Manchurian Candidate.* To support the idea that the character played by actress Meryl Streep resembled former first lady and current New York senator Hillary Clinton, Schneider read from what he called a "conservative website." He said, "There's no end of speculation about the villain in it, played by Meryl Streep. . . . Notice the haircut. One conservative website asks, 'diabolical, cold, manipulative member of the U.S. Senate. Any thoughts on a real-life middle-aged blonde who might fit the description?' "

In an onscreen graphic, viewers got to see a piece of my weekly column, "The Left Coast Report," where I typically do a little Tinseltown ribbing while providing the lowdown on the latest politically charged Hollywood stories. Schneider showed my jocular poke called "The Manchurian Senator" and shared this excerpt: "The *New York Daily News* reports that, much to the chagrin of Hollywood execs, Streep's character is frighteningly similar to a certain former first lady."

Brock's watchdog website picked up on the Schneider "Left Coast Report" inclusion and actually chastised the veteran analyst because he had "perpetuated—without offering refutation—the suggestion that Senator Hillary Clinton (D-NY) was the inspiration for the 'villain' character, played by Meryl Streep." Media Matters wrote that Streep herself had told the *New York Times* that she based the character on a host of women, including Bush adviser Karen Hughes, Republican senator Elizabeth Dole, conservative pundit Ann Coulter, *Wall Street Journal* columnist Peggy Noonan, and former British prime minister Margaret Thatcher.

In an apparent effort to create the impression that Schneider, a liberal, was really a conservative conspirator, Brock's site reminded readers that Schneider "is also a resident fellow at the American Enterprise Institute."

Bill Schneider a conservative? Yeah, and Ann Coulter's shy and retiring.

THE AIR AMERICA FIZZLE

As bizarre as the claims of "conservative media bias" might be, many on the Left have taken them quite seriously and have been spurred to action because of them. Brock's Media Matters is one well-funded example, but another, even more celebrated effort came right around the same time, when the Air America radio network went on the air. The Left wanted to bring to the national scene a left-of-center parallel to the highly successful conservative radio talk show universe.

On March 30, 2004, Air America held a posh soiree at Manhattan's trendy Maritime Hotel to celebrate the launch of the network. According to the *Wall Street Journal,* more than a thousand guests were present, including such celebrity lefties as Tim Robbins and Yoko Ono. The assembled libs accepted as true the idea that if only their message could get out to the people, network success would surely follow. Lefty leaders from Hollywood to Manhattan loved the idea of sticking it to Rush Limbaugh and his conservative radio cohorts.

With cash supplied by wealthy ideologues, the liberal radio network tried to get its entire twenty-four-hour lineup picked up by radio stations. But the reality is that station managers prefer to choose programming that best suits their particular markets, so the

Air America dilettantes hit a major snag, because the radio biz didn't work the way they thought it did.

The fledgling network tried to buy its way in to the big markets and attempted to purchase some radio stations outright. Not enough dough was available, though. Then it went the route of leasing airtime in some of the largest radio markets in the nation—New York, Chicago, and L.A. Ironically, committing to costly lease payments for unproven programming would later prove to be an unlucky gamble.

The lack of luck had nothing to do with a lack of help from the mainstream media. In fact, the media pushed the radio network with jet force. ABC featured it twice on *Good Morning America,* while Peter Jennings pitched it a couple of times on *World News Tonight* and Ted Koppel devoted an entire *Nightline* program to the new radio venture. NBC lent it some publicity with an interview on the *Today* show and a reporter's story on the *Nightly News.* CNN aired countless stories on it, including some in prime-time slots. NPR plugged it on *All Things Considered* and in an interview on its afternoon chat show *Talk of the Nation. Newsweek* covered it with an article and an interview with Al Franken. The *New York Times* spotlighted the network in a front-page piece on its first broadcast day and in a cover story in the *New York Times Magazine.* And the *Washington Post* reserved some front-page space for Air America on its launch day, as well as some room for it in the Sunday Style section.

Despite all the media help, Air America ran into some huge problems (which, by the way, were virtually ignored by the mainstream media). The quality of the programming was less than stellar. The all-star lib lineup didn't have the prerequisite radio experience. Instead of tapping the vast reservoir of radio talent that was already out there, Air America turned to the likes of *Saturday Night Live* alum and rock-throwing writer Al Franken, comedienne and actress Janeane Garofalo, and rapper Chuck D. The content mostly consisted of no-holds-barred hate. It was enough to make James Carville blush.

Things went downhill for the network pretty fast. The company was in poor financial health from the start, and before long Air America couldn't pay the sizable lease fees to its Chicago station, which was owned by MultiCultural Radio Broadcasting Inc. MultiCultural ended up having to lock Air America out of its studios and kick it off the air in Chicago and Los Angeles. Air America CEO Mark Walsh jumped overboard, and others in its management team eventually joined him.

Upon finding itself in this predicament, what did Air America do? It did what any lawyer-loving liberal would do having failed to succeed by conventional means—file a lawsuit.

Air America found a New York judge who would order Multi-Cultural to put the network back on the air in Chicago. The victory would be short-lived, though, because it would soon be bumped off again.

Investors in the network eventually set up a new entity called Piquant LLC. Piquant bought the assets of the old company and started over, allowing local stations to pick up whatever part of the lineup they wanted to.

The liberal media continued to try to coerce people into falling in love with the jilted suitor. To supplement the mainstream's bouquet of puff pieces for the public, HBO rushed in with an Air America box of candy in the form of a documentary called *Left of the Dial,* which it aired repeatedly in the spring of 2005.

As of this writing, Air America is on the air in New York, several other major markets, and a bunch of smaller ones. And Al Franken is still trying to paddle to the progressive promised land in his deflated inner tube.

To me, the whole liberal-network thing illustrates a basic free-market principle: supply and demand. The reason that radio and TV personalities like Rush Limbaugh and Sean Hannity, and websites like Drudge and NewsMax, are successful is that people love the shows and the sites and want more of what they have to offer. And the reason that Air America generally fails to cut the radio mustard is because neither the interest nor the demand for the delivery of the lib message in that format is there.

The fact of the matter is, liberals get their messages out in media venues galore. Pretty much everything they need and/or want to convey is already being transmitted via our mainstream information and entertainment fare.

Tonight Show host Jay Leno seems to understand it. When the idea of a liberal radio network first hit the news, Leno cracked, "According to the *New York Times,* a group of liberal venture capitalists are in the process of developing their own liberal radio network to counter conservative shows like Rush Limbaugh. They feel the liberal viewpoint is not being heard—except on TV, in the movies, in music, by comedians, magazines and newspapers. Other than that, it's not getting out!"

O'Reilly Factors In

Bill O'Reilly, the creator of the "No-Spin Zone," is a *New York Times* best-selling author many times over. He holds two master's degrees, one of which is from Harvard.

O'Reilly is a veteran journalist with experience at CBS and ABC and is the winner of numerous honors, including two Emmys and a National Headliner Award.

He joined Fox News Channel in 1996 and is the anchor and host of *The O'Reilly Factor,* the most-watched program on cable news.

I had the opportunity to chat with O'Reilly and find out, when it comes to the media, where the spin stops.[1]

HIRSEN: Fox is getting slammed by the elite press, by media critics, by the protesters, even by Hollywood now. There's a notion out there that somehow Fox is not objective. I wanted to get your take on that.

O'REILLY: The Left has had a monopoly on the broadcast media and much of the print media for decades. And now they are taking it on the chin because conservative and traditional Americans felt they were underrepresented in the press. So once Fox News came on and said, "We'll give voice to this point of view, this opinion, conservative and traditional as well as liberal too," I mean we do that as well, they didn't like it. They didn't like losing their monopoly.

The real tipping point was that the elite media—the *New York Times, L.A. Times,* network news, PBS, NPR, CNN—in the past had demeaned points of view which they disagreed with, actively demeaned them by ignoring them altogether or by putting people on and just scoffing at them.

Now that message got across. Once Fox got up and did *not* do that, did not demean the point of view of the pro-life people or the NRA, they didn't demean it—challenged it on occasion, but didn't demean it—then the lefties really got crazed, because they said, "Uh-oh, now we are in a position where we are going to be perceived as being one-sided. We can't have that, because our whole myth is that we are fair." But they aren't. They never have been.

So, of course, you attack the people that you fear the most. And that's why the terrorists attacked the U.S.A. That's why these left-wing people attack Fox. Even if Fox were a conservative channel—which it is not, it is a traditional channel, there's a big difference—even if it were conservative, so what? You've got at least a dozen left-wing outlets stacked up against one that doesn't see it that way. But they didn't want to be challenged, and that was the crux of the matter.

HIRSEN: I teach in a journalism school, and the academic world talks about objectivity as a virtue. The question is, Is there objectivity in the media? Is the elite media objective—the ones that are pointing the finger at Fox?

O'REILLY: Well, there has to be objectivity in presenting a news story by a reporter. If there isn't, then you're just not going to get the truth. I worked at ABC and CBS, and I didn't see a lot of slanting of the news by the reporters. I didn't see that. I saw a group-think mentality at ABC and CBS news that said, basically, "Our sensitivities and sensibilities are noble. And if you disagree with us, you're not noble." That's where it all came in. So at Fox, our reporters go out, they report the story. If I see any kind of slant on the story, believe me, I'm on them like crazy. So it is dangerous here to slant a story. When commentators come on, then obviously they are going to analyze from their point of view, which, of course, is what the op-ed pages do in the newspapers.

HIRSEN: How come there is not more public knowledge about your credentials and your pedigree? I find it strange that a comedy writer goes after you over an award, when you've won two Emmys and a Headliner. You are distinctive from a lot of these other voices out there, and yet people don't know about your background.

O'REILLY: Why would the propagandists want to lend legitimacy to a voice they want to silence? They wouldn't. There is no objectivity coming from the *New York Times*. I mean, I've had three number-one *New York Times* best-sellers. They haven't reviewed any of them, and each of them they miscategorize when they describe it in their little list.

So these people want me silenced. That's number one. Let's get him. Let's discredit him. Let's personally attack him. We don't want to hear what he has to say. The question is why? Because they fear me. And why do they fear me? Because I keep an eye on them. I am the *New York Times*'s worst nightmare. I am CNN's worst nightmare. I watch what they do. I criticize what they do openly. They have never been held accountable on television, *ever*, in the history of the media. Now they are being held accountable. You can imagine what kind of fear and loathing that engenders.

HIRSEN: I want to ask you about this, because one of the things that is talked about with Fox—there's a worry about the "Foxification" of cable news. It has been said that Fox is more entertaining than other cable news outlets, and that includes your show. Is there something wrong with news becoming entertaining? Is there a point where entertainment undermines reporting or even analysis?

O'REILLY: Well, sure, it could. If you become a caricature out there, then you are going to undermine the point you are trying to get

across. But the audience will know that, and the serious audience will leave when that happens. Morton Downey couldn't
sustain what he did because he was a cartoon. So he was on
the air for a year, year and a half. We've been on the air now
eight years. I try to present my material in a stimulating way
that a lot of people can identify with. And that means that I
get away from the very dry policy wording.

I write my own stuff. It's colorful language. But I'm not
changing the meaning of the story or the facts surrounding
the story. I am just doing it in a way that engages. And the
others either can't do it or won't do it. I think it's the former—
they can't do it. They just don't know how to do it. And particularly CNN and MSNBC, where they've got to know they
are both in desperate trouble. They just can't engage the audience. So they'll say, "Well, O'Reilly is this; O'Reilly is that."
You can say whatever you want. Our stories are accurate. Our
analyses are based on facts. And we've been around eight
years and that proves it.

HIRSEN: One of the things that I notice that you do is you communicate in a way that common folks can understand. Is that part
of your success? And is there a kind of snobbery toward that
kind of communication because it is perceived as anti-
intellectual?

O'REILLY: I don't think it is as much that as the fear factor. I think that a
lot of these people are snobs. If you saw Paul Krugman and I
go at it.

HIRSEN: I did.

O'REILLY: There was a great example of a guy who is a total snob.
When he was on, he just crumbled. He couldn't take the fire.
He couldn't make his points. He crumbled. And anybody
watching that would have known, Well, here's this street guy
O'Reilly against the Princeton pinhead, Krugman. Well, look
what happened.

There is some of that snobbery, but it's more of a fear of—
It's not that they object to my style, my populist style. They

object to the fact that I'm a watchdog, that I watch them. I don't hold them in awe. I feel that some of them are very dishonest. That's what they object to.

HIRSEN: You have become a famous guy yourself. Studs Terkel once said that journalism is a trade; it's not a profession. Do you find that the fame and the stardom and the entourage and all have affected your perspective?

O'REILLY: Well, I don't have an entourage, so—

It is easy for that to happen. I've seen it happen to a lot of people. But I do all my own work, and that's the difference between me and all the other anchor people. I write every word I say, and that includes a commentary on three minutes every day, a newspaper column once a week. I do it. I pick the stories. I'm the executive producer. So I'm actively working twelve hours a day. I don't have time, then, to be dealing with the fame aspect of it. I'm not out at the parties. I don't want to be there. I don't care about it. I don't have a PR agent drumming me up. All of that.

I do the same thing I did twenty-eight years ago when I started in Scranton, Pennsylvania. I write my own stories. I do my own work. And I'm kind of divorced from all the bells and whistles that go on around me. But, you know, you can easily become seduced by that.

HIRSEN: There was a big flap and still is about the wearing of flag pins, the use of certain terminology, the question of whether stories should be presented through the eyes of patriotism or not, political correctness in the coverage of war. What is your position?

O'REILLY: I never wore a flag pin, even though the *New York Post* said I did. I never once in my life have worn a flag pin or any other kind of pin. My job is to tell the folks what's going on in any situation, including a war.

That being said, I'd be dishonest if I didn't say I wanted the United States to win. Of course I do. And I don't make any pretense about that. I can say that as a commentator. And I think most of our reporters in the field want the United States to win as well, for their own protection. There is nothing wrong with that, as long as you are not shading the story. If the United States starts to lose and you keep saying they're winning, then you become Baghdad Bob. But we're human beings, too.

Now, on the Iraq situation, when I made a mistake, I said I made a mistake. Like the weapons of mass destruction. I should have been more skeptical about the CIA, which had booted three or four things before that. So why did I believe them when they said there were WMDs there? That was my mistake, and I went on and I said it was a mistake. Was that patriotism? I think that was just my probably being too easy on the federal government at that point. So you can say, yeah, maybe patriotism skewed my analysis out. But when I make a mistake, I say it and I correct it. And I don't make too many.

HIRSEN: What is taught in journalism school is that journalists should be detached—

O'REILLY: No, you can't. You just can't do that because then you have moral equivalencies going on. I mean, you have to decide if Saddam Hussein is a bad man or not. That's part of being a journalist, deciding what the field of battle is, what the theater is. You didn't send your reporters to World War II thinking, "Well, let's give Hitler a break. Let's give him the benefit of the doubt." That's ridiculous. You go in. You make determinations based upon what you know and what you see. And then you report what happens. And that's objectivity. But you don't go in like a zombie and say, "Gee, I think Goebbels has a point." That's ridiculous.

Journalists should be trained to evaluate all situations for what they *are.* That's accurate reporting. To make a moral equivalency between Saddam Hussein and George W. Bush— that's *insane.* That's what Michael Moore does. That's just propaganda garbage. You have to know what happened there. You have to make a journalistic judgment about who the bad guy is and who the good guy is.

HIRSEN: I have to ask you: All of the networks, local broadcasts, network broadcasts understand that sometimes you have to
grab attention. Every once in a while you have on your show
attractive women, foldouts, starlets, things like that. Is that an
intentional programming thing for you?

O'REILLY: I'll put on a subject like some bimbo who writes a book or
whatever, a porn star, if I feel that I can interview the person
in a way that people will get something out of it. So I'll put on
Pamela Anderson and usually give her a hard time, because
we do six segments a night. One of the segments is called the
"Back of the Book," and it's a lighter fare. If it's part of the
American landscape, I'll do it. But we usually have a point to
everything we do. We just don't throw people on there to
bloviate without a point.

HIRSEN: A few true or false. I just want to make sure some things are
true. Is it true that you are for gun control?

O'REILLY: I am for gun control in a reasonable way.

HIRSEN: So limited gun control?

O'REILLY: Right. I don't want assault weapons in private hands. I don't
think that's necessary.

HIRSEN: Is it true that you are for—these are things that have been reported in the *Boston Globe*—same-sex adoptions?

O'REILLY: If there are no other alternatives.

HIRSEN: That is an important qualification, I think.

O'REILLY: Right. I'd rather have a kid being in a loving home, where
people want him or her, rather than in the system. But you'd
have to go through the heterosexual thing first. I don't put
that on the same plane.

HIRSEN: They say you are for civil unions also.

O'REILLY: I am for civil unions, not based on sexuality. I think every
American should have an equal chance at pursuing happi-
ness. My two aunts were living together their whole lives,
and they never married. Why should they be penalized in
any way?

HIRSEN: As distinguished from gay marriage, civil unions?

O'REILLY: Civil unions—I mean, gay marriage to me, I don't care personally about it. But I don't think society is under any mandate to change the definition of a marriage to accommodate an alternative lifestyle. But I don't want any homosexuals deprived of any rights. So that fills the gap with the civil unions.

HIRSEN: They describe you as an environmentalist who accepts global warming.

O'REILLY: Correct.

HIRSEN: And they say you are against capital punishment.

O'REILLY: Correct. I don't think capital punishment is a deterrent. I would revamp the whole system of punishing criminals and do it in a classification that you would be really punished if you committed a violent crime or narcotics-related dealing situation. But if you killed somebody, you would be sentenced to hard labor. You would *wish* that you were dead when I got through with you.

HIRSEN: And you do not believe that abortion should be illegal, they report.

O'REILLY: No, I would not legislate against abortion. But I would try to take the politics out of it so that you would not have an encouragement of abortion. Because abortion is a human rights issue. It's not a political issue. It's been defined improperly by the liberal press as reproductive rights. That is absolutely false. This is a human rights issue, because now we know that at conception there is DNA. As soon as there is human DNA, you have human rights involved, whether you want to acknowledge it or not.

HIRSEN: So with these views, they call you a right-winger.

O'REILLY: They can call me anything they want but, again, they are not interested in getting the truth out. They don't care about that. What they want to do is keep me quiet or keep me on the defensive or whatever. These people have no—there is no sense of honor to them. They are just going to do what they can do to destroy anyone they perceive as being an opponent.

HIRSEN: According to the *Boston Globe,* in 1993 a coanchor named Susan Burke heard you say, "I'm not sure where the business is going, but my gut says it's going in the direction of Rush," meaning Rush Limbaugh, "and man I'm going to be there." True?

O'REILLY: I don't remember saying anything like that. Okay?

HIRSEN: Sound like a fantasy thing?

O'REILLY: Yeah. Yes, I mean, Susan is a nice girl, but I was never a Rush Limbaugh aficionado. I, of course, listened to him like everybody else. But he certainly wasn't anybody that I wanted to be like. So I'm not going to call the woman dishonest, but I don't remember ever saying anything like that. And it certainly wasn't in my game plan to be like Rush Limbaugh. If it were, I could have done talk radio a long time ago. I had tons of offers to do talk radio but always turned them down. So if I wanted to be like him, I would have got on that talk radio thing a long time ago.

HIRSEN: The other way your game plan was described was as a "populist *Nightline*." Correct?

O'REILLY: Yeah, I think that is true, but *Nightline* is pretty dispassionate, so we certainly weren't going to model this program after a dispassionate show. We believe emotion is very important in the presentation of this kind of journalism.

HIRSEN: My last question, Bill. Is it true that *Saturday Night Fever* is one of your favorite flicks?

O'REILLY: Absolutely. Great film. It captured that moment in time and the underclass of people that—

HIRSEN: Do you have a room with mirrors where you do the Travolta routines?

O'REILLY: Yeah, I can do Travolta as well as anybody.

5

THE GAME CHANGES

The idea that the media are now biased in favor of conservatives is as ridiculous as the notion that Hillary's a duck-shooting, pro-life-defending, tax-cutting, tobacco-chewing Southern evangelical. You know the argument about conservatives is flimsy when it's being lampooned by Jay Leno—the guy who went out of his way to establish his liberal bona fides after a reporter accused him of being too soft on Bush.

Coverage of events like the 2004 presidential race illustrates just how upside-down the talk of rightward media bias is. But as we shall see, while the mainstream media don't seem to be giving up on their semantic shuffle, some things are changing.

KITTY LITTER

Those who question claims of liberal media bias tend to focus on whether the members of the press throw Nerf balls at those they perceive to be on their team and shoot spitballs at ideological opponents. It's a superficial way of examining the issue, since bias doesn't always manifest itself so overtly and often involves subtleties like what stories news organizations choose to cover in the first place. Why does, say, homelessness become a big news item under a Republican administration but escape the notice of producers and journalists when a Dem takes over the White House?

Case in point: In 2004 there was a load of evidence that the media really did have their daggers out for George W. Bush and the Republicans.

It surfaced in one instance in the way NBC News rolled out the red carpet for Kitty Kelley and her nail-digging volume *The Family: The Real Story of the Bush Dynasty,* which was released in September, smack in the middle of the red-hot political campaign. The producers of the *Today* show didn't feel it was enough just to give Kelley one of the coveted spots on their highly rated morning show. They gave her *three straight days* on the show to make her outrageous claims.

Kelley took a swipe at the White House almost as soon as she turned up on the program. "Thanks for having me," she purred. "I really appreciate this because I know that the White House put great pressure on NBC not to have me, and I commend the president of your network and you for not caving."

But NBC would have had good reasons to back away from Kelley that had nothing to do with political pressure. The fact was, her book was based heavily on unnamed sources and was full of stories that were impossible to substantiate. That alone should have given NBC pause, but what should have been even more compelling was the fact that one of Kelley's primary named sources denied telling Kelley anything resembling what was printed in the book.

It wasn't just conservatives who recognized the serious flaws in Kelley's innuendo-laden piece. *Newsweek* had been given a chance to publish an excerpt from *The Family,* but it rejected the offer because it couldn't confirm key allegations Kelley had made in the book. And to his credit, CNN's Larry King—not usually one to shy away from celebrity-driven pseudo news—passed on the chance to interview Kelley, even though he had frequently invited her to be on his show in the past.

I guess at NBC News, a lack of sources wasn't going to get in the way of helping Dem friends.

While NBC was giving Kelley day after day on its celebrated morning show, it just couldn't seem to find any time to talk to another author who was raising serious questions about presidential candidate John Kerry. John O'Neill, the Swift Boat veteran who wrote the best-selling book *Unfit for Command* about Kerry's Vietnam service, never got the call to be on the *Today* show, or any other NBC program, for that matter.

Come to think of it, neither did any of the other Swift Boat veterans who spoke out against Kerry.

CROSSFIRE AT CROSS-PURPOSES

If in 2004 it looked like members of the liberal media were actually Democratic campaign operatives, sometimes it was because they really were. CNN actually allowed its employees to keep their TV posts while actively working to get John Kerry elected president.

It wasn't shocking that former Clinton aides James Carville and Paul Begala would go to work for the Kerry team. But it was perplexing that they saw no problem with simultaneously working for a TV news network. Begala and Carville hung on to their CNN gigs, and on the debate program *Crossfire* they were allowed to dispense the official Kerry campaign spin to the American viewing public.

Lots of other people saw problems with the dual duties, though. The editor of *American Journalism Review,* Rem Rieder, told the *Washingtonian* magazine, "This is an outrageous conflict of interest. Working as a commentator and advising a campaign at the same time is a really bad idea." And the managing editor of *U.S. News & World Report,* Brian Kelly, said, "This to me crosses a line beyond belief."

The *Washingtonian* summed it up perfectly: "There once was a line between those who worked for politicians and those who worked for the media. You were a flack or a hack. That line has all but disappeared."[1]

Unlike Begala and Carville, columnist Peggy Noonan announced that she was taking several months off from the *Wall Street Journal* to work on the Republican campaign.

When I spoke with Bill O'Reilly about what the CNN boys did, he told me that that kind of thing "would not be tolerated here at Fox News. Nobody could be employed under the banner of Fox News and work for a political campaign. It is against all journalistic ethics."[2]

I was thinking that the least CNN could have done was place a graphic on a certain forehead that read, "The statements emanating from the mouth below have been preapproved by the Kerry campaign."

MOORE COVERAGE

During the political conventions in the summer of 2004, the mainstream media showed once again that they hold conservatives to different standards. Muckraking filmmaker Michael Moore made big news because of his "documentary" *Fahrenheit 9/11,* which, as Chapter 8 will detail, was riddled with distortions. The fabrications in Moore's film didn't prevent the media from celebrating his role in the campaign. Moore, in fact, managed to get his puss plastered on TV at both political conventions.

First, in July, Moore was feted at the Dem fest in Boston. The Democrats treated Moore as an honored guest, seating him next to Jimmy Carter in the presidential box, where he earned lots of face time on TV. Somehow, mainstream reporters didn't make much of the Dems' celebration of a hallucinating lefty who had promoted conspiracy theories about President Bush, his family, and his associates. Dems were crazy about Moore's flick, thinking it would help their cause. (In fact, according to *Time* magazine, the normally frosty Tom Daschle, the Senate minority leader, gave Moore a little hug at the Washington premiere of *Fahrenheit 9/11*.)

During the convention, Moore ratcheted up the rhetoric. Speaking at a forum sponsored by the left-wing group Campaign for America's Future, Moore gave his fans some of his patented outrage. "The right wing is just a small minority of people who hate," he bellowed. "They hate. They exist in the politics of hate. They're not patriots, they're hate-triots, and they believe in the politics of hate-triotism. I mean, they are up at six in the morning trying to figure out which minority group they're going to screw today." He finished up with a record use of the "h" word, saying, "They hate, they eat [it] for breakfast. They are going to fight and they are going to smear, and they are going to lie, and they are going to hate."

Sounds like someone lost his rubber ducky.

USA Today was so taken with Moore that it hired him to cover the Republican National Convention in New York. But the paper was quick to say that it was respecting the idea of equal time. It chose conservative pundit Ann Coulter to cover the Dems' coronation of John Kerry.

Apparently, for *USA Today*, publishing conservative commentary seemed better in theory than in practice. The paper never ran any of Coulter's columns. The editors spiked her first piece, the stated reason being that "we had a disagreement over editing." Coulter had another explanation, telling the online edition of *Editor and Publisher* magazine, "*USA Today* doesn't like my 'tone,' humor, sarcasm, etc., which raises the intriguing question of why they hired me to write for them."[3]

Funny how *USA Today* had no "disagreements over editing" with the over-the-top Moore when he dished the applesauce on the Republican National Convention. But Republicans who were gathered at Madison Square Garden didn't give Moore the adulation he was accustomed to from Democrats and the media. On the first day of the Republican convention, Moore received the same audience feedback that he got when he accepted his Academy Award in 2003—a big bunch of boos. During his address, Senator John McCain of Arizona boldly reminded the delegates about "a disingenuous filmmaker who would have us believe that Saddam's Iraq was an oasis of peace." Everyone knew exactly who he was talking about. At first the audience cheered McCain, but the positive crowd reaction quickly became negative as the focus turned toward Moore. Moore taunted the delegates, grinning and flashing hand gestures, and the boos grew even louder. Eventually, though, the crowd shifted into a joyful Bush-oriented chant of "Four more years."

The Republican delegates seemed to realize that winning the election would be the best payback. They were right.

HOLLYWOOD GETS *OUTFOXED*

While Michael Moore getting booed by an arena full of Republicans isn't exactly earth-shaking news, the same convention did produce something that shocked some observers and may have changed the face of the news biz.

It turned out that a cable venue, Fox News, soundly thumped the Big Three broadcast networks in the prime-time ratings during the Republican National Convention. It was unprecedented.

Stunned network execs from CBS, NBC, and ABC struggled to come up with an explanation for their setbacks. Instead of recognizing the obvious—that their production may be stale and their priorities impaired, and that more and more folks believed they were biased—they chose to sing the same old refrain that the Left uses when fussing about Fox. They chalked up the loss to the notion that the cable network is biased to the right.

Hollywood had already set things up when, among other things, it poisoned the media atmosphere with *Outfoxed,* the so-called documentary that basically characterized the FNC as the RNC in disguise. One broadcast bigwig told the *Washington Post* that the "Fox News Channel doing a big number at the RNC is the least shocking thing that's happened all week," offering the analogy that "the Olympics are to NBC what the RNC is to Fox News." Another exec called Fox "the official channel of the GOP," adding that "if people didn't know it before they certainly know it now." And yet another executive said the reason for the cable network's unprecedented success was that Fox was an "in-house organ" of the Republicans.

Fox News Channel representative Paul Schur reacted this way: "It must be embarrassing to no end that they got beat by a cable news network." He then suggested, "These are the groans the dinosaurs made before they became extinct."[4]

CBS's Dan Rather appeared to be munching on sour grapes. Out of one side of the anchor's mouth came an apparent compliment, "I tip my cap to Fox." But before the positive statement could take root, the following words flew out of the other side of his mouth: "I'm sure people in the party are saying that's a great audience and on a channel that's friendly to us. But the wise ones know that this is preaching to the converted." In a seemingly defensive as well as self-promoting effort, Rather added, "If they want to reach independent or swing voters, the way to do that is through the over-the-air networks."[5]

Fox News anchors boldly defended their employer. Cable's top guy, Bill O'Reilly, said, "If Fox News is a conservative channel— and I'm going to use the word 'if'—so what? You've got 50 other media that are blatantly Left. Now, I don't think Fox is a conservative channel. I think it's a traditional channel. There's a difference. We are willing to hear points of view that you'll never hear on ABC, CBS, or NBC."[6]

Meanwhile, *Fox News Sunday* host Chris Wallace, who had spent fifteen years with ABC, declared, "The only marching order I've had is to do the best news show I can, and there's never been a single eyebrow raised about what we've done."[7]

Fox Report's Shepard Smith stated, "I swear I'm not biased, and I know that no one [at Fox] has ever told me what to say."[8]

And Jim Angle, who worked at ABC for three years and at NPR for nine years before becoming Fox's senior White House correspondent, contended that "the only time in my career that anyone ever told me I had to say something was when I was with a different organization."9

Admittedly, Fox News did much better in the ratings during the Republican convention than it did during the Democratic one. Fox's ratings were up 107 percent when compared with the Democratic convention. CNN, on the other hand, did 42 percent better during the Democratic convention than during the Republican one. These ratings support the findings of the Pew Research Center, which issued a report in 2004 showing that more Republicans watch Fox than CNN and more Democrats watch CNN than Fox. Interestingly, though, the Pew survey showed that Fox is hardly preaching to an all-Republican choir. In fact, only 41 percent of Republicans said they liked to watch Fox, while 25 percent said they actually preferred CNN. And a fairly sizable minority of Democrats, 29 percent, watched Fox, though 44 percent said they instead tune in to CNN.

Fox News's vice president of production, Bill Shine, pointed out that partisanship could not explain away the success of Fox. He noted that Fox has been at the top of the cable news charts for years because "we have a better, more interesting screen, and better, more interesting journalists."

Ratings data regarding another major news story seem to lend credence to Shine's assessment. It turns out that, in its coverage of Hurricane Charley, Fox earned better ratings than CNN and even the Weather Channel. As a result, Shine confidently quipped, "When someone can convince me that a hurricane hitting the coast of Florida has a Republican bent, let me know."10

60 MINUTES OF DON HEWITT BIAS

While folks on the Left like to claim that Fox News is a hotbed of conservatism, they bristle when anyone suggests that mainstream outlets are liberal brothels. For instance, any negative comment about CBS's 60 Minutes is usually dismissed out of hand, since that long-running program is often labeled the flagship of television journalism. But it's eye-opening to take a closer look at this supposedly middle-of-the-road broadcast. One way to do that is to look at the man who started it all, the show's creator, Don Hewitt.

In the spring of 2004, Hewitt gave an interview with CBS's MarketWatch.com's Jon Friedman in which he revealed a few things about himself and the leanings of his decades-old program. Emphasizing his supposed objectivity, Hewitt told Friedman that he is "not in anybody's pocket." Apparently he forgot about Viacom, the parent company of CBS and, coincidently, the parent company of the publishers of books by former treasury secretary Paul O'Neill, former White House counterterrorism coordinator Richard Clarke, and the *Washington Post's* Bob Woodward. One after another, these authors appeared on the "not in anybody's pocket" *60 Minutes* program to answer interview questions that looked suspiciously like they were lifted from a DNC-action alert. It was enough to make Ed Bradley's earring fall off.

Hewitt also claimed to be nonpartisan. "I don't vote parties," he alleged. "I'm an Eisenhower-Reagan Republican and a Roosevelt-Kennedy Democrat." Referring to the upcoming election, Hewitt said, "I would bet I'll probably vote for Kerry," then quickly tacked on the phrase "but I don't know that yet."

While Hewitt didn't yet know if he would toss his vote John Kerry's way, he seemed to be more sure-footed when it came to his Dubya decision. "I know why I don't want to vote for George Bush," Hewitt declared. "If I should hold anything against George Bush," it's that the war in Iraq has "created more terrorists," he contended.

Created more terrorists? That must have been a surprise to the knee-knocking, weapon-dismantling Muammar Qaddafi.

Despite Hewitt's claims about the political independence of his esteemed program, just months later an offshoot of the *60 Minutes* franchise would be nailed for trying to pull off a politically motivated journalistic hatchet job. It would become one of the most outrageous news scandals ever, but it would also produce some benefits—most notably, a shift in the media equation.

RATHERGATE

It seems that Bill Clinton has something in common with Kenny Rogers. They both know when to hold 'em and when to fold 'em.

Back when Clinton was mired in his Lewinsky scandal and he was confronted with a certain piece of blue clothing, he cut the stonewalling. Dan Rather, on the other hand, continued to wallow in Watergate-like denial when confronted with the overwhelming evidence that the documents he had presented to the nation in a story about President George W. Bush's National Guard service were not just questionable—they were patently fake.

Rather tried to sell the notion that it was somehow acceptable to forge the name of a dead man in order to smear a sitting president while in the midst of a war and a tight election as well. What made it okay? If the journalist in question trotted out an octogenarian former secretary to say that although she believed the documents were fake, she felt that the contents of the documents were factual. Putting it in Dan-speak, CBS attempted to sell the public more cow pies than a dunghill at a cattle ranch.

It all began in September of 2004, during a broadcast of the Wednesday edition of *60 Minutes,* when Rather presented a story about Bush's National Guard service that CBS, and the Democrats, believed would be a bombshell in the presidential race. CBS revealed documents purporting to show that Bush had received preferential treatment in the National Guard and avoided his military obligations. Rather's report claimed that the documents were from the personal files of the late Lieutenant Colonel Jerry B. Killian, Bush's squadron commander. Over and over, Terry McAuliffe and other Democrats had been saying, without proof, that Bush hadn't fulfilled his obligations in the National Guard and had gotten away with it because of his father's connections. The Dems were salivating at the prospect of a Republican candidate on the ropes.

Only one problem: The documents weren't real.

Soon after the story aired, a whole bunch of forensic document experts surfaced to challenge the authenticity of CBS's memos. The formerly under-the-radar Internet blogosphere flexed its media muscle. CBS News had posted the memos on its website, and within hours, bloggers were raising serious questions about the documents. For starters, they pointed out that the memos, supposedly typed in the early 1970s, looked as if they were created on modern-day word-processing software. In fact, they displayed many characteristics that couldn't have been produced by type-writers in use in that period.

At the time, CBS claimed to have relied on experts to determine the reliability of the documents. But one of the experts, Marcel Matley, publicly stated that he had verified only the signature and had said nothing about the validity of the document itself. Because the memos were copies, Matley in a later interview said, "There's no way that I, as a document expert, can authenticate them." CBS never had the originals. And document examiners are not able to authenticate a photocopy.

Soon two of the other CBS experts showed up on ABC News with additional revelations that splattered more egg on the faces of Rather & Co. One expert, Emily Will, stated that she had expressed unease about Killian's signature and the typography in the memos. The other, Linda James, said that she had "cautioned" CBS, warning the network that other document examiners would see the same problems that she had. James told CBS that she couldn't rule out that the memos had been "produced on a computer." It also came out that none of these experts had prepared a written report before the *60 Minutes* segment was aired.

Adding to Rather's quandary was the fact that Colonel Walter B. "Buck" Staudt, the man who was cited in one of the memos as putting on the pressure to "sugarcoat" Bush's record, wasn't even in the National Guard at the time; he had retired from the service a year and a half earlier.

CBS hunkered down and tried to mount a defense. It trotted out more experts to declare that the documents didn't come from a computer printer. But the new set of authenticators told the press that they were not document examiners. They had very specialized expertise in computer-typesetting technology and fonts. They were not certified by the American Board of Forensic Document Examiners, something that in a court case a seasoned lawyer would require.

Still others came forward to challenge the CBS report. Both Jerry Killian's widow and his son maintained that it was ridiculous to suggest that he had written these memos. The widow revealed that Killian didn't type or keep written files. And Killian's son, who had also served in the National Guard, stated, "No officer in his right mind would write a memo like that." And the daughter of a man who said he had thrown his weight around to get Bush into the National Guard, former Texas House Speaker Ben Barnes, said her father was a liar, and that he had admitted to her earlier that he had nothing to do with getting Bush favorable treatment.

As the evidence mounted against CBS's story, Dan Rather just dug in his snakeskin boots. At one point he defiantly told CBS viewers that the network had gotten the memos from "unimpeachable sources." The only reason these questions were getting play, he suggested, was that "partisan political operatives" were waging a campaign against CBS.

At the time I offered Dan some suggestions that he might consider using as excuses. I wrote the following memo of my own:

> Dan, about the forged documents flap. You're going about it all wrong. You need a better defense. Try giving a few of these a whirl.

> • About you not ever having the original documents, blame it on successor-hopeful John Roberts and make a big stink about him leaving them at Kinko's.
> • About when you said that the memos were from the personal files of the departed lieutenant colonel, but his widow and

son insisted that he kept no personal files and that Killian didn't type, say he was a closet typist like Joel Klein.

• About critics pointing out that the typing on the docs looked immaculate and that there were no errors, visible corrections, or misspellings, say that Killian had special-ops training in erasing.

• About the *Washington Times* and other media sources bringing in handwriting experts to look at the signatures and coming to the conclusion that they were counterfeit, take a dance break on top of an SUV.

• About your saying that Marcel Matley, the handwriting expert you used, authenticated the signature, but he wrote that he couldn't authenticate a copied signature, divert attention by asking if anyone remembers Marcel Marceau and his "Bip the clown" routine.

• About Colonel Walter Staudt not being able to pressure Killian because Staudt retired a year and a half before Killian's memo was written, launch into a rendition of "I'm a Little Teapot."

• About retired General Bobby Hodges authenticating the memos over the phone and then reneging, say that you heard he was offered a job at Halliburton.

• About not having talked to Killian's widow and son, change the subject. Pretend that you've got a Jolly Rancher stuck in your throat.

• About computer geeks pointing out that the memos exhibit things like variable line spacing, automatic word wrap, kerning, proportional spacing, superscripting, and precise centering and that no technology existed in 1972 or 1973 that could have accomplished all of these things simultaneously, tell them Killian was a fellow time traveler.

And then do your broadcast from Roswell.

Dan didn't take my suggestions. The tack he took was something the writers for *Mad TV* couldn't have thought up. Some brainiacs at CBS came up with a new theory that even if the papers were forged phonies, as long as the assertions in them might possibly be true, they were off the hook. So America watched as Rather asked leading questions of Marian Carr Knox, the eighty-six-year-old former secretary of Lieutenant Colonel Killian.

"I know that I didn't type them," Knox acknowledged. But she added that "the information in those is correct." Rather's follow-up questions failed to delve into how Knox had acquired that particular knowledge.

Rather and CBS tried to skate by. Predictably, though, Rather's peers, the blogosphere, and the public weren't buying the idea that "fake but real" could be used to defend anything other than the stylishly pouty-looking lips in Hollywood.

CBS News kept trying to build a barrier against the mounting criticism, and in doing so it took a page from some of the craftiest D.C. operatives. It decided to try to blame the White House. Reports from the *Los Angeles Times* indicated that although CBS news executives had entertained serious doubts over the authenticity of the photocopied documents, their concerns had been addressed when they heard about a single conversation. Here's what soothed the execs' doubts: In an interview with John Roberts, CBS's White House correspondent at the time, a presidential aide apparently hadn't *challenged* the authenticity of the documents. The thing is, though, the aide was not in a position to know anything about the documents, because they were supposedly from a third party's private files.

Information even came out about the "unimpeachable sources" who had provided the documents to CBS. As it happens, the person who had foisted the memos on CBS was a Texan named Bill Burkett. Far from being "unimpeachable," Burkett was actually known as a vociferous opponent of George W. Bush. A year and a half earlier, in fact, he had written an article on the website VeteransForPeace.org in which he compared Bush to Napoleon and Hitler.

Things really seemed to be caving in on Rather and the CBS team when the network's own Andy Rooney spoke out publicly. "I'm surprised at their reluctance to concede they're wrong," the

60 Minutes curmudgeon said. Rooney also had some thoughts on Rather's future at CBS—rather prescient ones, as it would turn out. Although he said he didn't believe the CBS suits would immediately remove Rather from the anchorman's chair, Rooney predicted that the phony memos "might have an effect on him six months from now."

Finally, after ten long days in which CBS's story had been completely exposed as a fraud, Rather issued a statement in which he acknowledged, "I no longer have the confidence in these documents that would allow us to continue vouching for them journalistically."

There it was, an admission that should have come days earlier, when it became obvious that the National Guard memos were fakes. But it was only a *partial* admission. Dan still wasn't willing to concede that the documents were phonies. When he was interviewed by the *Chicago Tribune,* Rather said, "Do I think they're forged? No."

Despite his refusal to own up to the forgeries, Rather just couldn't sidestep the blame for the National Guard story. He had been an anchor for longer than anyone in the network's history. So what was he supposed to do?

Well, for one thing, he should have immediately revealed the source of the fake memos. Those who commit fraud, or a crime like forgery, forfeit any confidentiality owed by journalists to their sources.

And there's something else he should have mused about. When NBC's *Dateline* used explosives to make it look as if the alleged flaws in the design of a truck caused a blast, the president of the NBC news division resigned.

And when a couple of writers from the *New York Times* and *USA Today* did a little fabricating, some high-level editors did a little resigning.

For a while, then, we listened to the ticking, waiting to see if and when the CBS eye would blink.

What did the network do? It hired two independent experts— former attorney general Richard Thornburgh and former Associated Press president Louis Boccardi—to figure out what went wrong.

Before the investigators could issue their report, Rather made an announcement of his own. In November 2004 he revealed that he would step down as anchor of the *CBS Evening News*. Interestingly, he gave up the anchor's chair on March 9, 2005—almost exactly six months after Rathergate erupted.

About that Rooney prediction, there were some rumors floating around that CBS execs had perused the phone bills and were surprised to find that somebody had been making calls to the Psychic Hotline.

THE CHANGING MEDIA LANDSCAPE

The ten days in September that became known as Rathergate were a remarkable turn of events. The "Tiffany Network" had been severely tarnished—mainly by people whom CNN executive Jonathan Klein famously dismissed as guys "sitting in [their] living room in [their] pajamas."

Our beloved bloggers, plus or minus their PJs, led the search for the truth, and in the process they exposed Rather, *60 Minutes,* and CBS News. These were individuals spread out across the country who did real legwork and investigation.

Without the New Media's valuable check-and-balance ability, things would have been very different. Had CBS run with this story in the 2000 election, it's conceivable that the forgeries wouldn't have been exposed. Why? Well, four years earlier the network of blogs wasn't nearly as developed as it was by 2004, meaning that information could not have been exchanged as easily and as systematically among various individuals sharing their research and investigation.

A story like this would not have been exposed in a pre-Internet age. CBS News posted the memos on its website, which allowed bloggers and journalists to examine them closely for themselves. Had a television news program run with forged documents only fifteen years earlier, it might have gotten away with it. Memos flashed on the TV screen for a bit wouldn't have been subject to real scrutiny.

But today the rules have been laid down for CBS and other media members. If bogus documents are used, the cyber-sleuths, radio P.I.s, and cable gumshoes will be there to blow the whistle.

It's a whole new media ballgame.

Crier Confab

Former prosecutor and judge and Emmy Award–winning journalist Catherine Crier has been an anchor on Court TV since 1999; she is now celebrating her fifth year as host of *Catherine Crier Live*. She began her television career at CNN and was coanchor of both *Inside Politics* and *The World Today,* the prime-time newscast of the cable network. She also hosted *Crier & Company,* a live half-hour news talk show featuring a panel of female policy experts.

Crier also has experience with a major broadcast network as well. She was a correspondent and recurring substitute anchor for Peter Jennings on ABC's *World News Tonight* as well as substitute anchor for Ted Koppel on *Nightline.* She also served as a correspondent on *20/20.* She then moved on to anchor her own show, *The Crier Report,* a live one-hour interview program for the Fox News Channel.

I talked with Crier and, among other things, got her perspective on the blurring of news and entertainment and Hollywood-style trappings as they relate to journalists.[1]

HIRSEN: Is there a possibility that, particularly with young people, they are no longer discerning the difference between entertainment and news?

CRIER: Well, I worry. I worry about that, and the great example is the

Oliver Stone story. Do we believe the JFK film, or do we go back and read history and come up with our own conclusions? Which is not to criticize one way or the other this movie, but there are too many people today, I think, who receive their cinematic version or their television news version of events and take that as fact and history. And most of the time it's not.

That's not necessarily attributing bad motives to people who are putting out the information. But we know that when you are relying on very few sources nowadays, when you're not getting historical perspective, when you're not putting things in context and you're also chasing a moving target as events unfold, you aren't delivering enough substance for people to say, "Here is the reality. Here is sort of truth with a capital 'T' to the best that I can discern it." You can't get that from television, and I think whether it's documentaries or film, sophisticated viewers have to understand that there's a point of view, there's a perspective, there's usually an angle. And I don't care who's delivering it, Right, Left, or Center. You've got to go back and be a student of history and read the weeklies, the monthlies, and your books, and then figure out what truth is.

HIRSEN: James Fallows pointed out that we now have superstar journalists who get lecture fees from organizations and write and sell books. They go on one show as a commentator and on another show as a journalist. Do you see any problems with this?

CRIER: Oh, we could point to so many professions and say there are problems. I think the problem comes if you're not candid about your position. You know, I've been sitting on the bench, I've been a news anchor, and I'm also now doing a talk show. And I give my opinions now but I make it clear, "This is just my opinion and this could be wrong." Sort of like what Bill O'Reilly does, which I think he does well, "Tell me why I'm wrong." You've got to have enough integrity to step up to the plate and say, "This may be a bias, this is my own position, this is the reason I came to this conclusion, and I could be wrong." And if people are unwilling to do that, then I think they ought to be called on it.

HIRSEN: Out here in Hollywood, we have people who have reached a level of notoriety where they are surrounded by an entourage that is so thick with yes people that it insulates them from the outside world. They even have difficulty getting objective opinions about their ideas. To some extent we have journalists now who have achieved this same kind of celebrity. Do you think this takes away from the ability to be a journalist?

CRIER: Well, I'm a bit of a Studs Terkel sort. I love the notion that journalism reporting was a trade and not a "profession." In other words, you got out on the street and you got to know people when you ferreted out your stories and you really were a man or woman *of* the people. And I don't mean that to oppose the "elite," but you knew your country and you knew your community and you were out there working the stories.

I tend to agree with what I'm hearing in your question, and that is, I don't know that that's a good thing. If you're really going to be sort of a morning personality—and I don't mean to pick on the morning shows, but whatever show—then we've got to be careful because you are utilizing personality to sell as much as you are delivering information. Some of that is unavoidable given the exposure that you get, particularly through television.

But I think you've got to keep reminding yourself who you are, what you are, keeping in touch. And just like I don't approve of CEOs necessarily making $423 million a year—I think some of the salaries and attention are kind of wild—but we're in a capitalist country and if I'm going to say you can't pay a talk show host that, then I'll have to argue that you can't pay the baseball player and you can't pay the CEO.

And do we really want some external force telling us what the value is in a country that is supposed to gauge value by a kind of supply and demand and all the rest of that business?

But I know for me—and this is going to sound a bit, you know, patting myself on the back—but I come in and I do my job. And I go home and I clean up after six dogs and four horses. And I play in the countryside and I grocery shop for myself and I drive my Honda hybrid. Ha, Ha, see I'm Hollywood. [Laughs] I sold my Mercedes and bought a hybrid.

HIRSEN: You've been on the list of so-called "info babes." Is there a pressure now to be concerned with image?

CRIER: Of course, it's always been that way in television, whether it's movies, television, television news. I think I was looking in *USA Today* and the cover of, I think it was the Lifestyle section, was how middle-class America is now finding their way to the cosmetic surgeons on a regular basis. The country is obsessed with that sort of thing.

My first job was prosecutor in the DA's office, and then I ended up on the bench before I came here, so I understand that—you know, I want to thank my parents for genetic contribution [Laughs] and I really appreciate that—but I also think I've tried very hard to have the intellectual background and [I am] determined to try and make that contribution, so I hope my head is kind of balanced. If they come in one day and say, You look too old to do this, well then I'm writing books and I'm lecturing and I'll go do something else.

But I feel bad when I see people who feel that they're in a box. We've been doing this long enough, and people like Barbara Walters, for women, have come on through. But I really think the pipeline is opening up where it's becoming much more what you contribute. But you better stay on top of that game, because otherwise cosmetics can overtake substance. I think as long as people, men and women, really have the substance and have something to offer, then the other remains secondary.

6

ENTER STAGE LEFT

The more things change, the more they stay the same. At least that's how it looks as I scan the tilted terrain of Tinseltown.

In Hollywood, most of the money goes to the Dems and has for a long stretch. Oscar winners provide a good indication of where Tinseltown's political sympathies lie: According to Federal Election Commission records, Academy Award winners gave about *forty times* as much to Democrats and Greens in the 2000 presidential campaign as to Republicans. On the whole, over the past several years more than 70 percent of the cash from Hollywood has gone to the Democrats. In 2000, for instance, the entertainment industry channeled 64 percent of its contributions to Dems. The figure went up to 78 percent in 2002 and hung in there at 69 percent for the 2004 election cycle.

We're talking about a lot of dough here. Hollywood is one of the nation's largest sources of money for federal campaigns, according to the Center for Responsive Politics.[1]

A big Democrat donor in Tinseltown, Haim Saban, explained why the Dems always come west to seek cash. "They come where they know, as a matter of principle, they have great support. They're not going to go to Mississippi," he cracked.[2]

527 HEAVEN

Hollywood fund-raising isn't quite as simple as it used to be. Huge gifts like Saban's $7 million donation to the Democratic Party in 2002 have been banned under the McCain-Feingold campaign finance reform law. The new rules prohibit an individual from giving a candidate more than $2,000 at a pop.[3]

But that doesn't mean the Hollywood pipeline to the Democrats has been shut off. Dems and deep-pocketed Tinseltown donors quickly figured out ways around the new laws. The same individual who earlier wrote a check directly to the Democratic National Committee can still give a gazillion dollars to benefit his or her candidate of choice, as long as the money is funneled through something called a 527 group. (The term *527* refers to the section of the IRS code that allows these entities to get around campaign finance laws and raise "soft" money.)

Anyone smell money being laundered?

The Democrats really figured out how to game the system in the 2004 election. According to the nonprofit Center for Public Integrity, Democratic-supporting 527s spent three times as much on the 2004 presidential race as did GOP-supporting 527s.[4] As the presidential campaign heated up, John McCaslin of the *Washington Times* quoted Larry Purpuro, founding partner of Rightclick Strategies (an online solutions developer), speaking on a panel on the election. "If you look at the list of all 527s to date," Purpuro pointed out, "the top 20, 18 of them are clearly left of center. Two would arguably be on the Republican side. . . . If you've looked at their expenditures, the top 20 committees alone have spent almost $100 million as of the last reporting requirement, which is no small piece of change."

I still haven't figured out how soft money ceases to be evil only when it's financing the Left.

In any case, the Dems learned how to do the soft-money merengue—with some fancy dance lessons from the entertainment industry. One Dem pot of soft-money gold arrived courtesy of Bruce Springsteen and other musicians during the 2004 campaign. To support the John Kerry camp and to try to help defeat George W. Bush, Springsteen joined forces with the Dixie Chicks, R.E.M., James Taylor, Jurassic 5, the Dave Matthews Band, Keb' Mo', John Mellencamp, Bonnie Raitt, and Jackson Browne in what was called the Vote for Change tour, a series of concerts that went through nine swing states. MoveOn PAC, the electoral wing of the rabidly liberal group MoveOn.org, presented the shows. The money generated went to the Democratic 527 group America Coming Together (ACT). In case there was ever any doubt about ACT's politics, in August 2003, George Soros—the hedge fund investor and multibillionaire (with a "b") who ended up giving some $27 million in the effort to defeat President Bush—issued a statement saying, "The fate of the world depends on the United States and President Bush is leading us in the wrong direction. ACT is an effective way to mobilize civil society, to convince people to go to the polls and vote for candidates who will reassert the values of the greatest open society in the world."

Saturday Night Live alum Will Ferrell also joined in the fund-raising efforts. Ferrell is a likable guy who's great at portraying harebrained dullards and dizzy dimwits. ACT enlisted him to do his Bush impersonation for a sham campaign commercial called "White House West." The anti-Bush organization posted the commercial on its website and used it to ask visitors to sign a petition to the Federal Communications Commission. "Join ACT and our friend Will Ferrell for a behind-the-scenes look at 'White House West,' " the site stated. "We promise it's the best commercial you'll see this election. Help stop the Republicans' fraud by joining ACT today and signing our petition to the FCC."

The plea to the FCC read, "Americans must be able to trust the facts in political ads. Every voter has the right to truthful advertising. Free speech is no defense to massive, purposeful fraud. You, the FCC, have an obligation to ensure that broadcast stations around the country do not transmit misleading, deceptive and fraudulent advertising. We, the undersigned American citizens, demand that you require proof of fact before airing political advertisements. Laws must change to protect our democracy."

So basically ACT wanted to modify the law to get rid of "Republican" fraud. Apparently, this is the Left's idea of free speech. Maybe their motto ought to be "You're only free to agree with me."

Plenty of other celebrities joined MoveOn.org's campaign to toss President Bush out of the White House. MoveOn PAC amassed big-name Hollywood troops to produce campaign ads attacking Bush and assisting John Kerry. Rob Reiner directed an ad written by *West Wing* creator Aaron Sorkin. Literary mudslinger Al Franken wrote copy. Comic Margaret Cho wrote and directed a piece. Danny Glover made a splash. Alicia Silverstone did an appearance. Woody Harrelson scripted and directed a spot. There was even an animated bit that used the voices of Kevin Bacon, Ed Asner, and Scarlett Johansson. The ads were reportedly tested on focus groups so MoveOn could determine the best timing and location for each bitter broadcast.

At the time I was wondering if the darn things were going to pop up on the 2 A.M. replays of *Punk'd*.

THE HOLLYWOOD ASSAULT
ON THE FOX NEWS CHANNEL

The Hollywood Left struck again in the summer of 2004, and this time the target was the Fox News Channel. Leading the partisan attack was Robert Greenwald Productions, whose previous flicks included *Steal This Movie*, a biography of the late arch-radical activist Abbie Hoffman; *Crooked E*, a made-for-TV film about the Enron scandal; and *Uncovered: The Whole Truth About the Iraq War*. *Outfoxed: Rupert Murdoch's War on Journalism*, which premiered in the summer of 2004, was allegedly an exposé of how Fox News was biased toward the conservative viewpoint of Rupert Murdoch. It featured leaked policy memos, footage of FNC anchors in action, and interviews with former Fox employees.

Greenwald told MSNBC's Keith Olbermann that "the level of fear about Roger Ailes and FNC was as extreme as I've ever seen. People hung up the phone on me. People told me that their e-mail was being read. . . . People told me to lose their numbers. They feared for their jobs."

The film used intercepted material from satellite feeds that was not intended for public broadcast. One of the segments showed FNC's Carl Cameron talking to President Bush about Cameron's wife having a delightful time campaigning with the president's sister. The movie also revealed memos from a senior FNC vice president instructing journalists on how to report about U.S. fatalities in Iraq. "Do not fall into the easy trap of mourning the loss of U.S. lives," the memo said. Another memo referred to coverage of the U.S. military's siege of Fallujah. "It won't be long before some people start to decry the use of 'excessive force,'" the memo read. "We won't be among that group." A third memo on the 9/11 Commission stated, "The fact that former Clinton and both former and current Bush administration officials are testifying gives it a certain tension, but this is not 'what did he know and when did he know it' stuff. Do not turn this into Watergate."

Greenwald said that one of the reasons he made the flick was that he "wanted to start a campaign to free the reporters at Fox News."

Well, I guess someone had to do something about those poor Fox News journalists who are stuck working on the number-one-rated cable news station in the country.

Greenwald marketed his movie with some significant lefty assistance, especially from MoveOn.org, which distributed DVDs directly to his audience and even covered a significant part of the cost of the film. The support for Greenwald's film was part and parcel of MoveOn's campaign against the Fox News Channel. MoveOn, along with the like-minded group Common Cause, petitioned the FTC to compel Fox to get rid of the cable network's slogan "Fair and Balanced." The petition read, "I believe the Federal Trade Commission and Congress must act to prevent Fox News from using the deceptive and misleading trademark 'Fair and Balanced.' "

MoveOn's chief media reform spokesperson, Noah T. Winer, revealed to *Media Life* magazine the motivation behind the legal challenge against Fox News. Winer claimed that Fox was misrepresenting itself by using the phrase "Fair and Balanced" because "it's a partisan network interested in repackaging and broadcasting Republican values. It's not fair in a democratic society to present your opinion as fact." When Winer whimpered, "What's happening at FNC is part of a larger trend that needs to be addressed," it was a signal to hold on to our First Amendment hats. He maintained that this larger trend was the "disintegration of journalism."

With the advent of talk radio, the Internet, and cable news, though, I venture to say that most folks see a greater opportunity for free flow of communication than ever before, and they also recognize that there are more info-providing venues from which to choose.

If that's disintegration, let's keep up the decline.

FESTIVAL FOLLIES

Other Hollywood libs picked up Greenwald and MoveOn's attack on Fox News. At the 2004 Venice Film Festival, for example, director Spike Lee admitted that Tinseltown personalities wanted to affect the political debate. "People are trying to have an influence," he confessed, but he claimed that was only fair, since "Bush has Fox News."

Lee was right about politics being in the air at Venice. Tim Robbins was at the festival to show a low-budget digital film version of his tedious, Iraq war–distorting play, *Embedded.* Robbins told the assembled entertainment press, "The last nine months, there has been a reaction to the deception that led us into war."

On the second day of the festival, director Jonathan Demme, while pushing his flawed flick *The Manchurian Candidate,* gave a news conference on a nonfilm subject. He was apparently in a geopolitical mood as well. "As an American, I really feel my country is in a lot of trouble," Demme unloaded, adding that "I think our leaders have taken us in a really bad direction on so many levels."

Demme gave a couple of reasons why he thought our leaders were headed the wrong way and why he believed they actually wanted to take over the world. "I feel that our leaders really want to own the world for two reasons," Demme surmised. "One, there are endless profits from owning the entire world, and because if you own and control the world, there is a relief from fear."

Which got me thinking: How can our leaders ever "own the world" unless George Soros decides to sell it to them?

ROBERT REDFORD'S CHE CHATTER

Tree-whisperer Robert Redford went after the Bush administration in 2004 as well, implying that it was somehow for dirtier air and water. Speaking at an event sponsored by the Environmental Accountability Fund, a political action committee, Redford blubbered, "Sadly, the erosion [in environmental policy] that's occurred is disastrous, frightening, and dangerous." The actor also howled that the administration was "intentionally blind" to the nation's environmental needs.

Actually, Redford seemed to be blind about some things himself. The celluloid Sundancer produced a film called *The Motorcycle Diaries,* a biopic about revolutionary Che Guevara's early years. The flick tells the story of the journeys of Guevara and his biker buddy, fellow Argentine Alberto Granado, during the 1950s, as they traveled across Latin America on a Norton motorbike.

Sort of a commie version of *Easy Rider.*

Redford went to Cuba in January 2004 to give comrade Fidel Castro and Guevara's relatives a private screening. "[Castro] came to me," Redford told Reuters. "He seemed to be in good health, good humor, good spirit."

Good grief. Apparently, Redford thinks a guy who puts dissenters in prison—or worse yet, in coffins—is worthy of neighborly concern.

"I came to present the film that I produced on Che Guevara and I am very happy to be in Cuba," Redford cheerily said.

NewsMax columnist Humberto Fontova offered a different perspective. "Che's true legacy is simply one of terror and murder," he wrote. "That dreaded midnight knock. Wives and daughters screaming in rage and panic as Che's goons drag off their dads and husbands—that's the real Che legacy."

Today in Cuba you can find children dressed in Fidel-style uniforms chanting in school each day, "We will be like Che," as they pledge to be "pioneers for communism." Pictures of Guevara are everywhere. They hang in schools, medical clinics, and food ration centers. His image also appears on a three-peso coin along with the words "Homeland or Death."

Redford's flick was shown at the actor's own Sundance Film Festival, where left-leaning fare is the norm and fair play never seems to see the light of day. And sadly, in La La Land, where lefty dreams come true, it took the Oscar for Best Song in 2005.

RICHARD CLARKE'S AGENT STUNNER

In the spring of 2004, Hollywood's interest in the Bush-bashing book *Against All Enemies* had Richard Clarke's agent and publisher feeling kind of flabbergasted. Clarke's business associates were apparently unaware of the amount of Bush antipathy in Tinseltown. Clarke's literary agent, Len Sherman, told the *New York Times* that he was shocked at how far the book had gone in such a short time period.

"He wrote the book to get the story out, he wasn't really thinking about the movies," Sherman disclosed. "Even the publishing house wasn't thinking that this would be a movie. It's a nonfiction, policy-driven book. But it became an inevitability."

Actually, there was a fairly simple explanation for why cinematic hearts in Tinseltown were aflutter. The book slapped the president around in a major way. Ron Bernstein, Clarke's film agent, was deluged with requests from executives, agents, and producers for copies of the book. "A million people called," Bernstein explained, including "almost every studio" and "every major production company."

Although HBO and a division of Universal wanted the rights to the Clarke manuscript, Sony Pictures Entertainment ended up making the deal. Sources indicated that Clarke sold the story for an amount in the low six figures.

Hollywood film companies often buy the rights to books that never make it to the screen. But because former Sony chairman John Calley is slated to develop and produce the celluloid Bush-basher, it's likely to become a reality. Calley has some experience with politically lopsided films. He was an executive at Warner Bros. and oversaw the production of *All the President's Men*.

Hey, Calley, how about this for a title of the screen version of Clarke's book—*All the President's Turncoats*?

I'm actually surprised Hollywood didn't option more Bush-bashing tomes. There were plenty to choose from in 2004. In an unfortunate sign of the times, some bookstores set up whole "I Hate Bush" sections, featuring an array of anger-laced selections, from *The I Hate George W. Bush Reader* to *The Bush-Hater's Handbook*. One novel, Nicholson Baker's *Checkpoint*, featured the nasty dialogue of two guys in a hotel room who were plotting the assassination of President Bush.

And wouldn't you know it? In an age when fiction takes the Documentary Oscar and Yasir Arafat snags the Nobel Peace Prize, Baker got plenty of kudos from both the glitterati and literati.

REVERSE BLACKLISTING

With so many outspoken liberals in Tinseltown, it turns out that conservatives can often get the cold shoulder. In my first book, *Tales from the Left Coast*, I coined the term "reverse blacklisting" and even included a whole chapter on the concept. Simply put, those in Hollywood with conservative leanings are hesitant to express their ideas publicly, because if they do, it can be detrimental to their careers.

Now, if you go out looking for a blacklist dispatch, chances are you're not going to find one. And it's unlikely that we'll be seeing SAG hearings held on the subject anytime soon. But I know from my research and firsthand experience—and the tons of personal communication I've had with those who have truly suffered, are afraid they may suffer, or have suffered mistakenly—that reverse blacklisting is very real and potentially devastating.

That industry folks would contact me over the years with the proviso that I keep their names private is understandable, given the way Republicans, libertarians, patriots, and people of traditional faith are treated by the Hollywood establishment. The discovery that a person has such tendencies can quickly land him or her on the Tinseltown rebuff list. There are, of course, several members of the Hollywood community who are outspoken about their beliefs and quite frankly don't give a rip, but they're usually the ones who have already achieved the level of success that affords them the luxury of thumbing their noses.

It just so happens that in its September 2004 issue, *Details* magazine outed some Hollywood Republican sympathizers. The magazine claimed that in order to address the celebrity deficit that the GOP was experiencing, the Republican National Committee had unveiled a list of stars who veer toward the Republican side of the aisle. Some of those listed, like Jessica Simpson and Shannen Doherty, had already been fingered as conservatives. But others were more unexpected, like Adam Sandler and Freddie Prinze Jr., although Prinze's wife, Sarah Michelle Gellar, has been known to lean right in the past.

In a related article, Sony producer Mike DeLuca stepped up and acknowledged his Republican affiliation, describing the reaction in Hollywood as the equivalent of being "exposed as a serial killer." DeLuca pointed out some lefty hypocrisy by saying, "They scream about the environment before they hop onto their private jets and blow 8,000 pounds of fuel getting to the Hamptons."

One of the celebs named in the *Details* article responded to the outing incident via her publicist and did so in an entertaining and quasi-historical manner. The star was Mandy Moore, and the *New York Post* reported the response as "Mandy is not, nor has she ever been, a Republican."

I was half expecting to wake up the next day to a news flash that had Mandy asking the prying reporters of *Details* magazine, "Have you no decency?"

Another actress, Patricia Heaton, described how one time she "was at a dinner party and someone made a snide comment about the current administration [George W. Bush's]. And I just wanted to lay it out there that not everyone agrees, just because you're sitting at a dinner party in Beverly Hills. And I said, 'Oh gosh, I love President Bush. My husband and I voted for him.' And literally, you thought I had crapped in the middle of the table. Sorry to be vulgar, but the reaction was so . . ." Heaton let out a gasp.[5]

Faith-filled individuals often have isolating encounters of their own in Hollywood. Actress Morgan Brittany knows firsthand. She told me this little neck-wrenching story. "There is an extreme dislike for anyone who wants to talk about religion," she explains. "I was told by a manager—I walked into his office and I'm wearing my cross necklace. He picks it up off my neck and says, 'You are going to have to lose that.' I said, 'Excuse me?' and he said, 'If I am going to represent you or you are going to work in Hollywood, you better lose that, and you better not *ever* mention religion.' I said, 'Well, you know what? I don't think this is going to work. This is just not going to work, because I'm not going to hide who I am.' He said, 'Well, have a good life.' Basically, You're out of here."

Of course, a dirty little secret of Hollywood is that not all faiths are equal. While Brittany has learned that she simply cannot discuss her religion in Tinseltown, if she had followed another, "acceptable" spiritual path, she would have had no problem. In fact, some alternative religions have become downright trendy.

CELEBRITY KABBALAH

What do Madonna, Guy Ritchie, Britney Spears, Gwyneth Paltrow, Demi Moore, Ashton Kutcher, Rob Lowe, Roseanne Barr, Elizabeth Taylor, Courtney Love, Sandra Bernhard, Paris Hilton, Paul Newman, Naomi Campbell, Mick Jagger, Rosie O'Donnell, Brittany Murphy, Winona Ryder, Sharon Osbourne, Jeff Goldblum, Laura Dern, Barbra Streisand, Diane Ladd, Monica Lewinsky, Marla Maples, and Dan Aykroyd have in common? They're among the celebs who have expressed an interest in the hottest Hollywood faith of late—Kabbalah.

Evidently, an insurance salesman from Brooklyn named Yahuda Berg has been able to convince the famous Tinseltowners that an ancient Jewish mystical teaching can supply them with the spirituality they crave.

The international headquarters of the Kabbalah Centre is located in Los Angeles. The Centre has taken the ancient teachings of Kabbalah and converted them into a New Age mystical philosophy promising improved sex, immortality, and a changed world. According to the Centre's website, it is "a miraculous source of power" studied by everyone from Jesus to Shakespeare. Followers scan the text of the Zohar, the Kabbalist commentary on the Bible, for protection. They also wear red strings around their wrists in order to keep the evil eye away.

According to the Centre, the Zohar is beneficial to the reader even if he or she has no inkling of what the Hebrew means.

Beneficial? Well, maybe not to the reader's wallet. The complete text sells for more than $400.

Madonna apparently believes in Kabbalah so much, she's helped to underwrite the organization's efforts by giving millions of dollars to the Centre.

I wonder if Berg has any P. T. Barnum books on his shelf.

Noonan Time

Peggy Noonan is a *New York Times* best-selling author and a contributing editor of the *Wall Street Journal, Time* magazine, and *Good Housekeeping.* She served as special assistant to the late President Ronald Reagan and chief speechwriter for Vice President George H. W. Bush as he ran for the presidency in 1988. Before entering the Reagan White House, Noonan was a producer at CBS News in New York, where she wrote and produced Dan Rather's daily radio commentary. She also wrote television news specials for CBS News. Noonan was an adjunct professor of journalism at New York University in 1978 and 1979.

Noonan shared her thoughts on the New Media, old Hollywood, and a timeless story.[1]

HIRSEN: A lot of television journalists, commentators, and analysts seem to have become stars in their own right, with the accompanying fame, salary, and lifestyle of Hollywood celebrities. Do you think this has had an effect on journalism or on the media in general?

NOONAN: Yes, but this has been true for the past fifty years, since the advent of television. The reporters FDR dealt with were working guys in bad hats whose suits hadn't been cleaned in a while and who smelled like tobacco. They were guys, not stars, and they had a craft, like being a good electrician. They were in touch with the common concerns of common men because they were common men. By the time Dick Nixon was dealing with reporters, they were richer than he was. By the time Reagan was dealing with them they were what I called the millionaires in the front row—the major network stars seated up front at the news conferences. It was then that it occurred to me that presidents come and go but anchors are forever. That's when it occurred to anchors, too. They became conceited about it, and quite vain, and it showed in their work.

HIRSEN: Much like the entertainment arena, looks, youth, and image seem to be becoming increasingly important in the TV news and information delivery world. What's your take?

NOONAN: Oh, that's life, isn't it? When I was in high school the most popular kids were pretty teenagers and handsome football players. TV is just an extension of life in this regard. But yes, a case can be made that Douglas Edwards and Walter Cronkite and Richard C. Hottelet were *not* hired because they were attractive. And your local anchors since the 1970s have mostly been hired because they're more attractive than the average bear. But here's a funny twist: the old lions like Cronkite became fiercely political and ideological. Young anchorwoman Tammy on WOOO in Tuscaloosa is less likely to be an ideological jerk slanting the news. She's more likely to be grateful she's there, and respectful of diversity, which is the holding of different views by others. Go figure.

HIRSEN: After 9/11, there was a controversy over whether television journalists, analysts, etc., should wear flag pins. This raised the issue of the use of terms such as "terrorists," "Muslim extremists," etc., and whether a patriotic reporter can be an objective one. What are your thoughts?

NOONAN: I'm with Zell Miller: reporters didn't win for us the right of freedom of speech, soldiers did. If a reporter can't feel and therefore show a minimal appreciation of that fact and this country, then he's probably not too mature and not too bright. I don't think anyone has to wear a pin of any kind. But I think it's sad if you want to wear a flag pin and feel you can't. You should do it anyway.

HIRSEN: Do you have any reflections on the Dan Rather memo flap?

NOONAN: It's the historic moment in which Old Media got defeated by New Media. It was the Agincourt of the Internet Age—the old aristocracy cut down by the new weaponry of the lowly yeomen of England. Only twenty years ago a major network could put forth as legitimate a forged political document and it would be months or years before they got nailed, if they got nailed. But certainly they wouldn't get caught until the damage had long been done. This time they got caught within twelve hours by an "intellectual entrepreneur"—i.e., a yeoman of England; i.e., a digger in pajamas; i.e., a blogger. Hooray. Big media isn't the only game in town anymore. Used to be the *New York Times* could do an unfair, badly reported piece and if you didn't like it you could write a letter to the editor that they wouldn't publish. Now the badly reported piece gets exposed in the next news cycle. May a million voices speak—ten million, a hundred. There will be a downside—there always is—and foolish and wicked things will be reported and said on the Internet. But the *New York Times* can always catch 'em and expose 'em down the line, so there you are. We live in great days.

HIRSEN: Hollywood is playing journalist with movies like *The Day After Tomorrow* and *Fahrenheit 9/11*. How do you think these types of cinema are impacting public perception?

NOONAN: I don't know. I suspect those inclined to believe a certain kind of propaganda come away reinforced. I suspect some who aren't too informed find themselves impressed. I suspect some know that Hollywood these days is always pushing an agenda, and are not impressed by the propaganda but enjoy the entertainment. And I suspect a lot of people just don't go. *Fahrenheit* was big for a documentary but not big for a movie. *Day After Tomorrow* I think kind of flopped but I sort of liked it because I liked the tale of survival part. But this all comes with the territory of freedom of speech.

HIRSEN: Many in the media displayed an antagonistic response to Mel Gibson's *The Passion of the Christ.* In your opinion what accounts for the hostility shown with regard to the film?

NOONAN: Well, Christ himself is controversial—he's either the son of God and God or he's not. He either spoke the greatest truths ever spoken or didn't. That's a controversy for you. A movie that says he is God will be controversial. What's different about the reaction to Gibson's film this time is the number of people who thought that to make an explicitly faithful and religious film was a faux pas at best and an incitement at worst. When did that happen? I don't know. Fifty and seventy-five years ago Sam Goldwyn and Harry Cohn, the old buccaneers who invented Hollywood, were making *Song of Bernadette* and *The Last Days of Pompeii* and *King of Kings.* They were feeding a market—and they had no fear, none, of bankrolling a story they didn't believe in. They were open-minded and noncensorious about others' beliefs, and they didn't feel acknowledging those beliefs compromised their own Judaism in any way. And they were right. I miss those guys. They also loved America so much. We don't appreciate enough who they were.

7

TINSELTOWN TAMPERING

These days it seems that Hollywood is poking its glitzy nose into every aspect of modern life. Though we expect our music, TV, and film to be Hollywood-ized, something else is being Tinseled up. More and more of what we think of as journalism is being turned into big- and little-screen entertainment.

Lost in all the debate about media bias is the fact that lots of people are now getting their scoops and forming their opinions courtesy of the entertainment industry. So while we need to take a look at the liberal twirlings of the David Brocks and Eric Altermans—the kind of stuff we saw in Chapter 4—we also need to eyeball the entertainment industry's ever growing urge to do some spinning and grinning.

The reality is that decision makers in the entertainment community now have a lot of power because they've jumped into the business of presenting what appears to be factual information.

And with Hollywood being as saturated as it is with liberal doc-
trine, films and TV shows are getting the full lefty treatment.

What's most troubling is that even though conservatives have
had some success in recent years documenting the liberal bias in
the news media, bigwigs in the entertainment field are essentially
making an end run around the news and planting their political
messages in supposed entertainment products.

LEFT COAST CREED

In addition to Hollywood celebs spending their time and money
campaigning for liberal pols and causes, more and more we see
that they're using their creative endeavors to promote a cockeyed
worldview. Some in the entertainment biz recognize the influence
of TV and films and want a liberally sanctioned message to get out
to the American people. Their shows and movies often betray
their politics.

Consider the long-running NBC drama *The West Wing* (known
to conservative wags as "The Left Wing"). In the program's 2003
season finale, the obnoxious Republican speaker of the House
character, played by John Goodman, temporarily ascended to the
presidency. To compensate for making a Republican the leader of
the free world, the writers made the character appear even more
revolting than usual.

While appearing on ABC's coffee klatch *The View,* actor John
Spencer, who plays *The West Wing*'s White House chief of staff,
Leo McGarry, said he saw no need to avoid the liberal prejudice of
the show. He commented, "I know myself, as a left-of-center liberal Democrat, I like to watch Fox and yell at all those people, you
know. And with 20 million viewers we must have some Republicans, I mean, you know, and I would think that they would love to
watch us and scream back."

Lawrence O'Donnell, a consultant on *The West Wing* and an
executive producer of the critically acclaimed but short-lived
NBC show *Mister Sterling,* offered an even more candid analysis

while appearing on CNN's *Reliable Sources*. Host Howard Kurtz brought up the lack of conservative characters on TV shows, saying, "One thing these programs have in common: Conservatives are practically invisible. President Bartlet in *The West Wing* is a Democrat. Martin Sheen [who plays Bartlet], in fact, made antiwar ads before the invasion of Iraq. *Mister Sterling* is a California liberal based loosely on Jerry Brown." Then Kurtz asked, "Why aren't there any Republicans?"

O'Donnell's answer was direct and honest. "You will never get that TV show. You'll never, ever get the Republican TV show. The Writers Guild of America, my union, is at a minimum, 99 percent leftist liberal. . . . And we don't know how to write it. We don't."

When I spoke with O'Donnell, I brought up that statement. He reflected on it and made a minor adjustment. Very minor. "I might have exaggerated," he told me. "It might be 90 [percent liberal]." But as to the fact that these writers are truly liberal, he said, "I mean it." That makes a real difference in the creative output, O'Donnell explained, since Tinseltown plots are based on the writers' personal experiences and feelings. "So there is that fictional scripted world, which is fueled by—basically, all of the fuel for that comes entirely from the creative members of the Writers Guild. And that is the group that I'm saying is 90 percent liberal," he stated. "And so they, of course, write what they know and what they feel, which is all you would ever ask a writer to do."[1]

Well, you might ask a writer to take off the "blue state" blinders once in a blue moon.

THE DOCUDRAMA BOOM

One way that Hollywood shapes the message is through the docudrama, and interestingly, a lot of TV writers, as well as filmmakers, are looking to history and current events to get their inspirations and plotlines. Today, reality-based narratives born of popular news stories are some of the hottest tickets in town.

Docudramas vary in type, scope, and approach. They can take the form of a dramatization of an actual occurrence, a historical reenactment, or a biopic. Examples of these kinds of docs include *JFK, Malcolm X, Reds, Mississippi Burning, The Insider, Apollo 13,* and *Nixon.*

Often we find that the works are multifaceted in nature: they may have a journalistic function, by conveying factual information, and also a dramatic function, since they spring from a writer's imagination. Good docudramas provide insight and expand our knowledge of the human condition, like *Roots, Schindler's List,* and *Braveheart.*

We have to keep in mind, though, that producers, directors, and creators of docudramas have discretion as to how much they care to dramatize aspects of their works or how much reality they wish to ignore or downplay. Writers, in particular, must fill in story gaps, which may take some heavy speculating. And character development is a world unto itself, with inner thoughts and feelings frequently being expressed through conjecture and fantasy in an effort to produce believable dialogue. The more a filmmaker departs from the historical record, the more subjective imagination directs the ultimate interpretation of reality. So film creators must be willing to interpret events in a balanced way, or else history and accuracy can be compromised.

Then there's the competitive pressure in the entertainment industry, especially on television. If the public is captivated by a story that's making headlines, network TV and cable execs will invariably turn out a docudrama on the news theme. And in the race to be first to get the story, there's a risk that accuracy gets sacrificed for ratings.

Just look at what happens during the all-important rating sweeps periods, in November, February, and May, when advertising rates are determined. The made-for-TV docudrama is a network favorite during these months.

"Ripped-from-the-headlines" crime cases are especially popular. For example, the trial of Lyle and Erik Menendez produced two TV flicks, *Menendez: A Killing in Beverly Hills* and *Honor Thy Father and Mother: The True Story of the Menendez Murders.* And when CBS figured that we hadn't seen enough of the O.J. Simpson trial, it gave us *American Tragedy,* a two-part miniseries.

Within a single week, no less than three TV movies—*The Amy Fisher Story, Amy Fisher: My Story,* and *Casualties of Love: The Long Island Lolita Story*—came out and told the story of the seventeen-year-old Long Island girl who had an affair with a married auto mechanic and ultimately shot the mechanic's wife.

A couple of docu-versions—*Perfect Town, Perfect Murder* and *Getting Away with Murder: The JonBenet Ramsey Story*—detailed the tragic killing of the little girl. The latter had three different endings with three different murderers.

Only a month after the raid on the Branch Davidians in Waco, Texas, one could see *In the Line of Duty: Ambush in Waco,* which dramatized the tale of the religious group's standoff with the government and the horrible way the men, women, and children met their deaths.

Just in time for the November 2003 sweeps period, and even before the start of the trials for John Muhammad and John Lee Malvo, the USA Network brought us *D.C. Sniper: 23 Days of Fear,* a two-hour film about the three-week shooting spree that claimed thirteen lives. The movie was told from the perspective of Maryland police official Charles Moose, who became an instant celebrity.

When a ten-year-old Cuban boy made it to freedom while his mother lost her life trying to bring him to safety in the United States, Hollywood execs turned the real-life drama into a made-for-TV doc called *The Elian Gonzalez Story.*

How could the networks resist bringing us the account of a young, beautiful, and highly successful Hollywood business-woman? They couldn't. TV viewers were treated to *Call Me: The Rise and Fall of Heidi Fleiss.*

And who could forget the story of Tonya Harding, who used to be a bit too competitive in the sport of Olympic ice skating and later turned to celebrity boxing? NBC capitalized on the saga with *Tonya and Nancy: The Inside Story.*

The fluff stuff may be incidental. But when entertainment divisions looking to get rights to a docudrama start teaming up with sister news organizations to try to score the best deal possible, things can get a bit bizarre. It seems like the long-established wall between television news and entertainment divisions is breaking down. And this can't help but affect the way that the public becomes informed—or not.

One of the most dramatic examples of the newfound "synergy" between news and entertainment divisions came in 2003, when all the networks were tripping over themselves to get the story of Private Jessica Lynch, the former prisoner of war in Iraq. A big topic of conversation among TV execs is something called the "get," which is industry speak for bagging an exclusive guest. In the mad dash for exclusivity on the Lynch story, CBS pushed the bounds of journalistic ethics.

CBS News exec Betsy West sent a letter outlining the full supply of sweets available from the Viacom candy store. "Attached you will find the outlines of a proposal that includes ideas from CBS News, CBS Entertainment, MTV networks and Simon & Schuster publishers," West wrote to Private Lynch's military representatives. "From the distinguished reporting of CBS News to the youthful reach of MTV, we believe this is a unique combination of projects that will do justice to Jessica's inspiring story." The letter also stated that the executives at CBS Entertainment had said that "this would be the highest priority for the CBS movie division, which specializes in inspirational stories of courage." West assured them that Simon & Schuster "is extremely interested in discussing the possibilities for a book based on Jessica's journey from Palestine, West Virginia, to deep inside Iraq." Finally, CBS suggested that Jessica and her friends could be the cohosts of an hour-long music video program on MTV2. The hit show *Total Request Live,* hosted by teen idol Carson Daly, would have a special edition of the show in Lynch's honor. According to the letter, "This special would include a concert performance in Palestine, West Va., by a current star act such as Ashanti, and perhaps Ja Rule."[2]

Media critics were disturbed by CBS's multimedia carrot. The periodical of the Society of Professional Journalists was pretty brutal in its disapproval, saying, "The bloated expectations of the national marketplace have been fed in part by news media that continue to try to satisfy an appetite that is none of their business. Journalists' core business is news, not entertainment. They should not be cooking up stories with one eye focused on whether they will become network sweeps-week specials."[3] This lent even more fuel to conglomerate-conspiracy theorists who everywhere they look seem to see multinational corporations attempting to dominate the media.

In the end, Lynch didn't even accept CBS's lavish offer—though she did, of course, secure a lucrative book deal and end up all over TV to promote it.

The crumbling wall between news and entertainment also means that entertainment products can be cannibalized into "news" pieces. When CBS shelled out big bucks for the rights to the authorized version of kidnapping victim Elizabeth Smart's story, the network figured that it would get the first shot at an interview with the family. But the Smarts' book publisher chose to schmooze with NBC's Katie Couric instead. So CBS simply took a Smart interview it already possessed for the made-for-TV movie and turned it into a TV special containing the "first" interview. CBS beat NBC by a week.

GIPPER MAKEOVER

As much as studios and networks like to lift their docudramas from the headlines, they also like to make films on important historical figures. And here's where there are ample opportunities to telegraph their worldview.

The most dramatic example of this came in the fall of 2003, when CBS produced a docudrama about Ronald Reagan's presidency entitled *The Reagans*. That piece of CBS "entertainment" was essentially a prolonged attack on Reagan, full of distortions and invented scenarios meant to confirm the creators' view that Reagan was a first-rate dunce and dangerous leader.

Of course, when word of the planned assault on Reagan

got out to the public, it prompted an outcry from millions of Americans.

People first got nervous when it was announced that Barbra Streisand's hubby, James Brolin, had snagged the starring role in the CBS miniseries. When asked about the miniseries on the *Oprah Winfrey Show,* Streisand offered little comfort. Oprah asked her how she felt about the content of the film with the tease "How is that for you, Miss Democrat?" The audience laughed as Streisand impishly grinned. She claimed that she'd have no problem "as long as they tell the truth about Ronald Reagan."

Well, conservatives were concerned, and their uneasiness turned out to be justified. CBS was about to depict one of the greatest American presidents as a forgetful, inattentive, callous lout who royally bumbled his way through eight years in the Oval Office with a domineering, pill-popping spouse at his side.

Evidently, CBS planned on leaving out any reference to the Gipper's infectious optimism and underplaying the 1980s boom that conquered the Jimmy Carter malaise, ended the gasoline lines, and salvaged the economy. Ironically, the man known as the "Great Communicator" was, at that time, in the grips of Alzheimer's disease and couldn't speak for himself. That cruel fact made the very idea of a miniseries of its nature all the more heinous.

Some of the key players in the made-for-TV Reagan rewrite have backgrounds that explain the final product. Leslie Moonves, chairman of CBS, has spent time with overweight overlord Fidel Castro and schmoozed at Renaissance Weekends with the Clintons. James Brolin, who played Reagan, is the hubby of Babs, the Democratic Party's virtual ATM machine. Brolin already had some practice playing a reprehensible Republican when he appeared on *The West Wing.* He was also one of the Left Coast liberals who signed on the anti-recall dotted line to try to keep California governor Gray Davis afloat. And he referred to Reagan as "a naive innocent."[4] Meanwhile, his costar, the Australian actress Judy Davis, who played Nancy Reagan, stated publicly, "If this film can help create a bit more questioning in the public about the direction America has been going in since the 1970s, I guess then I think it will be doing a service."

When CBS first announced it would air *The Reagans,* it tried to pawn the program off as a love story between Ronald and Nancy. Despite the CBS pitch, conservatives were determined to keep the historical record accurate and protect the legacy of the man with the fighter's resolve, commander's confidence, and leading man's charm. A nationwide movement sprang up to persuade CBS not to run *The Reagans.*

Streisand jumped into the squabble. In one of her Web "truth alerts," the political crooner rushed to defend the CBS miniseries. On her site, she proceeded to set NewsMax.com and other sources straight. She wrote that she was on the CBS set to watch her hubby for "a total of only 4 hours of one day," as opposed to the "weeks on the set" reported by what Streisand called "the Republican spin machine." She also wrote that she had never read the script, had never seen the film, and was "not responsible for what is depicted in it." But in the next breath, she declared that "the Republicans, who deify President Reagan, cannot stand that some of the more unpleasant truths about his character and presidency might be depicted in the movie, along with his positive actions." Streisand went on to describe the made-for-TV flick that she supposedly had never seen as "a balanced portrait of a complicated man."

Apparently she's a bit of a left-wing psychic, too.

In a world according to Babs, millions of Americans adored Ronald Reagan because no one else with noteworthy GOP credentials was available. She sneered that Reagan was "glorified by conservatives because what other Republican leader of recent history are they going to point towards? Richard Nixon? George H. W. Bush? Newt Gingrich? Are these men worthy of exalt?"

If you look at events through Funny Girl goggles, Reagan accomplished nothing of substance, but Bill Clinton was a leader for the ages—the same fellow who brought us Travelgate, Filegate,

Chinagate, and Pardongate, who turned down the opportunity to nab Osama bin Laden, and who was impeached, held in contempt by a federal judge, and kicked out of the Supreme Court bar. Donning her economist hat, Streisand blogged that "conservatives love to boast of the 16 million jobs Reagan's economic policies generated" but that he had actually "created record budget deficits, increased inequality and tripled the national debt." She concluded, "Reagan proponents would have to admit that Bill Clinton, who generated 23 million new jobs in the same amount of time in office and also turned a major deficit into the largest surplus ever, was a more successful president."

Streisand explained that "the Right Wing" will "spread vicious lies and attacks and scream and yell until they get their way." Ultimately, she brushed aside the criticisms of the miniseries and urged the public to tune in to CBS's ill-timed fib fest.

Despite Babs's e-yammering, CBS eventually admitted that *The Reagans* was biased. The network stated that "although the miniseries features impressive production values and acting performances, and although the producers have sources to verify each scene in the script, we believe it does not present a balanced portrayal of the Reagans for CBS and its audience." But apparently the miniseries wasn't too biased for CBS's sister channel Showtime. In the same statement, CBS announced that the unbalanced portrayal would air on the cable network, which, like CBS, is owned by Viacom.

Streisand wasn't happy. "Today marks a sad day for artistic freedom—one of the most important elements of an open and democratic society," she declared.

Her comments completely overlooked the legitimate inaccuracies in the production, ones so blatant that CBS finally had to acknowledge them. The production history of *The Reagans* was telling. ABC had rejected the project because it was, according to one network executive, "very soft; it was not controversial in the least." CBS bought the $16 million production only after the filmmakers made it "controversial" enough.

And as *New York Times* critic Alessandra Stanley pointed out, the stars of the miniseries "gloated about how controversial their film would be. James Brolin said his portrayal of Mr. Reagan was partly inspired by the Reagan puppet on the British satirical show 'Spitting Image.' Judy Davis, who played Nancy Reagan, pompously said she hoped the film would teach Americans to scrutinize their elected leaders more carefully." According to Stanley, "Producers appear to have sacrificed showmanship to self-righteousness, adopting a preachy, liberal agenda."

Respected authorities on the Reagan legacy spoke out about the CBS miniseries. Reagan confidant Martin Anderson, who served as domestic policy adviser in the Reagan White House, proclaimed the film "a lie" and "basically a hit piece." Anderson could point to specific fabrications to support his contention. One of the scriptwriters on The Reagans, Anderson noted, admitted to having made up the words about AIDS that she put in Reagan's mouth, "They that live in sin shall die in sin." The truth is that at a time when the disease was not widely understood, the Reagan administration determined that AIDS patients were entitled to protection from discrimination. Anderson told NewsMax.com, "You know, they can lie all they want. But they cannot tell us it's the truth. And coming from a major network, I'm very surprised that they think they can get away with this, and tell the American people that something is true when they know it's not true."

It wasn't just Reagan supporters who denounced the CBS hatchet job. Journalist Lou Cannon, who covered Reagan for thirty years and wrote two Reagan biographies, said that the film didn't reflect the real man. For example, he cited the fact that, far from being "homophobic," Reagan, against the advice of some advisers, opposed a 1978 California initiative that would have discriminated against homosexual teachers.

Longtime California news anchor George Putnam, who knew Reagan personally, dismissed the CBS presentation for perpetuating the myth that Reagan lacked intelligence and was some sort of dolt. "In fact," Putnam told me, "he was highly intelligent, studied issues deeply, knew exactly what his agenda was, and implemented his ideas with utmost care and consideration." He added that both *Reagan: A Life in Letters* and *Reagan: In His Own Hand,* compilations of his writings, reveal that "he was intimately concerned and knowledgeable." Putnam also argued that the CBS miniseries attacked Reagan by presenting "manufactured myths," such as that the former president was "inattentive to his staff, hard-hearted, neglectful of the AIDS epidemic" and that Nancy Reagan was "a bossy wife."

Leave it to the 2004 Emmy nominations to try to revise the historical record. Even though *The Reagans* had to be shuttled from CBS to Showtime because of adverse public reaction to the cinematic maligning of one of the most beloved presidents and his wife, the film received a preposterous seven Emmy nominations, including Outstanding Movie, Lead Actor, and Lead Actress—this despite the fact that a whole lot of critics slammed the TV miniseries for its weak writing, poor acting, and makeup that mimicked Al Gore's airbrushed mortuary look from the 2000 presidential campaign. It ended up winning the Emmy for, of all things, hairstyling, for what many critics referred to as the "blockhead" look.

Ultimately, though, a measly Emmy for hairstyling couldn't make up for the gross distortions the creators of the miniseries tried to get away with. The story of *The Reagans* showed that liberal propaganda doesn't always have to rule the day. And flyover country showed how to win one for the Gipper.

HOLLYWOOD'S GREEN EYESHADES

Conservatives could take some solace in the fact that the creators of *The Reagans* were caught in many of their inaccuracies, and a TV channel-changing victory was scored. But more liberal slop was ready to plop.

One piece of propaganda came in the summer of 2004, when Hollywood released a PC piece of celluloid called *The Day After Tomorrow,* which purported to show America what global warming is all about.

In terms of disasters, *The Day After Tomorrow* had them all—storms, floods, tornadoes, tidal waves, blizzards, and more.

Actually, the thing was a rollicking comedy. Or at least that's how it hit me. While watching, I found myself alternating between restrained chuckles and outright guffaws. I'd suspected it might be a sidesplitter when I heard that a certain snarling ex-veep had endorsed it.

For those of you who may have actually thought that the film was serious, I have to tell you it had scenes that could only be there for laughs. Apparently filmmaker Roland Emmerich relied on his prior *Godzilla* experiences for the project, because it contained the same kitschy quality of the original Japanese monster flick and generated about as much fear as his 1998 remake.

Tidal waves crashed against Manhattan's skyscrapers. Huge balls of hail knocked over billboards, bent steel frames, and crunched cars, as crowds of people screamed and ran for cover. Twisters descended on Los Angeles, devouring the Hollywood sign and the Capitol Records building. A super fast-freezing storm encased New York in ice.

Characters were heard prattling on endlessly about how we got ourselves into the frosty mess. Being a science fiction buff, I found myself wondering how the writers could think they could pull off such a snow job, believing no one would recall that the climate change of eons ago had zip to do with greenhouse gases or SUVs. Maybe they were under the illusion that agenda-driven science fiction doesn't have to be consistent.

The movie brought up the Kyoto Protocol more than once—in reverential terms, of course. (You remember Kyoto, the UN treaty that the Democratic-controlled Senate under Bill Clinton voted down 95 to nothing.)

And there was a presidential character who was a Dubya look-alike. The guy became a victim of greenie circumstance and was killed off. Shortly afterward, a veep-turned-prez Cheney replica apologized to the world for not having seen the enviro light sooner.

As I watched the film, I couldn't help but connect with reality for a moment. Despite what Al Gore would have us believe, the science on global warming is far from settled. The temperature on the ground shows that there's only been warming of a little more than one degree over the past one hundred years. But even with that, ground measurements have been discredited by new equipment. Satellite and weather balloon measurements are considered to be more accurate and show that very little warming has occurred since they were first used. It seemed to me that there had to be a heck of lot more warming before the climate would go bonkers and we'd all become Popsicles.

Still, there was no denying that many people wanted to use *The Day After Tomorrow* for political purposes. Some greenies actually hoped that the film would produce new support for the McCain-Lieberman Climate Stewardship Act, which would force Kyoto down our throats via legislation.

As for me, I was hoping that Woody Allen would consider re-dubbing the flick for a *What's Up with the Weather* release the day after tomorrow of the week before yesterday of next year.

KINSEY ATTIRE

If one Hollywood trick is to smear conservative figures like Ronald Reagan, another is to whitewash the stories of liberal icons.

In 2004 writer and director Bill Condon, whose previous work was *Gods and Monsters,* did a biopic called *Kinsey,* which actually could have been tagged with the same title. The film was about a man, Alfred Kinsey, who in some folks' minds still stands as a god but who in reality was a monster.

Had Condon's film been honest, it could have been thought-provoking, meaningful, and maybe even instructive. Instead it was a tedious, pretentious, and pseudo-intellectual work of pseudo-art. It was also a blatant attempt to snag some awards. The marketing plan had been fairly transparent with its super-limited release and poster that trumpeted the message "instant Oscar contender."

And what better way to get attention and accolades than to profile one of Hollywood's counterculture idols?

The real Kinsey was an entomologist who in the 1940s and 1950s transitioned his research from insects to humans because, as he stated, "Human beings are just bigger, more complicated gall wasps." Rejecting morals and viewing sex as merely a biological function, he was the catalyst for the so-called sexual revolution. I guess we're supposed to thank him for that.

In the film, Liam Neeson played the part of Kinsey. Neeson showed the professor (in the name of research, of course) prying into the sexual history of everyone he came into contact with, writing a best-seller, and eventually becoming a celebrity. The actor rendered a stilted performance, wearing pretty much the same frozen expression throughout the film. Perhaps in an attempt to reproduce the scientific stare, Neeson inadvertently captured the pre-Pepto pose.

John Lithgow played Kinsey's father, depicting him as a Hollywood version of the "universal Christian"—you know, repressed, mean-spirited, and fanatical, with the attendant mental defects as defined in the Tinseltown handbook.

Tim Curry rounded out the cast. He played a morality professor who was laced up so tight he made the Puritans look like party animals.

The film was a robust effort to celebrate Kinsey's bisexuality and included what has become almost obligatory in Tinseltown: the same-sex love scene. It occurred between Neeson's character and *Garden State*'s Peter Sarsgaard.

The movie portrayed America as a repressed, prudish culture and Kinsey as a passionate proponent of the high Hollywood virtues of tolerance, diversity, and adultery. And apparently in the name of a couple of other Hollywood virtues—relativism and nonjudgmentalism—all allegations of pedophilia were left out.

In my opinion, a soft trap was set in an effort to sell the film, and a lot of critics appeared to fall for it. It's one that was woven into the screenplay and it goes like this: If you don't like what you're watching, you're obviously missing something in the intellect department.

But to me there was an "emperor's new clothes" thing going on, and we weren't supposed to tell what we saw—that once again Hollywood was trying to work through its problems on the big screen, and Tinseltown therapy was what was on display.

Well, here goes. *Kinsey* had no clothes. It had no merit either.

ALEXANDER THE GRATE

Another movie that came out in 2004 offered the same "enlightened" take on sexuality that Hollywood feels is so important to preach to the masses. The only trouble was that Oliver Stone's big-budget *Alexander* didn't turn out to be a blockbuster; it was simply a bore.

Alexander reportedly had a tab somewhere in the neighborhood of $200 million. My hunch is that the most sizable portion of the costs went to foot the mascara bill for the guys in the flick.

The casting of the movie was pathetic. Colin Farrell snagged the lead role, but it appeared as if he couldn't seem to remember whether he was in a History Channel special or an *SNL* spoof. The fiercest battle looked like it was going on in his head, with surfer dude expressions that betrayed an inner struggle—"Did Ollie say warrior conqueror or B.C. comic?"

Angelina Jolie played Alexander the Great's mom. While the age discrepancy was bothersome enough in and of itself, somehow Stone must have directed her to offset Farrell's Irish brogue with some Transylvania diction.

Rounding out the miscast was Hannibal-in-a-toga Anthony Hopkins and Batman-in-a-crown Val Kilmer. Hopkins played Ptolemy, the senior reminiscer who made long-winded speeches about Alexander's conquests. Kilmer was Alexander's dad and apparently studied with the same speech coach as Madonna.

The *Toronto Star* called the film "not just a bad movie but a bad movie of truly epic proportions."

The *Washington Post* said that "as expressed through the weepy histrionics of Colin Farrell," Stone's main character was "more like a desperate housewife than a soldier."

The *Northwest Herald* warned that the flick often seemed "a couple of heartbeats away from turning into a gay porno film."

The *New York Times* said Stone's work contained "puerile writing, confused plotting and shockingly off-note performances."

The *Los Angeles Times* described the movie as an "indifferent epic" and a "plodding endeavor."

The *Boston Globe* said that the film was "full of brilliant highlights" which were "all in Colin Farrell's hair."

Don't feel too bad for Stone, though. He sought redemption for *Alexander* from the Michael Moore fans in Europe. Stone tried to get America haters abroad to ratchet up ticket sales, boost disappointing box office receipts, and help him save some *Alexander* face.

While receiving a lifetime achievement award at the Stockholm International Film Festival, Stone remarked, "I think one of the reasons I am being honored here is Europeans tend to see me a little differently than they do in the U.S."

Get this. He talked about the "incredible parallels" between the ancient Macedonian conqueror and President George W. Bush. Evidently, he was trying to fuel the kooky European sentiments by comparing Alexander the Great's efforts to expand his empire into the Middle East to President Bush's invasion of Iraq.

I have to say that Stone did accomplish something with *Alexander.* He solidified his place in history as a rock-solid revisionist.

KINGDOM OF HEAVEN—TRUTH IN LIMBO

Why is it that when Hollywood meets history these days, history seems to get the squeeze? In spring 2005, it was the factually challenged movie *Kingdom of Heaven* whose historical content got schmushed.

Kingdom of Heaven's director, Ridley Scott, took a cue from

Cecil B. DeMille and chose the Crusades as the subject of his epic. This is the same fellow who brought us *Gladiator* and *Blade Runner,* which made me wonder: How did a talented filmmaker like Scott get stuck with an incoherent script like this one?

It's understandable that a film dealing with the ancient battles that took place between European Christians and followers of Islam might seek to make some modern-day comparisons. But is it really necessary to stuff the screen with the kind of pseudo-humanistic claptrap that could make a knight dump his armor on eBay?

As is typical of today's Tinseltown chronicling, *Kingdom of Heaven* fuses fiction with fact, much to the chagrin of the more informed filmgoer. The movie takes place in 1184, some time between the Second and Third Crusade. At the top of the film the audience is introduced to a young blacksmith named Balian (played by Orlando Bloom). Balian receives a visit from Godfrey of Ibelin (played by Liam Neeson), who claims to have fathered him and is seeking forgiveness for having done so illegitimately.

After a few conversations with Godfrey, Balian switches out of his horse-shoeing duds and opts for Crusader couture instead. In a Middle Age minute, the guy transforms himself into the most formidable knight in town. He also starts stealing a page from MoveOn.org and some guidance counseling tips from Dr. Phil.

While on his deathbed, Godfrey knights Balian and instructs him to pursue the vision of a "kingdom of heaven," where Christians, Muslims, and Jews can peacefully party together. Balian eventually finds himself as a stand-in for the king of Jerusalem and in a position to surrender the city to the Muslim army. But this doesn't happen until he's killed a creepy priest, given up on organized religion, tossed his faith out the door, and joined the ranks of the "can't we all just get along" crowd.

The film has a certain cinematic allure for some. If you like lots of head-splitting, side-piercing, gut-wrenching, limb-flying battling between foes, then this flick is for you. If you like a hefty dose of accuracy with your historically based entertainment, then it's not. In part, here's why.

The film depicts Muslim leader Saladin's conquest of Jerusalem, with his forces breaking through the wall of the city during the final battle. But the actual battle was outside the city in a place known as Hattin. That's why it's called the Battle of Hattin. Also, in the movie, the knights knock off Saladin's sister in order to provoke him. The truth is she was held up but never snuffed out.

But to me, the real problem with the movie's authenticity is the way it interjects sappy messages into the story line. Exceedingly clear is who the heroes are, and likewise who the villains are. Saladin (who in one scene repectfully cradles a fallen cross) is portrayed as a wise, seasoned, and noble leader. In contrast, Guy de Lusignan, crony Sir Reynald, and the Knights Templar are shown as bloodthirsty, empty-headed warmongers. And as you might have predicted, the Christian clergy are cast as cowardly hypocrites who want to kill "infidels."

Many who see *Kingdom of Heaven* may not realize that the Crusades were actually defensive in nature. Christians didn't act until the Muslims had conquered two-thirds of the Western world, and the Crusaders believed they were restoring formerly Christian territories to their rightful status.

In the film, the only Christian good guys are Balian, leper-King of Jerusalem Baldwin IV, and his minister Tiberius. But unlike other Christians in the flick, these folks aren't motivated by religious faith. Instead they spout a form of modernist egalitarian drivel that sounds like it was written by Bill Moyers.

Balian makes a dramatic speech before the final battle in which he tells the assembled throng that the Muslim army, which is about to attack and kill all of them, has just as much right to rule as its Christian counterpart does. Rather than a call to arms, Balian gives his troops a call to multiculturalism. If a real medieval commander would have given such a speech, he'd have been chopped into tiny little pieces.

Which is probably what should have happened to that section of the footage, along with all the other PC portions.

GORY GLORY

Even when films don't have overtly political messages, Hollywood can still show off the sorts of lifestyles and values it feels we should all respect and uphold. And it sometimes puts out amoral products that are supposed to be important simply by virtue of being "edgy" and "innovative."

In this regard, Tinseltown gets a lot of help from the critic community. As much success as Hollywood has had with classic plots involving love, rivalry, courage, betrayal, and self-sacrifice, certain critics seem to have become jaded and have essentially developed a disdain for the conventional. These "enabler critics" embolden Hollywood to pump out films that are short on meaning and long on mayhem. *Kill Bill* and *The Texas Chainsaw Massacre* were recent examples of the Tinseltown severed-arms race.

The problem is that movies like these amount to what in the law is called an "attractive nuisance." Here's what I mean. Quentin Tarantino's *Kill Bill* combined the look of a video game and the allure of martial arts, sprinkled with some Japanese animation. All these elements drew in a youthful audience. Tarantino himself said, "If you are a twelve-year-old girl or boy, you must go and see *Kill Bill,* and you will have a damn good time. Boys will have a great time, girls will have a dose of girl power. If you are a cool parent out there, go take your kids to the movie."

Tarantino received some big-name help on his gory hike from critics in the mainstream press who raved about the film's stupefying violence. Roger Ebert claimed that Tarantino's work was "so effortlessly and brilliantly in command of his technique that he reminds me of a virtuoso violinist racing through 'Flight of the Bumble Bee.'" Jeffrey M. Anderson of the *San Francisco Examiner* wrote that "'Kill Bill' takes a cue from spaghetti-western master Sergio Leone and turns every little twist and turn into a giant-sized operatic odyssey." Mark Caro of the *Chicago Tribune* gushed that the flick was "the most gorgeous B-movie ever made." Stephen Hunter of the *Washington Post,* with whom I appeared on

MSNBC's *Buchanan and Press,* said that Tarantino "delivered with such high panache and brio, it's mesmerizing."

With regard to the remake of *The Texas Chainsaw Massacre,* the movie had a young cast and an adolescent's dream actress in the form of Jessica Biel. It was designed to reel in the puberty crowd. And like *Kill Bill,* the gory flick had far too many respected authorities throwing superlatives at it. Once again, Stephen Hunter praised the mindless violence, writing, "Realize how hard this is on me, to have to tell you what a superb job director Marcus Nispel has done re-creating, yet also revising, 1974's grisly, gristly, protein-centric masterpiece." Hunter apparently thought that depictions of splattered brain matter and twitching limbs qualified the film for the "masterpiece" category.

And Terry Lawson of the *Detroit Free Press* focused on the teenage male angle, writing that the remake "is nearly as tense and nasty as the original and, to be fair, features far better acting, most notably by Jessica Biel, who is compelling even when she isn't about to burst out of her wet T-shirt."

At least Robert K. Elder of the *Chicago Tribune* got it half-right when, while praising the film, he classified it correctly. He called *Chainsaw* "an effectively scary slasher film."

Oh yeah, as opposed to an ineffectively scary slasher film.

PG LONGINGS

The awards handed out at the 2004 Venice Film Festival illustrated the warped ideology of the entertainment elite. *Vera Drake,* a film that venerated abortion, won the Golden Lion for Best Picture, and that movie's lead, Imelda Staunton, won Best Actress. The runner-up flick, *Mar Adentro,* exalted the other side of the culture of death: euthanasia. Its lead, Javier Bardem, was given the award for Best Actor.

Ironically, while festival judges were giving awards out to this kind of fare, and jaded critics were hailing the flicks as "fresh" and "edgy," the public seemed to hold a different opinion. In fact, films that presented a traditional moral universe, with distinctions between good and evil, were going over big with average folks. Of the more than 280 movies that came to multiplexes in 2004, films with a "very strong Judeo-Christian morality" made an average of $107.7 million; according to a report prepared by the Christian Film and Television Commission. The commission also reported that in 2003, films that emphasized "strong moral content" on average earned *six times* as much as motion pictures with an "immoral, negative content." And movies rated G and PG earned two or three times as much as those movies rated R. (A notable exception in 2004: Mel Gibson's R-rated but reverent *The Passion of the Christ*.)

Some in the industry seem to be catching on to the market reality. A group called the Family Friendly Programming Forum has been created using financing from a group of forty major national advertisers, all members of the Association of National Advertisers who are taking positive steps to increase family-friendly programming choices on television. And with *The Passion* and the success of Christian music, a resurgence of interest in religion in the media is taking place.

Still, the major networks don't employ full-time religion reporters. In addition, generally when religion is covered on TV, the same nonbelieving liberal academics are brought out to trash traditional faith.

I imagine that some of these academics have an aversion to sunlight, can't stand the smell of garlic, and routinely make their beds in a coffin.

DOCU WARP

Hollywood has figured out another way to blur the boundaries between news and entertainment. Filmmakers have gone beyond the docudrama and incorporated documentary techniques into fictional setups.

The 2004 shark flick *Open Water*, for example, was a piece of fiction that was partially based on a true story and made to appear as a documentary. In the movie, a scuba-diving couple discovers that the boat that brought them to their diving location is gone, and when sharks arrive, they have no way to escape. Director Chris Kentis used digital video cameras to film the actors, who were really in the water and really swimming with the sharks.

Incident at Loch Ness had the look and feel of a documentary, too. It involved the making of a film about the making of a movie that focuses on the making of another movie. In the movie, German filmmaker Werner Herzog takes an assignment from producer-writer Zak Penn to go to Scotland to shoot a documentary called *The Enigma of Loch Ness,* about the fabled Loch Ness monster. Another filmmaker, John Bailey, accompanies Herzog to shoot yet another flick about Herzog shooting his flick. Herzog suspects that Penn had an agenda other than the described reason given for the film when Herzog finds out that a sonar engineer used to be a *Playboy* pinup. If this seems confusing, imagine the audience's difficulty in sorting out the fact from the fiction.

Another invented saga, *September Tapes,* purported to describe the search for Osama bin Laden. It featured some actual documentary footage shot in Afghanistan, but with a twist: A single actor with scripted lines was surrounded by real people who were really reacting to those lines. Director Christian Johnston had to modify his script to conform to real situations that he and his team came across, including live ammunition and bounty hunters. The Department of Defense ended up requesting a full review of the footage because of the possibility of classified information being compromised.

These kinds of flicks are a cross between the traditional narrative and the documentary. They go by a number of names: reality fiction, hybrid films, and even faux films. The goal of a filmmaker in this genre is generally to confuse the audience into mistaking fantasy for reality and vice versa.

There is, of course, a concern about whether the hybrid form is going to harm the credibility of the traditional factually based documentary.

But no real need to worry. These days you can't find a whole lot of those in Hollywood anyway, as we'll see in the next chapter.

Morris Musings

Dick Morris, one of America's best-known political consultants, helped guide President Bill Clinton to a stunning comeback reelection victory in 1996. In addition to assisting Clinton, Morris has handled the winning campaigns for more than thirty senators or governors, including former Senate majority leader Trent Lott and former governors Bill Weld of Massachusetts and Pete Wilson of California. He's also a *New York Times* best-selling author, a commentator for the Fox News Channel, and a columnist for the *New York Post;* the *Hill,* a newspaper about Congress; and Canada's *National Post.*

When I interviewed Morris, we talked about everything from nepotism to narcissism.[1]

HIRSEN: One of the journalistic pundits has decried the fact that news and entertainment are becoming blurred. What effect, if any, is this having on the coverage of the political world?

MORRIS: Well, give me a break. I mean, for goodness' sakes, when Bill Clinton and Monica Lewinsky are the front-page news for a year and a half, how can you tell the difference between news and entertainment? Try news and pornography. Of course it's blurred. And reality TV I think is blurring it. But I think that

that's appropriate. I think that's good. I think that when you have voter turnout at 50 percent, and 65 million people vote for *American Idol,* and a hundred million vote for president of the United States, it's good to confuse news with entertainment so we can get some popular interest in government.

HIRSEN: [William] McGowan had this book *Coloring the News,* where he talked about how the pursuit of diversity and multiculturalism has affected the way journalists cover the news. We saw this in the aversion to wearing flag pins and the reluctance to call terrorists "terrorists." What's your view on that?

MORRIS: Well, first let me just spend a moment on the idea of journalistic bias. Most reporters are liberal, and most reporters voted for Gore as opposed to Bush [in 2000]. . . . But I don't believe that the news media is primarily motivated by ideology. I think they march to the beat of their own drummer, and they have their own code that relates to the pendulum.

So I think you go back to the Kennedy era and the journalists were very softball. And then they said, "Oh, my goodness, we let Johnson and Nixon get away with Vietnam." So then they became hardball. They threw out Nixon. They doomed Carter to one term. They defeated Ford. And then Reagan got elected and they said, "You know, we're being too hard on presidents. We're creating one-term presidencies. We've got to go easier." So they gave Reagan a much easier time. And then just after Iran Contra, and after the [George H. W.] Bush administration, they said, "You know, we have given these presidents too easy of a ride." So they gave Clinton an incredibly hard time. Every other minute was about scandals. Some of them richly deserved. Still, it was there. And then after 9/11, they said, "Well, you know, we're being much too tough on presidents. Look at all we did with Clinton." And they gave Bush a much easier ride after 9/11.

Now they are saying, "You know, we were way too easy on Bush after 9/11. We let him do all kinds of stuff that we think was wrong. Now we've got to come down on him like a ton of bricks." So I think it's less a question of ideology than a question of overreacting and then compensating.

HIRSEN: Is it really possible for a journalist to express information without coloring it with his or her personal views?

MORRIS: No. And I think the beauty of the Fox News Channel, that I love to appear on, is that it doesn't pretend not to be colored by personal views. It just puts on the Left personal view and the Right personal view and lets them fight about it. The reason it gets better ratings than CNN is CNN says, "We are impartial. We are just going to put on one person who's going to tell you the truth." And everybody who sees through it says, "Hey, this guy is biased." But Fox News sort of understands that you are biased, and they put you on the air expecting you to be biased.

HIRSEN: Should journalists be biased toward their own nation?

MORRIS: Well, yes, I think they should. I think that, but I think that probably they have different views of how to serve the nation. I don't think that those people who expose, you know, the Iraq prison stuff are unpatriotic. I do think there are reporters who are unpatriotic. Peter Arnett. I mean that's outrageous to go to Baghdad in the middle of a war and give aid and comfort to the enemy. That's ridiculous. But I do feel that the journalists are much more reacting to the pressure of their peer groups than they are to their own bias. I think that sometimes they were very rough on Democrats. I think they were fierce to Bill Clinton. On the other hand, I think he probably deserved most of the attacks he got, but certainly you can't say they gave him a free ride.

HIRSEN: Our culture seems to be celebrity-obsessed. You've had this long career where you've had to create media-generated images of your clients. Do you take into account this celebrity obsession in your political calculus?

MORRIS: Yes. I think that we are going into a very dangerous period of celebrity obsession. Eleven out of the hundred members of the United States Senate were preceded in the body by their fathers, or their brothers, or their husbands. And we're developing something where it becomes almost a hereditary monarchy, or a hereditary political class, or hereditary aristocracy would be a better way to put it.

When Gore runs against Bush, both sons have famous fathers and neither of them would be candidate for president if their father had not been prominent. And you're getting the wives of the last two presidential candidates, [Hillary] Clinton and [Elizabeth] Dole, sitting next to each other in the U.S. Senate. I think that we're getting to a point where politicians become brands, and the brand carries through to the spouses and to the descendants. And I think that's a real serious problem. I think that that is the sort of celebrity, if you will, "branding obsession," that I think is really creating what the founding fathers were very much afraid of—an aristocracy. John Adams said to Thomas Jefferson, "You fear the one. I fear the few." Jefferson was afraid of a monarchy. Adams was afraid of an aristocracy. And they were both right.

HIRSEN: As a political consultant, you're forced to jump into that playing field. You used the term "branding"—the creation of a secondary meaning for a product as you would with advertising. Would that be a correct way to put it?

MORRIS: Yes. I think the way to understand branding is that when you do something, like let's say you crack a joke, people think that you were funny. Then if you would do it several times, they think you are funny, that it's a trait. And then if you keep doing it, it becomes a characteristic that then becomes a reputation. And when you sell it, it becomes a brand.

So I think that everybody in life, in a sense, is their own brand. I think it's fine to do that. I think that's how we see politicians, and I think it's appropriate. We see Bill Clinton as a certain brand. We see him as brainy and focused on the economy. We see him as gluttonous and overly self-indulgent. And we have a whole sense of what the Bill Clinton brand is.

HIRSEN: Hollywood's number-one political icon is JFK. But a very close second is Bill Clinton. When you were working with Bill, did he speak about this relationship with Hollywood?

MORRIS: Yes, we spoke about it at length because he would always take summer vacations in Martha's Vineyard because he loved hobnobbing with celebrities. I urged him and got him to stop vacationing in Martha's Vineyard and instead to go to the Rocky Mountains and go hiking for his vacation, because politically it was better for him.

But the whole point is Bill Clinton, like Hollywood celebrities, only exist in their own eyes when somebody is looking at them adoringly. That's the characteristic of a narcissist. They cannot internally generate their own self-image. That's why he wants popularity. And it's the derivation of his promiscuity, because when the band stops playing and the press conference is over, he needs the adoration or the stimulus of another human being looking at him and that leads to the promiscuity. So Clinton is really a constant narcissist.

And narcissism is present in probably about half of American politicians. But it's present in like 98 percent of Hollywood people. The reason you become an actor and actress is because you are a narcissist. You have no character. You assume the character of the person you are playing and you look for approbation from the audience, and that approbation sees you and empowers you to play that character. So basically narcissists attract because they can be mirrors for each other. And that's why Bill Clinton got along with Hollywood, and Hollywood got along with Bill Clinton. They could look at each other and say, "My, how beautiful and smart we both are."

HIRSEN: That's a tremendous observation, Dick. The classic mythology of falling in love with your reflection in the pond, and there's an affinity between D.C. and Hollywood, the two worlds of narcissism loving each other's reflections.

MORRIS: Now, of course, if you look back over the presidents in our history, some are narcissists, some are not. John Kennedy clearly was. Lyndon Johnson obviously was. Richard Nixon probably was. Gerry Ford obviously was not. Jimmy Carter was not. Ronald Reagan probably in a strange way was not, because he probably got the narcissism out of his system by the time he was president, and he had become his reflection and didn't need it anymore. George [H. W.] Bush, of course, was not a narcissist. Bill Clinton obviously was. And Bush Jr. obviously isn't. But it's a very important distinction. And when I worked for a politician, almost the first thing I'd ask myself is "Is this person a narcissist or not?"

HIRSEN: And that can change your strategy, I suppose.

MORRIS: Yes, of course. It's not just the strategy in handling him with the voters, but more important, a strategy in handling him by himself, because if you are dealing with a narcissist you have to feed that. That's how they get power. A narcissist is a little bit like a cold-blooded animal that cannot internally generate body warmth but requires the sun to do so. The other metaphor I use is a headlight reflector on the highway, or a solar battery. When you are shining on it, it gives you energy. Otherwise, it's a cold lump of metal.

8

MEDIA MINDBEND

In July 2004 Peter Jennings, Ted Koppel, and George Stephanopoulos appeared on a panel together in front of an audience of media critics. Jennings and Koppel were trying to make the case for the importance of reliable hard news. Then Stephanopoulos launched a word-of-mouth missile that caused considerable discomfort among panelists and audience members alike. What did the former Clinton adviser–turned-Sunday-morning moderator say to get folks fidgeting? He told a story about how he'd asked some people who had gone to see *Fahrenheit 9/11,* Michael Moore's so-called documentary, why they'd decided to watch the flick. Their answer was "Because we wanted to get the facts."

Stephanopoulos's tale illustrates just how big a player Hollywood has become in the "factual" presentation business. The quotation marks that cup the word are important, because few things can be as potent and/or potentially corrupting as the blurring of entertainment and quasi news, contorted news, or, worst of all, falsified news.

PROPAGANDA DELIGHT

When we look at the documentary, we see that it can be an effective vehicle of propaganda. A documentary with journalistic shading can offer a false window to the world and slyly shape a worldview. Despots in history have understood this.

The word *propaganda* has negative overtones because often it has been associated with media operations used to assist the worst totalitarian regimes in history. Josef Goebbels, one of the monstrous figures of the Nazi regime, had the official title of Minister of Propaganda and National Enlightenment. He used his office to make sure Germans were inundated with messages that were favorable to the Nazis. Under his direction, books were burned in bonfires, and unfavorable media were demonized and censored.

Perhaps the most famous cinematic piece of propaganda was the 1934 film *Triumph of the Will*. The Leni Riefenstahl documentary is often cited for its filmmaking technique, despite the fact that it boosted the Third Reich. In fact, the darn thing continues to garner attention. As recently as 2004, the Academy Awards saw fit to honor the Hitler-helping filmmaker. More than a few viewers were utterly astounded when it came time for the Academy to give its perfunctory yearly tribute to a movie great who had passed away during the prior year and Riefenstahl's name was announced. To be fair, Riefenstahl's camera work, editing, and lighting techniques were admired separate and apart from her content and purpose. Still, the ability to ignore its insidious function was disturbing. Clearly, the movie's motive runs contrary to the moral compass of every decent human being, including all the decent-minded in Hollywood. But somehow the Academy members were able to "compartmentalize," separating their moral sensibilities from their artistic ones.

I've been known to characterize Michael Moore of Oscar boo fame as a modern master of propaganda, and that's not meant to be a compliment. In my opinion and others', Moore has only an arm's-length relationship with the truth. For example, as reputable critics have documented, in his Oscar-winning "documentary" *Bowling for Columbine,* Moore pawned off staged events as spontaneous, and the flick contained many serious factual errors. The movie exploited the 1999 tragedy that took place in the suburban town of Littleton, Colorado, where two high school seniors, Dylan Klebold and Eric Harris, enacted an all-out assault on Columbine High School. *Bowling* implied that Harris and Klebold had violent tendencies because of the "weapons of mass destruction" produced at a Lockheed Martin plant in Littleton. But the truth was that Lockheed Martin's Littleton plant produced space launch vehicles for TV satellites, not weapons.

Moore also scripted an event at a bank in Michigan's Traverse City, claiming that opening an account would allow a customer to stroll out of the bank carrying a free firearm. The film showed Moore filling out some paperwork and receiving his free rifle. The truth here was the bank didn't hand over guns when an account was opened. No one was able to walk in or out of the bank with a firearm. The rifle was one of several premiums that customers could select for opening a CD account. If a customer made such a selection, he or she had to pass a firearms background check and could only pick up the gift from a licensed gun dealer.

Another particularly vicious Moore fabrication involved legendary Hollywood personality and producer Dick Clark. Moore confronted Clark and accused him of being responsible for a fatal shooting of a six-year-old girl by a classmate. In a ridiculously remote causation daisy chain, Moore also blamed the shooting on Michigan's work-to-welfare program, which he claimed prevented the shooter's mother from spending time with her son. The link to Clark was that the mother had been given a work-to-welfare job at Clark's American Bandstand restaurant in the local shopping mall.

The point is that Moore had been placed on notice that he ought to do some diligent fact checking for his next film.

Who knew that as his fact checker he'd use Al Jazeera?

CROCK-UMENTARY

Michael Moore's preelection conditioner *Fahrenheit 9/11* turned out to be one of the clearest examples of modern-day propaganda. The supposed documentary broke a host of box-office records. But it also broke records for its lack of truth, discretion, and entertainment value.

The flick was an overt attempt to indict the Bush administration and the United States of America. It was replete with heart-tugging scenes of Iraqi casualties and footage of victims' families rebuking the American military. No surprise, then, that it got a glowing endorsement from Hezbollah. The thing actually would've made an ideal recruiting film for terrorist organizations.

Although I took issue with *Bowling for Columbine,* I at least had to acknowledge that it displayed some cinematic imagination. I couldn't really say that this time around. Maybe Moore had gotten complacent going from the budget of $160,000 for his first film, *Roger & Me,* to the $3 million for *Bowling for Columbine* to the $6 million he boasted about getting for *Fahrenheit 9/11,* because basically the film was lousy. It wasn't informative. It wasn't thought-provoking. It wasn't original. And Moore broke the cardinal rule of filmmaking—the movie was just plain boring. The editing had about as much rhythm as Bill Gates at a hip-hop concert. And the attempts at humor were largely adolescent.

Fahrenheit was loaded with urban legends that were presented with Moore's accompanying postnasal-drip narration. And it was chock-full of sound bites from such empty founts of wisdom as Congressman Jim McDermott, the Democrat who buzzed over to Baghdad in 2003 to proclaim that President Bush was lying to the American people in order to justify war and who later accused the president of timing Saddam Hussein's capture for political gain.

In describing his work, Moore sometimes called the film a documentary. Other times he referred to it as an op-ed. He said it was "just a movie" but then admitted he hoped that it would turn the election. The problem was that the imposter-documentary was filled with gaffes, flubs, goof-ups, and all-out howlers. I present to you a partial list of things that make you go "oops!"

• Moore claimed that Bush was having difficulty getting his legislation passed prior to September 11.

Oops! Both houses of Congress passed Bush's tax cut—you know, the one that resulted in the greatest economic growth rate in two decades.

• According to Moore, the war in Afghanistan had nothing to do with the fact that the Taliban harbored the terrorists who had attacked us. Rather, the Bush administration went to war to protect a pipeline being built through Afghanistan in order to bring natural gas from the Caspian Sea. The scheme, Moore alleged, involved a dark cadre of companies led by the oil giant Unocal.

Oops! Unocal dumped the pipeline idea back in the late 1990s.

• The film indicated that, in the days following 9/11, some Saudis, including a few who bore the last name of bin Laden, were allowed to fly out of the country when other air traffic was grounded.

Oops! The flights actually occurred after the aircraft ban was lifted. And the guy who made the decision to let the bin Ladens go was one of Moore's soul mates—Bush's former counterterrorism chief, Richard Clarke.

• Moore claimed that Saddam Hussein never threatened, attacked, or killed any Americans.

Oops! For an entire decade Saddam tried to shoot down American planes as our pilots patrolled the no-fly zones over Iraq. And he offered rewards to the families of suicide bombers in Israel. And he tried to assassinate former president George H. W. Bush. And he gave safe haven to the notorious Abu Nidal, a terrorist whose group has been blamed for attacks in more than twenty countries.

Rather than distance themselves from the flimsy flick and its famed fabricator, Democrats wrapped their arms around Moore. Then–Democratic National Committee chairman Terry McAuliffe and other prominent Dems cozied up to the film and its creator, thinking that it would help them politically. Moore sat in the place of honor at the Democratic National Convention next to President Jimmy Carter. Moore was one of the most visible faces on cable and network television during the convention coverage. Is he worthy of such treatment?

Well, he fabricated an interview with Fred Barnes. He publicly badmouthed Pete Townshend when he couldn't get rights for a Who tune for *Fahrenheit*. And he deleted from the film Congressman Mark Kennedy's response to a question, apparently because it didn't fit neatly into the message he was trying to deliver to the audience. When he asked Kennedy for help in recruiting kids of members of Congress to participate in the war on terror, Kennedy agreed to pass out Moore's recruiting petition and even pointed out that he had a nephew in the military who was heading off to Afghanistan. But as Kennedy later told NBC News, "He [Moore] didn't like that answer, so he didn't include it."

Moore has uttered one outrageous statement after another, claiming that the United States brings "sadness and misery to places around the globe"; that Americans are "possibly the dumbest people on the planet"; that Bush knows "where Osama bin Laden is but won't go after him"; that the idea of a terrorist threat in this country is the "biggest lie we've been told"; that the self-sacrificing souls of Flight 93 were "scaredy-cats" because they were white; that those who kill our soldiers and saw off heads are revolutionaries and "Minutemen," that "their numbers will grow"— and that "they will win." Not exactly ambassador material.

In June 2004 I appeared on MSNBC's *Hardball* opposite former New York governor Mario Cuomo, who, amazingly, was appearing on behalf of the film. *Fahrenheit 9/11*'s distributors had retained Cuomo to try to get the movie's rating changed from R to PG-13. But he was also on TV to hype the flick.

When Cuomo was asked whether the film was a lighthearted,

satiric look at Washington, he answered, "These documentaries are filled with pictures, with real evidence. They're not aspirations, they're not speeches. They're real evidence. That's the kind of debate we should have."

More important, when asked whether he thought the movie hit the target in terms of being serious and accurate, Cuomo responded, "Oh, very definitely. Very definitely." He added, "It's a documentary. It is not a novel. It is not nonfiction. It is a documentary."

I had to wonder whether the former governor had seen the same film I had.

A STUDY IN MEDIA CONTRASTS

When *Fahrenheit 9/11* hit the screens, the media outpouring was remarkably different from that which a few months earlier had surrounded Mel Gibson's *The Passion of the Christ*. Both films did gain publicity from controversy, but the assessments from the most prominent reviewers at elite publications could not have been more opposite. Take a gander:

• The *New York Times*'s A. O. Scott noted, "Moore's populist instincts have never been sharper. . . . He is a credit to the republic."

But Scott wrote that Gibson had "exploited the popular appetite for terror and gore for what he and his allies see as a higher end."

• The *New York Daily News*'s Jami Bernard sobbed at the beauty of Moore's work. "I was in tears after first seeing 'Fahrenheit' at Cannes," he confessed.

But Bernard had no such soppy sentiment for Gibson, calling *The Passion* "the most virulently anti-Semitic movie made since the German propaganda films of World War II."

• The *Washington Post*'s Ann Hornaday praised Moore for exercising "admirable forbearance" and called *Fahrenheit* "his finest artistic moment."

But she saw no artistic split seconds in *The Passion* and chastised Gibson for exhibiting "a startling lack of concern for historical context."

• The *Los Angeles Times*'s Kenneth Turan congratulated Moore for making "a persuasive and unrelenting case that there is another way to look at things beyond the version we've been given."

But Turan turned 180 degrees and criticized Gibson's work as "a film so narrowly focused as to be inaccessible for all but the devout."

• The *Boston Globe*'s Ty Burr urged readers to go see Moore's flick "because it takes off the gloves and wades into the fray, because it synthesizes the anti-Bush argument like no other work before it, and because it forces you to decide for yourself exactly where passion starts to warp point of view."

But Burr frigidly warned those who ventured to see Gibson's film, "If you come seeking theological subtlety, let alone such modern inventions as psychological depth, you'll walk away battered and empty-handed."

• The *Boston Herald*'s James Verniere wrote, "At a time when the film industry is turning out sugarcoated, content-free junk, Moore has given American viewers a renewed taste for raw meat."

But Verniere said Gibson's movie was "an exercise in sadomasochistic bullying."

• The *Chicago Tribune*'s Michael Wilmington defensively declared that "it wasn't because of some clichéd French antipathy to America" that "*Fahrenheit* received the first prize and the longest continuous standing ovation in the history of the Cannes Film Festival."

But according to Wilmington, Gibson's work lacked "artistic and even spiritual balance."

• The *New York Observer*'s Rex Reed raved that Moore had created "multitudes of shattering, seminal moments in his brilliant Bush-whacking documentary."

But Reed yawningly dismissed Gibson's film as "a movie that doesn't say much of anything new. Been there, done that, and you know how it all comes out already."

• The *Houston Chronicle*'s Eric Harrison glowingly called Moore "an indispensable treasure," adding that "his imperfections are part of the reason, because they mark him as real."

But Harrison had a different take on Gibson's "imperfections," calling *The Passion* "awful because everything he knows about storytelling has been swept aside by proselytizing zeal."

• The *Toronto Star*'s Geoff Pevre dubbed Moore's work "a plea for America's deliverance. . . . It may not be an argument one agrees with, and it may be unbalanced and propagandistic, but it is both convincingly argued and sincerely motivated."

But Pevre wrote off Gibson's cinema as "a work of fundamentalist pornography."

• The *Detroit News*'s Tom Long argued that *Fahrenheit* was "a film every citizen of voting age in America should see."

But Long gave Gibson's work short shrift, writing that it was "the feel-awful movie of a lifetime, a filmed bloodletting like no other on record."

• The *Philadelphia Inquirer*'s Carrie Rickey saw Moore's film simply as "a magnificent piece of filmmaking."

But Rickey called Gibson's film "the first spiritual splatter film."

• The *Christian Science Monitor*'s David Sterrit defended the use of the term *documentary* as appropriate for Moore's fantasy flick, writing that "of course it is, unless you cling to some idealized notion of 'objective' film."

But Sterrit saw little merit in Gibson's film, complaining that "the highly selective screenplay includes only a few of Jesus' words, spoken in occasional flashback scenes."

• The *Village Voice*'s J. Hoberman evidently felt that Moore could accomplish what *Saturday Night Live*'s Dana Carvey once did, saying, "Let us not forget that Dana Carvey did more than anyone in America, save Ross Perot, to drive Bush père from the White House. There are sequences in 'Fahrenheit 9/11' so devastatingly on target as to inspire the thought that Moore might similarly help evict the son."

But J. Hoberman watched *The Passion* and saw "garishly staged suffering" in which "one might well ponder the millions of people—victims of crusades, inquisitions, colonial conquests, the slave trade, political terror, and genocide—who have been tortured and killed in Christ's name."

• The *Greenwich Village Gazette*'s Eric Lurio ordered every independent voter to "see this movie and vote for Kerry."

But Lurio luridly described *The Passion* as "a snuff film."

Reviews like these make me think that any vestige of fairness and objectivity in the mainstream-media film critic community is what's really been snuffed out.

RHOADS SCHOLAR

How could it be that reviewers were doing cartwheels over *Fahrenheit 9/11*? Well, when I saw the film, I thought I saw Moore using a variety of well-established propaganda devices. To see if my hunches were correct I sought out a specialist on the subject, Dr. Kelton Rhoads.[1]

Rhoads teaches at the University of Southern California's Annenberg School for Communication at the U.S. Air Force's Joint Special Operations University. He has also served as senior mentor for psychological-operations forces at the JFK Special Warfare Center and School in Fort Bragg, North Carolina. He works with industry, government and defense agencies, and political candidates, providing advice on the principles of influence.

Rhoads is particularly interested in the way we process narratives or stories. He describes two different types of discourse: one he calls "polemic" and the other "narrative." We see polemic discourse all the time on cable news shows, where two or more folks with differing ideas have a quarrel of sorts. The attacks are obvious and readily observable.

The narrative stands in complete contrast. In a narrative, people aren't concentrating on their defenses. In fact, research shows that when we read or view a narrative, the brain suppresses cognitive defenses that it normally puts up to stop material we disagree with. "So you can run stuff in a narrative, and people will just drink it in," Rhoads explains. He adds that "narrative is sort of a stealth technology of persuasion."

According to Rhoads, if narrative is presented in a compelling way and seems as if it could be true, it becomes the equivalent of truth. "It is the feeling that it could be true," he says, "so if you do a narrative well enough, it has this feeling of truth, and that is this elusive, slippery term that those of us in the sciences don't like. What is a feeling of truth? How do I measure that? Well, that is where the creative genius of the storyteller comes in. A storyteller can get you into that suspension, what they call 'transport.'"

Transport is Rhoads's term for what happens when you see a movie or television show and you "kind of leave your space and get into the story." When that happens, Rhoads tells me, "people aren't able to distinguish the fact from the fiction once they get back to normal life."

This is particularly effective when the form used is labeled a documentary or a docudrama. "You get images into your head, and once you can picture them, they have this feeling of truth. And, again, it keeps coming back to this 'feeling' of truth, rather than truth itself," Rhoads informs me.

In addition to using narrative, Moore's *Fahrenheit 9/11* uses classic propaganda techniques to enhance its persuasive potential. When Rhoads saw Moore's film, it had an effect even on him. "I found that the film had moved me several notches leftward after seeing it. I went in and I thought, 'I've been hearing so much about this movie.' I went in to watch it, and I came out with less confidence in Bush and more questions about going to war."

But Rhoads knew that some things in the film weren't quite right. "I thought that there were things that I had never heard in any other sources," Rhoads observes. He found himself having "a lot of uncertainty and doubt." He recognizes the feelings as some of the goals that propagandists in the military seek to elicit from recipients. There's even an acronym that the military uses for the targeted emotional response—FUD, which stands for fear, uncertainty, and doubt.

Unlike the average moviegoer, when Rhoads got out of the

theater he decided to fact-check the film himself. "I started seeing that it was like a house of cards," he remarks. "I decided that I was going to roll up my sleeves and really take a look at it to see what was really underneath it. Once I started examining the claims that were in there, I started recognizing a lot of the tactics that propagandists use."

Rhoads identifies numerous propaganda techniques employed in *Fahrenheit*. Moore used *omissions* quite frequently. Some of the omissions were so obvious that only the most naïve would be taken in. For instance, when Moore did a roll call of the countries that were part of the coalition of the willing that had invaded Iraq, he showed only a few of the smaller nations.

Seems to me that Spain and Great Britain were pretty big omissions there.

Moore also used a very sophisticated technique that Rhoads calls the *convert communicator*. "That is somebody who used to believe one way and now has turned 180 degrees and believes something else," according to Rhoads. Moore sometimes coupled this technique with *modeling*. Using modeling, a narrative encourages the audience to emulate the actions and beliefs of a character. Rhoads argues that Moore combined these approaches most effectively when he featured Lila Lipscomb. As Rob Borsellino of the *Des Moines Register* described the scene, "Lipscomb, a self-described moderate who had 'contempt for anti-war activists,' talked about how she found out her son was killed in a helicopter crash. She was home alone when she got the call from the Defense Department. She fell to the floor and crawled across the room. She cried and talked about how parents are not supposed to bury their children. She cried and asked, 'Why my son? He was a good person.' "[2] According to Rhoads, that section of the film had "all the emotional arguments in it as well. And emotional arguments—how do you defeat those?"

Rhoads speaks of a technique that's sometimes employed in which "you show a sympathetic heroine, and you bring the audience along the same path that you bring your heroine. You get people to like the heroine. Then you show the heroine changing from one behavior to another behavior and you draw your audience along with it."

In Moore's film, Lipscomb was depicted as religious and patriotic. She displayed a U.S. flag in front of her home and referred to herself as conservative. On his website's blog, Moore wrote of Lipscomb, "She's a conservative, and that should be made note of." Moore's images created the impression that she slowly changed her political beliefs as she mourned her son's death. After the audience watched Lipscomb trek to Washington, she was shown collapsing in grief. At that point Moore came in with a narration. He said, "I was tired of seeing people like Mrs. Lipscomb suffer."

Rhoads says that the power of this technique rests in the communicator being perceived as having made a complete U-turn in his or her beliefs. But in reality, Lipscomb actually voted for Bill Clinton and Al Gore in their presidential runs.[3] She had told the *Guardian* of London that her son was against the war in Iraq. "I so vividly remember. I walked out of my bedroom and we have a long hallway upstairs and he was standing there and he said he would have to go to Kuwait and then to Baghdad. And he said he didn't support the war, that he didn't know why he had to go over there. We talked about fear. I was petrified, because in my mind I was thinking that's where bin Laden is, because that's what we'd been told."[4]

Rhoads tells me of two other propaganda tools called *pacing* and *distraction*, which are used to overload the mind. He explains that "modern life is taxing for modern brains. The human brain hasn't kept up the pace with modern society, so our brains have to deal with so much more information than they would have even fifty, sixty, or seventy years ago."

Apparently, the more complicated the technology, the greater the load on the brain. Rhoads says, "As life gets more complex, it fragments attention. We've got more and more things we have to pay attention to. The more things you have to pay attention to, and you're still using the same kind of underpowered computer as your brain, you have to start coming up with shortcuts."

Rhoads offers the example of going to a store to purchase

an orbital exerciser. If you didn't know much about the piece of equipment, and the shop offered several alternatives to choose from, you would have to find a way to decide which one to purchase. The comprehensive way to accomplish this would be to base your determination on the way the product was engineered. Since a consumer doesn't have the time to obtain an engineering degree, he or she would, by necessity, make up his or her mind based on other things like product information, price, or sales pitch.

The kinds of things that can overload the brain's ability to process include elements like switching contexts, scenes, music, and voiceovers. "When the film starts getting that cluttered feeling, that is a sign that you are getting distracted," Rhoads explains.

Fahrenheit 9/11 used voiceovers, cartoons, fast cuts, and newspaper clips that were flashed up on the screen. In many cases, viewers had only an instant to analyze the material before the scene shifted. This is an illustration of distraction.

"In contrast, the scenes with Lila Lipscomb contained virtually no distractions," Rhoads says. "The pacing got slower and you were able to concentrate on it more. Anytime that you have strong arguments, you want to slow down so people can process them. But when you have weak arguments, you want to speed up so people don't process them." Rhoads also notes that if "one person has one argument and the other person has twelve arguments, if you are rushed you are going to choose the person with the twelve arguments and say they were more persuasive."

One other propaganda technique Moore used is called *priming*. Priming is the phenomenon that occurs when a concept is activated in the mind and is timed to affect another concept that follows in sequence. Rhoads describes how researchers study priming: "You bring somebody into a laboratory and you show them something called a tachistoscope, a computer screen that can flash on words so fast that it is below the level of awareness, so it is nonconscious."

If you're like me, you think about "subliminal" advertising when you hear that comment from Rhoads. A few years back, rumors floated around that advertisers were placing persuasive thoughts into people's heads without their knowledge. Movie theaters were supposedly flashing the word *popcorn* on their screens to prompt audiences to robotically consume more of the stuff. Given my own popcorn proclivity, it still has me wondering.

But Rhoads tells me about a kind of nonconscious communication of the more real kind, saying, "They'll flash on words like bravery. You sit there and look at the screen. You see a little blip, but you don't know what it is. Nonetheless, your mind is able to recognize it." He explains how an audience will be "picking up these words like *bravery* and *proud* and *duty,* and all these other things that are related to bravery," and then when an ambiguous narrative about an individual is given, "if people have been exposed to the bravery word, they will view that person as being more brave."

According to Rhoads, the reason priming works is that "once we get a structure activated in our minds and, in this case, the structure is bravery, it doesn't just die out immediately. It colors the next thing that we see, and that is what the priming hypothesis is all about."

After talking to Rhoads, I had a whole new understanding of what *Fahrenheit 9/11* was really all about. It sure wasn't something to see if you "wanted to get the facts."

HUNTING FOR BUBBA

In 2004 lefties must have felt as if they'd died and gone to political movie paradise.

In addition to Michael Moore's feature-length DNC campaign ad, *The Hunting of the President* was in the liberal nirvana lineup. Many of the same celebrity libs turned out for screenings of the two flicks. High-profile viewers of both films included Glenn Close, Mike Myers, Lauren Hutton, Moby, Tina Brown, and Al Franken.

Press releases called *The Hunting of the President* a "groundbreaking political documentary" that focused "on the smear campaign against [Bill] Clinton from his days as Governor leading up to and including his impeachment trial." The film's press material also backed up Hillary's claims of a "vast right-wing conspiracy," saying it was an authentic "campaign to systematically destroy the political legacy of the Clintons."

Given the film's nakedly pro-Clinton approach, it may not surprise you to learn that *Hunting*'s director, Harry Thomason, is a longtime friend of the Clintons. In fact, he and his wife, Linda Bloodworth-Thomason, produced campaign films for Bill Clinton and also chaired the 1993 Clinton inauguration.

In an effort to keep the political momentum going and stoke the Dem embers, at one of the *Hunting* screenings organizers came up with the added incentive of having a special guest star in the mix. They managed to get Bill Clinton himself to show up. There was supposed to be a panel discussion at the event, with *The Week*'s Harold Evans acting as moderator. But surprise, surprise, the roundtable never happened. Bubba did show up, but apparently he wouldn't shut up.

Bill accused his enemies of seeking "to consolidate power and wealth in their own hands." Seems to me there was a little $12 million consolidation of the guy's own making in the form of *My Life,* Clinton's autobiography (which the *New York Times* described as "eye-crossingly dull"). The ex-prez explained that "when the Berlin Wall fell, the perpetual right in America, which always needs an enemy, didn't have an enemy anymore." He then boohooed that he "had to serve as the next best thing."

No wonder Hollywood loves Bubba so much. They're both used to crying on cue.

Miller Speak

Dennis Miller is a guy who walks an eclectic path. Over the years, the King of Quip has traveled from the *Saturday Night Live* soundstage to the HBO family to the ABC *Monday Night Football* booth. He's managed to snag five Emmy Awards along the way. He recently had a prime-time show on CNBC that was a blend of simile-laden monologues, in-depth interviews, and "varsity panel" discussions.

Miller also is somewhat unorthodox in that he's someone who hasn't been shy about talking about his conservative views. That doesn't happen too often in Tinseltown, where parroting Dem talking points is considered chic. He dumbfounds the Hollywood Left.

In chatting with Miller, I asked him about his political transformation.[1]

HIRSEN: What made you slide over to the right side of the political spectrum?

MILLER: I view it not as a slide, but rather an ascension. [Laughs] Slide has a negative connotation. By viewing this as a "Chutes and Ladders" game, I'm saying that I stepped up after 9/11 to a more serious approach to protecting this country.

HIRSEN: That leads to another question. Since you made your "ascension," have you been treated . . .

MILLER: By ascension, I don't mean like I'm imbued or anything. I don't want to sound like it's too ethereal. I just mean I don't like slides.

HIRSEN: But since you made the change—that is, moved on certain issues to the right—have you been treated differently?

MILLER: I don't notice it. Occasionally I've been called "naïve" at a party, but that's the extent of it so far. I would say three times I've been at a Hollywood party and three times people I've talked to have said, "You are so naïve." But that's pretty easy. I take it with a grain of salt. Most people have been very civil and very understanding about it. They don't agree with it, but at least they are my friends, and they think, "Well, whatever. At least you read up on it." They know I'm not completely uninformed on it. I at least try to read.

HIRSEN: You were called an iconoclastic liberal. Do you ever look back on the things you've said and now, post-9/11, do you ever regret any of it?

MILLER: No.

HIRSEN: Regrets, I have none?

MILLER: Well, I don't know. Am I going to go back and process jokes that I told in the mid-'90s and say, "God, I wish I hadn't said that."? You know, I've poked fun at every president who is in there, and indeed I've made the same hay off of Bush's malaprops as anybody else. But I think he's doing a pretty good job right now, and I'm on the other side.

Would I start poking fun at him again if we completely peel off of each other, belief-wise? Yes. I'm not a lifer. I respect him because I respect him, and that should be all any candidate or president would ask out of somebody. I'm not saying I'm there for life. If I didn't respect him, I wouldn't. I'm not blind about it.

HIRSEN: Since you are based in Hollywood and are a Republican, you could have done what Republicans in Hollywood do: become an action hero.

MILLER: [Laughs]

HIRSEN: So why did you choose . . .

MILLER: I'm too bulked up.

HIRSEN: [Laughs] So why did you choose to do a talk show, a daily TV talk show? You had other options.

MILLER: Well, that's not true. I have one monkey trick. It's sort of my opinion, and I deliver it in a reasonably sardonic manner. That's the only thing I have in my talent portfolio.

HIRSEN: You majored in journalism. Was the show sort of going back to your roots?

MILLER: No, I have no urge to be a journalist. [Laughs] I don't. That's nothing that interests me. [My] act is my belief. I just change the format. I go from a football booth, to cable, to a twenty-four-hour news network. I'll tell you what. I'm not very much on self-backslapping, but one thing I'll say is at least I step into different worlds and take my medicine if I have to.

9

MEL MUTINY

It was late March 2003. I was working at home when I received a phone call. On the other end of the line was a representative from Icon Productions, Mel Gibson's film company. Since January I had been reporting on a new movie that Gibson was directing, a film dealing with the life of Jesus Christ. Gibson himself came on the line. He told me he'd read my most recent NewsMax article, where I had discussed some of the early attacks on the film—attacks that came even before anyone had seen the movie. Little did I know at the time, but the phone conversation would lead to many others. In fact, in the coming weeks and months I would visit Icon's offices on numerous occasions and would be in close contact with Mel and his associates.

The movie, which would eventually be titled *The Passion of the Christ,* would become one of the most controversial films and also one of the most successful ever. I would be fortunate enough to have a behind-the-scenes view of the attacks, the challenges and counterchallenges, and ultimately, the Gibson victory.

The controversy surrounding the making of *The Passion of the Christ* makes for a fascinating story. But the saga also tells us something important about our Hollywood Nation. For starters, the story of *The Passion* shows that some renegades in the news and entertainment businesses are standing up and challenging the conventional liberal orthodoxy. Those who do sometimes pay a price, as the mainstream media's and the Hollywood establishment's approaches to *The Passion* indicate. The incredible success of the film, however, is a testament to the fact that those who for years have been disproportionately in control of the message are losing their precious monopoly.

JUMP START ON A CONTROVERSY

I took a particular interest in Mel Gibson's movie well before I began speaking with Icon Productions. I knew Gibson was one of the few Hollywood folks who had a worldview that was similar to mine, and he wasn't afraid to express it on film—*Braveheart, Signs, We Were Soldiers, The Patriot.* It was a pattern I'd long admired and, to me, the choice of his new project indicated that once again he was going to edify.

My information at the time was that Gibson's project didn't have name stars and that he was going to direct but would, by Hollywood standards, use a relatively low budget. I also understood that the film was being done in the classic languages of Aramaic and Latin.

In *Variety* magazine Peter Bart reported that the movie was probably going to be a small art film. That was my understanding, too. But as the year developed, something far different emerged.

I had a friend and source who was working on the production site in Rome, so even though I wasn't physically present, I had "eyes and ears." I received a call in early January 2003. My friend told me that a freelance journalist had begun to ask very private and personal questions and was looking into Gibson's finances, family, religious beliefs, and political affiliations for the purpose of an article that was to appear in the *New York Times Magazine.*

As I looked closer into the matter, I began asking questions and started to write a series of pieces for NewsMax. I was one of the first in the media to cover the story. One source notified me that Gibson was going to make an appearance on Bill O'Reilly's Fox News Channel program to discuss what had been going on. Sure enough, Gibson appeared on *The O'Reilly Factor* on January 17, 2003.

It turned out that freelance writer Christopher Noxon had indeed been digging for dirt on Gibson. Ultimately, Noxon's article appeared in the *New York Times Magazine* on March 9, 2003. The article contained a whole series of mischaracterizations and accusations. Noxon had spent months working on the story about the film, about a church Gibson was building near his home, and about his faith.

Meanwhile, a group of ad hoc experts claiming to be "interfaith scholars" began making demands on Gibson to change his movie. Long after production on the film had wrapped up, the so-called scholars wrote a letter to Gibson essentially saying that his idea of focusing on the Passion of Jesus Christ was wrong. They insisted that he needed to broaden his subject matter to include the "overall ministry of Jesus Christ," meaning he should scrap his own personal perspective and artistic vision and do a movie that met with their approval.

With the help of an individual who was dubbed in an e-mail "our Deep Throat," the group of academics got hold of a stolen draft of a confidential script. Using ideas and notes from the pilfered preliminary screenplay, the group generated a supposedly confidential report that twisted the film's message. Somehow the report landed in the hands of the news media. A number of its authors appeared delighted to have their criticisms aired in public, despite the fact that the report was based on incomplete, dated, confidential, and pirated material.

In addition to theft, it seems that falsification was also part of the unscholarly game. The group tried to pawn itself off as an official body of the United States Conference of Catholic Bishops, but the USCCB subsequently issued a statement denying a connection with the anti-Gibson group.

Boston University's Paula Fredriksen was a particularly high-profile player in the film-dissing drama. On previous occasions, Fredriksen had referred to Scripture as "a kind of religious advertisement." She had promoted the idea that the Gospels "proclaim their individual author's interpretation of the Christian message through the device of using Jesus of Nazareth as a spokesperson for the evangelist's position." On December 22, 2001, the *Washington Post* had even delivered a sort of un-Christmas present from Fredriksen in the form of a comment about the trustworthiness of the New Testament. Fredriksen was quoted by the *Post* as saying, "I can't think of any New Testament scholar who takes [the Gospel accounts of Jesus' birth] to be historically reliable," adding that most scholars believe that Christ was not born in Bethlehem.

It appeared to me as though Fredriksen and friends were on a mission to deconstruct the Gospels. They prattled on about "progressive interpretation" and "historical context" when it seemed as though what they really wanted was a rewrite of the Good Book. Could it be that their real beef with Mel Gibson had to do with the fact that he had based his movie on the writings of Matthew, Mark, Luke, and John?

The saga continued as film-snuffing sights were set on a potential distributor. This was the beginning of an unprecedented attempt to stop Gibson from releasing the film. My own familiarity with the Hollywood industry told me that a giant double standard was under way.

CINE-MAGIC

I attended an early screening of *The Passion of the Christ* along with a diverse group of people. The version we viewed was not the final. It didn't have its completed sound track, effects, or final editing. But it didn't matter. Even in its unfinished form, it was extraordinary.

The look of the film was compelling in its dimension of color, light, and texture. Mel described it as "a moving Caravaggio."

The idea of a moving work of Baroque art that is realistic in its portrayal was born of a change in Gibson's view of the Passion story. Mel said that when he was younger, he thought of it as distant and sanitized, like a "fairy tale." He later came to realize that the story was real. It was then that he began to think of it in terms of a film.

Gibson wanted to remind people of the reality of Christ's physical torment. He said that "we have gotten used to seeing pretty crucifixes on the wall and we forget what really happened."

Mel had trodden on this ground before. His directorial triumph *Braveheart* featured a suffering Christ-like figure in the visage of William Wallace. And although other movies on the life of Christ had been made, he didn't believe that they "tapped into the real force of this story."

Gibson said that with this film he intended "to create a lasting work of art." He added that "this is a movie about faith, hope, love, and forgiveness—something sorely needed in these times."

Everything was as he described. After viewing the film, the audience was silent for a spell, the breathing uneven, the air thick with emotion. Mel walked in and casually sat on the floor. He spoke quietly but intensely about his film, its cinematic elements, its characters, his goals in making it. He invited comments and listened with an intellectual's curiosity, a director's perceptiveness, and an artist's confidence. With his distinctive gestures, expressions, and style, he partly instructed, partly just conversed, gracefully accepting praise, fielding questions, challenging thoughts, cataloguing comments. It was a unique and remarkable experience.

After the discussion was done, I walked over to meet the filmmaker in person. I shook his hand, introduced myself, and saw the lightbulb of recognition go off. We talked for a bit. Mel commented about the universality of the film. He told me that the film had themes that everyone could relate to. And he pointed out that "the struggle between good and evil, and the power of love, go beyond race and culture."

The words would stick with me.

A PASSIONATE CALLING

After having screened the film, I was in a unique position to talk about it publicly, since few had yet seen it. I regularly go on radio and TV as an analyst and commentator, but now requests for my input multiplied as the buzz over the film grew. In many instances I was booked to debate individuals who were accusing Gibson of anti-Semitism. I kept in touch with my sources at Icon Productions to get updates on the latest developments as they occurred.

In one TV appearance I did with Tony Snow on the Fox News Network, I was able to explain that the detractors were misjudging the film. Since it was not one of those argumentative debate segments, my presentation was comprehensive and upbeat.

A couple of days later I checked in at Icon and was able to meet with Gibson. Mel had a light schedule that day and so did I. I stayed longer, and time allowed for more leisurely conversation. We spoke at length about philosophy, theology, the news of the day, and, of course, his project.

He expressed to me many of the things that he would later go public with. He told me that he knew he was entering territory that would lead to a lot of criticism. He also told me that friends of his said the project had the potential to be a "career killer." He semi-jokingly admitted, "I'm not sure I'll ever work again," but he added, "It doesn't matter." He felt that there was a higher calling involved.

Gibson is thoughtful, imaginative, and actually a fairly reserved guy. He doesn't like to preach and prefers to let his work speak for itself. But the deceptive attacks on his family and on his project made it necessary for him to take some extraordinary steps professionally, ones he'd never before engaged in.

Here he was this huge movie star and Oscar-winning director, yet he traveled all over the country to screen his film for small gatherings of folks—people who gave meaningful feedback and who were not predisposed to reject the work's premise.

I noted that Gibson's beliefs were not something he had arrived at casually. He was extremely well read and had thought things through when it came to his faith. As he explained to me, it was his faith that saved him from a path that was leading to destruction. His marriage, his livelihood, and even his life might have been lost were it not for the faith he uncovered. It is this faith that moved him to make *The Passion of the Christ.* It was also this faith he chose to communicate to the audience at each screening. He personally interacted and connected with the individuals present.

Gibson, I learned, had carried the zeal in his heart for this particular project for about a dozen years. Steve McEveety, one of Mel's key colleagues and a coproducer of *The Passion,* recalled that Mel had brought the film idea up over and over again, sometimes in the midst of other projects. During the filming of the critically acclaimed Vietnam War epic *We Were Soldiers,* McEveety explained, Gibson (who portrayed Lieutenant Colonel Hal Moore) raised the subject immediately after shooting a violent battle scene. McEveety told me, "Viet Cong soldiers were running down the hill blasting fire at him. The director yells, 'Cut,' and Mel walks directly over to me and says, 'We have to make *The Passion.*' "

Gibson's colleagues understood that *The Passion* referred to Mel's longtime desire to create this film. "Out of the blue, every now and then, every couple of months, Mel would mention it," McEveety said.

Once the preparation for the film began, things started to come together in some serendipitous and rather miraculous ways. Gibson and his team described the film as both the easiest film they ever worked on and yet, in many ways, the most difficult. Since he had carried the concept with him for so long, it was inevitable that this would be the first film Gibson would direct but not star in. To work with Mel on the script, McEveety brought in Benedict Fitzgerald, who turned out to be the ideal cowriter for bringing the Gospels to the big screen.

Choosing the actors who would play Jesus and Mary would, of course, be pivotal. The roles were ultimately filled by two individuals who, in this observer's opinion, are the best casting match this side of Heaven.

FINDING JESUS

Gibson has his own way of choosing an actor for a film. Rather than having a prospective actor read from a script, he looks at past work and engages in one-on-one conversation—meaning he does his homework and then follows his instincts. In the year 2000, Gibson and McEveety went to Tunisia and Morocco to scout locations. On the flight home, Mel showed McEveety a magazine that he'd gotten a hold of. He opened it to a page that included a tiny picture of an actor who had appeared in films like *The Thin Red Line, The Count of Monte Cristo,* and *Angel Eyes* with Jennifer Lopez. In an unequivocal tone, Gibson remarked to McEveety, "This is the only guy in the world who could play Jesus."

The conversation was laid aside until years later, when director Kevin Reynolds, who had read a script for a film dealing with surfers, suggested that Gibson and McEveety meet an actor he thought would be perfect for the beach production. They held the meeting at a little burger stand that's frequented by bikers. The young actor was quiet and slow-moving. McEveety recalls thinking that the actor's demeanor was a bit unusual, and when asked for his first impression, he suggested to Mel that the fellow might not be completely there. In a very brief time, McEveety did a 180. At a singularly startling moment, the actor told Gibson, "Somebody told me a month ago that Mel Gibson's going to ask you to play Jesus."

The actor was Jim Caviezel. The conversation on the plane suddenly became eerily relevant.

The meeting at the burger stand ultimately led to Caviezel's taking on the most demanding and fulfilling role of his career. The physical pain, time-consuming makeup applications, far-off locations, inclement weather, and magnitude of the role were some of the challenges Caviezel faced head-on. For many of the shoots, the young actor endured more than six hours of cosmetic preparation. He often slept in full makeup so as to be ready at dawn to act out a scene. One day the cold winds almost blew the cross that he was attached to off a cliff. He sometimes found himself hanging in freezing cold temperatures, without the benefit of much in the way of clothing. At one point he suffered a separated shoulder.

Gibson was aware of how Caviezel suffered. And he marveled at his perseverance. "He was in a lot of pain and discomfort, but he was very patient during the whole thing," Mel noted.

A few more mystical elements of surprise. At the time of the film shoot, Caviezel was thirty-three years old—the same age as Jesus in the real life Passion. And his initials just happen to be J.C.

MOTHER MORGENSTERN

Mel Gibson was viewing a videotape of a small film released nearly a decade earlier. As he watched the movie, he focused on the star, a Romanian actress.

"She's Mary," Mel stated without hesitation.

The actress was Maia Morgenstern. The 1995 film was *The Seventh Room*. It was about a Catholic convert, Edith Stein, who is now known as Saint Teresa Benedicta of the Cross.

Very simply, what happened was that Gibson saw a movie about one of the most famous Jewish converts, played by a Jewish actress, and decided to cast that actress in the most important film of his career. The result, in a word, was exquisite. While editing one of Morgenstern's scenes, Mel told me, "She is absolutely amazing. No matter what scene she is in, she is always on."

Folks who see *The Passion* often remark about its authenticity. It's no accident that this Mary and Jesus, in contrast to those in other movies, look like a Jewish mother and son.

When I saw the movie, I felt as if I were peering into a time portal. Mel himself described his work as "like traveling back in time and watching the events unfold exactly as they occurred."

LIGHTNING STRIKES

Extraordinary events occurred after filming began. Gibson said that people working on *The Passion* were "touched and changed by the experience." For instance, the six-year-old daughter of someone working on the film no longer had symptoms of epilepsy, which the girl had apparently had since birth. "A couple of people," Mel said, "have had sight and hearing restored," and he added that "another guy was struck by lightning while we were filming the crucifixion scene and he just got up and walked away."

The lightning reference is quite a story. It was the final day of shooting in Golgotha, the place where Jesus Christ was crucified. The beauty was breathtaking, but the cast and crew were fatigued and desperately wanted to finish up. As clouds began to form and the wind kicked up, one of the grips—who no one suspected spoke English—said, "I think we better get out of here." Everyone realized it was time to make a run for it. They sprinted toward the vehicles to seek shelter as the rain started pouring down and the thunder and lightning began their furious tear. Seeing a female crew member struggle, an assistant director came out with an umbrella to shelter her. Suddenly a huge bolt of lightning—"the biggest I've ever seen," McEveety recalled—hit the assistant director and went straight through his body.

Although he was shaken by the incident, he had only some minor burns on his hands.

Several months later, the production staff and crew were in Rome fine-tuning the scene depicting the Sermon on the Mount. Though Italy was in the midst of a long drought, it began to rain. Jim Caviezel continued the scene, with an assistant director holding an umbrella to keep him dry. Suddenly a bolt of lightning hit the assistant director at the same time as it hit Caviezel. Amazingly, neither man was hurt.

It was the same assistant director who had been hit the time before. Again he walked away unharmed.

When alone I think about the supernatural overtones and ask myself, What are the chances that a superstar can make a film about the final hours of Jesus Christ, survive attacks on his character and his family, and wind up with a critically acclaimed blockbuster to his credit?

About the same as lightning striking the same guy twice.

ARTFUL PLAY

The more time I spent at Icon, the more I came to understand how Gibson created such a powerful film.

To get the terrific performances that characterize *The Passion,* Mel used humor to cut the tension. Stories about Gibson cracking jokes, making sound effects with his bullhorn, threatening to nail Caviezel to the cross for real, and wearing a clown's nose abound.

It was revealing to watch Gibson relate to his employees. One time when I was over at the offices, I saw Mel stunting with one of his staffers. He pretended to be slammed up against the wall, only to recover from his fall at the last moment. It became clear that he treats the guy or gal who sweeps the floor the same way he treats a visiting Hollywood mogul. In fact, a number of my students have interned for Icon and they invariably tell me the same thing—that a very special corporate culture exists at the company, and that it comes from the top down.

On one very memorable occasion when I was at the Icon studios, Mel grabbed me by the shoulders and asked, "Do you want to hear the voice of the devil?" With my bravest expression and boldest posture I answered, "Sure."

Lucky for me it was only a movie.

I followed Mel down a long corridor and we strolled into a well-equipped editing room. An editor sat at an instrument panel that had a series of dedicated computer controls. Digital images of *The Passion of the Christ* were moving rapidly across an enormous screen. The temporary sound track filled the room. We watched a scene depicting Satan, and I listened to a bunch of alternative voices for the prince of darkness.

"Which one do you like?" Mel asked. They all scared the Hades out of me. But I mentioned my favorite, humbled to be asked for my input. Mel reviewed the scene over and over again, slightly altering the sequence of the images or the duration of the camera's focal point. It reminded me of the rhythm and harmony of symphonic music. I was awestruck at his ability to ratchet up the quality of a given scene.

Once again I saw on display the formidable people skills that Gibson possesses. It was quickly apparent that a surplus of camaraderie existed between this director and his editor. No matter how intricate the task or how many repetitions were necessary, each undertaking was completed with persistence and fluidity.

Gibson's mastery of the medium was far-reaching. He knew how many frames per second were passing by at any given time. He knew every beat of every scene, every expression on every face, and every word of the dialogue in the ancient tongues of Latin and Aramaic. As I watched hour after hour, scenes were slowly improved by the most subtle of changes. It was very late in the evening when I left, but the director and his editor remained focused on their work, seeming to possess an unlimited amount of energy.

When Gibson said goodbye, I heard the trace of an Aussie upbringing. "Cheers," he said.

BITTER BATTLE

Early on, the conventional wisdom in Hollywood was that, as *Variety*'s Peter Bart wrote, not a lot of people would go see a movie on the suffering and death of Jesus Christ, without big-name stars and in dead languages. In due time, he would be proven very wrong. Meanwhile, though, a group was organizing to attempt to stop *anyone* from seeing the film.

A small group of naysayers, with big media assistance, continued the relentless attack that had begun from the first moment they heard about Gibson's plans. These attackers found themselves thwarted at every turn, so much so that their stubborn pursuit looked like a Wile E. Coyote cartoon chase. Mel told me that although he had anticipated he would be attacked for the movie, he was surprised by the viciousness of those initiating the arguments.

Critics claimed that the movie was anti-Semitic. They were still basing their angry attacks on that stolen early script. Big media and even politicians joined the battle to keep the film from getting a distributor. New York assemblyman Dov Hikind scheduled a press conference and demonstration in front of the Manhattan headquarters of Rupert Murdoch's News Corporation. Murdoch's Twentieth Century Fox usually distributed Gibson's movies, but as it turned out in *The Passion* instance, it went with a thumbs-down. The *New York Times,* which described the film as chronicling "in bloody detail" the last hours of Jesus' life, called it "potentially inflammatory" and "not commercial enough for a high-profile mainstream studio like Fox." According to the *New York Daily News,* other Hollywood studios were also less than enthusiastic about taking on the project.

Gibson and the crew simply gripped the wheel, rode out the bumps, and ultimately found a distributor, Newmarket Films, which had only been launched in August 2002.

Unfortunately, more trouble lay ahead.

PASSION PIRACY

One evening as I was sitting in the offices of Icon, word came down that the *New York Post* had illegally obtained a pirated videotape of Gibson's film. Although this revelation was extraordinary in its own right, it's what the newspaper did with the tape that made ignoble cinematic history.

Months before the film was scheduled to be released, the *Post* displayed the grainy second-generation videotape to its own assembled panel of critics. Four of the five reviewers proceeded to slam the film in the pages of the paper.

Oscar-winning director Sydney Pollack put feelings into words this way. He told E! Online News, "If I had made that picture, I would have felt raped."

Evidently, the shenanigan wasn't just outrageous, it was also illegal. The *Los Angeles Times* reported that federal authorities were
launching a probe into the matter. But nothing ever came of the
investigation.

Around the same time, the Anti-Defamation League let loose
with one of the ugliest assaults on Gibson. At the organization's
annual meeting in New York, ADL national director Abraham
Foxman said, "I think he's [Gibson's] infected—seriously
infected—with some very, very serious anti-Semitic views." These
words spewed forth from the leader of an organization that purportedly stands for tolerance. Ironically, instead of modeling a
virtue, Foxman ended up demonstrating exactly what hate speech
sounds like.

A short time later some uninvited ADL officials registered for
a Christian pastors' conference where Gibson's film would be
shown. They used the fabricated name "The Church of Truth" to
gain entry to the event. After seeing the film, the ADL issued a
strongly worded statement that called Gibson's picture a "painful
portrayal" and a "commercial crusade to the church community."
Foxman requested that Gibson attach a personal disclaimer (drafted
by Foxman) denouncing any bigoted interpretation of his Passion
narrative.

That's when the mainstream media began piling on. *New York
Times* Arts columnist Frank Rich geared up the sleaze machine
several times over. In one column, Rich apparently got stuck in
sludge-slinging overdrive. He wrote that Gibson and his organization had been "baiting Jews," that Matt Drudge was a "token Jew,"
that traditionalist Catholics were a "fringe church," that Rupert
Murdoch was a "conservative non-Jew," that the *New Yorker*'s
Peter J. Boyer—one of the few mainstream journalists to write
sympathetically about Gibson—"sanitizes" Mel's father, that Bill
O'Reilly was "being paid" to defend Gibson, and that Gibson
spokesman Alan Nierob "plays bizarre games with the Holocaust."
(Rich evidently missed the fact that Nierob is a second-generation
Holocaust survivor and a founding member of the U.S. Holocaust
Museum.) Rich even took a swipe at yours truly. He claimed to

"decode" a section of my first book, *Tales from the Left Coast,* in which I supposedly displayed "a fetish of repeating Bob Dylan's original name."

In another column the Jayson Blair understudy heaved some more rubbish in Gibson's direction. After a Vatican official, who happened to be on the short list of papal prospects, raved about Gibson's movie and dismissed concerns over bigotry, Rich changed his focus. Instead of going after the *Passion* product, he attacked the *Passion* process. He wrote, "Intentionally or not, the contentious rollout of 'The Passion' has resembled a political campaign, from its start on 'The O'Reilly Factor.' "

Getting little traction with that one, Rich tried to jump into a story involving a higher authority.

THE PASSION AND THE POPE

In late 2003 I received a phone call from a source working closely with the Gibson organization. My contact called me from a special cell phone and informed me that he was in Rome and that the pope might view the film.

The papal screening did indeed take place. First, Peggy Noonan of the *Wall Street Journal* reported that Pope John Paul II had seen Gibson's movie and had made this statement about the film: "It is as it was." Noonan had received written confirmation for the quote from the pope's official spokesperson via e-mail. The same day, the *National Catholic Reporter's* main man at the Vatican, John Allen, reported the identical quote and attributed it to the pontiff. An unnamed senior Vatican official confirmed the statement for Allen. The following day, Reuters cited an unnamed Vatican source verifying the quote. The *Los Angeles Times,* too, received its own independent corroboration for the story.

But then the Catholic News Service's Cindy Wooden claimed to have talked to "a senior Vatican official close to the pope" who said that the pontiff had never said those words. John Allen, however, reported that he'd double-checked his original source and that the pope had indeed said, "It is as it was."

Enter once again Frank Rich. He tossed some more journalistic mud pies and accused Gibson and McEveety of using the pope to make money.

The next day the Catholic News Service reported that the pope's personal secretary said that "the Holy Father made no declaration" about the Gibson film. Two days later, *Los Angeles Times* columnist Tim Rutten apparently signed up to be Rich's Left Coast cohort. He wrote a vile piece that began, "A good Hollywood publicity campaign does not stumble over technicalities—like the truth. Still, it takes a particular sort of chutzpah to put a phony quote in the mouth of Pope John Paul II."

Actually it takes a particular sort of chutzpah for a columnist to forget to check his own paper's records before he writes on a subject. In a hard-news article, the *Times* admitted that "the ailing pontiff was quoted as having said after a private screening of the film 'it is as it was.'" The paper added that when asked "whether the quote was reliable, Vatican press secretary Joaquin Navarro-Valls told the *Times,* "'I think you can consider that quote as accurate.'"

Lost amid all the controversy was the truth: From the beginning, Icon had written authorization to go public with the pope's remarks on *The Passion of the Christ.* My sources allowed me to confirm the graphic nod with my own eyes. After the media started questioning the quote's authenticity, Icon immediately e-mailed the official Vatican press secretary and offered to discourage use of the quote. Navarro-Valls responded with an e-mail not only reaffirming that use of the quote was fine but also advising Icon to use the phrase "again and again and again." Even the *New York Times* wrote, "One prominent Roman Catholic official close to the Vatican said today, 'I have reason to believe—and I think—that the pope probably said it.'"

So we had four separate respected news organizations getting independent verification, and Icon Productions getting confirmation, authorization, and encouragement, to use the pope's "It is as it was" statement. The Icon team held fast to the truth and endured the personal insults, stolen scripts, threats of demonstration, pirated prints, and dire predictions.

Gibson did receive an endorsement of sorts from two prominent Vatican officials. Archbishop John P. Foley of the Catholic Church's social-communications office called the movie "an excellent film," reiterating how "there's nothing in the film that doesn't come from the Gospel accounts." And Cardinal Darío Castrillón Hoyos, prefect of the Congregation for the Clergy for the Vatican and one of the leading candidates to succeed Pope John Paul II, said in an interview that "Gibson's artistic choices make the film faithful to the meaning of the Gospels, as understood by the Church."

Positive statements from Gibson's peers in Hollywood rolled in, too. Jack Valenti, then head of the Motion Picture Association of America, called the movie an "impressive piece of art." Film critic Michael Medved said it was "by far the most moving, substantive, and artistically successful adaptation of Biblical material ever attempted by Hollywood." And the man who scared us half to death with *The Exorcist,* William Peter Blatty, dubbed the film "a masterpiece."

After the series of remarkable public messages from unanticipated quarters, Gibson and his Icon colleagues felt they could actually focus on what needed to be done—finish the film.

PASSIONATE OUTPOURING

I had the good fortune of being invited to a prerelease premiere of the film. It was a screening for the cast, crew, family, and friends of Mel. The movie would be released the next day—Ash Wednesday 2004.

A feeling of joy and release was in the air, as everyone knew that the film would finally be seen as it was meant to be seen. A bit of war-weariness was also present. Once again, I got to witness

Mel interfacing with the cast and crew and some of his employees. Many of the folks had flown in from Italy to be there. I watched as they expressed so much affection for this man.

As the screening was about to begin, Mel approached the front of the auditorium. He introduced and acknowledged some of the folks who had worked on the project and said a few words to his guests.

The lights dimmed, and the cinematic event of a lifetime began. Viewers experienced every emotion imaginable on the auditory and visual journey. Grown men felt at ease to cry. All felt at ease to rejoice as well. The film exceeded everyone's expectations, even those closest to its production.

As the movie closed, attendees sat in awed silence. Then the crowd unleashed another burst of emotion, rising out of their seats and erupting in thunderous applause. It was an unbridled display of gratitude for the man who had suffered deep personal trials, emerged triumphant, and was now poised to bring the magnificent work of art and object of unparalleled importance to so many.

It would be seen by millions. From the first day of the film's release it was clear that *The Passion of the Christ* would soar to blockbuster heights. A couple of days after the opening, I was at Icon and witnessed the loose buoyancy of emancipated spirits among Gibson and his close associates. Gibson showed me the gifts and piles of congratulatory letters that had poured in from the general public and from a broad array of colleagues—actors, actresses, writers, producers, and directors.

Sadly, however, the media were busy concocting their own sordid story.

SHAMEFUL EXPRESSIONS

Although *The Passion* experienced phenomenal box-office success and received amazing expressions of popular support, the mainstream media reacted in peculiar fashion. The reviews and press coverage were filled with hysteria and hyperbole. As the attacks failed to gain traction or stop the interest in the film, the language became increasingly shrill.

Catholic priest and author Andrew Greeley labeled it "sadomasochistic and pornographic." Christopher Hitchens wrote that it was "an exercise in lurid sadomasochism." A former Catholic priest, John Dominic Crossan, claimed that it was "pornographic." So did the *New York Post*'s Jonathan Foreman and columnist Andrew Sullivan. James Rudin, a rabbi I debated on television, said that Mel's work was "sadomasochistic." *USA Today*'s Al Neuharth referred to it as a "wasted exercise in sadomasochism." The *New York Times*'s A. O. Scott saw some "high-minded sadomasochism." *Newsweek*'s David Ansen was distressed by the "sadism." The *New Republic*'s Leon Wieseltier described it as a "repulsive masochistic fantasy" and a "sacred snuff film." The *Daily News*'s Jami Bernard claimed that the movie "would horrify the regulars at an S&M club." The *New Yorker*'s David Denby warned that the film was "extremely sadistic." *Slate*'s David Edelstein called it an "exercise in sadomasochism."

Who describes a cinematic rendering of the Gospels as pornographic or sadomasochistic? These sorts of reactions, quite frankly, were sickening to observe.

In my continued TV appearances, I debated detractors who were predicting that *The Passion* was going to result in pogroms and violence. What happened, in reality, is that the film was shown throughout the world, and the only consequence to the massive numbers of people seeing it was an outbreak of faith.

AMEN

The Passion, of course, went on to become one of the most successful films in history. First it earned over $600 million worldwide, and then it became a landmark success on DVD as well. The popularity of the movie didn't help, though, when it came to awards time. The 77th Annual Academy Awards continued the same egregious pattern established by the critics and the pre-Oscar award shows. *The Passion* was shut out of the three categories it was nominated for: Makeup, Score, and Cinematography. Mel was unfazed, but the snub served to highlight the mainstream media's and Hollywood's disconnect with the people.

Months after the film's release, Gibson told me that he had learned a lot about the media and that now he "knows the media better." But he was also able to draw positives from his experiences. "Even bad experiences, in retrospect, can be good," he said. He remarked that "even though "people said the film was going to cause violence, in the U.S. and in Europe, it didn't happen."

The backstory of *The Passion* tells us something about the current status of the liberal establishment: It's losing its stranglehold on information. Yes, many mainstream media outlets trumpeted the outlandish claims of interest groups opposing Gibson and went to great lengths to smear the *The Passion* and the filmmaker himself. But the effort didn't pay off. In the end, Gibson and his team circumvented traditional outlets and defeated opponents.

It's telling that when the controversy first emerged, back in early 2003, Gibson chose a venue where he knew he had a fair shot at getting his side of the story out: the Fox News Channel's *O'Reilly Factor.* And despite what the *New York Times*'s Frank Rich suggested, it wasn't because Bill O'Reilly was "being paid" to defend Gibson. Rich's overheated reaction said more about his frustration that publications like the *Times* could no longer set the terms of debate—and keep voices like Gibson's from being heard—than it did about the movie.

Long after *The Passion of the Christ*'s release, I asked Mel Gibson to assess the effects of the film. He used the same phrase that he had when he first described what he was trying to accomplish, bringing up those four simple virtues that are so familiar, so elusive, and so desperately needed. "This was about faith, hope, love, and forgiveness," he told me.

To which I continue to answer, "Amen."

Dayna *Extra*

Dayna Devon is a ten-year veteran of television news. From assignment reporter to anchor at affiliates of ABC and CBS, she has extensive experience in news reporting. Devon has been with *Extra* since 1999, serving as weekend coanchor and primary weekday correspondent before being named anchor in 2003. She also does commentary on entertainment-related subjects on a regular basis for CNN and MSNBC.

In my conversation with Devon we discussed the coverage of celebrities and the Hollywood influence that's all around us.[1]

HIRSEN: You primarily cover celebrities on *Extra*. How does it differ from your previous work as an anchor and reporter covering general news, or is it the same?

DEVON: Well, I think, generally speaking, you have about the same time restraints. So whether you're talking about tax fraud or a city election or Halle Berry in *Catwoman*, you still have about the same amount of time. The mission, I think, at *Extra* is you try and create a moment with that person. You try and show the viewer who that person is in a small amount of time. Everybody knows the public veneer that these people have. Our efforts are to get in a little bit behind that and get them to reveal a little bit about who they are, when they're not saying the standard lines to promote their movies. I think that's where it would differ.

HIRSEN: You know Andy Warhol's famous line about the fifteen minutes of fame, and how he coined the term *superstar.* You've been covering the famous for a long time. Do you feel that our society has become more obsessed with celebrity?

DEVON: Yes. If you think back even just to the 1980s. I remember being a teenager and I would go in the grocery store and I was obsessed, just like every girl was, with models and makeup and hair and all those things. I would look at the covers of magazines. There was Linda Evangelista, Naomi Campbell, Cindy Crawford, all of those girls. If you go on the magazine stands and you look now, they're all celebrities. We're completely insatiable as a society, I think, with celebrity.

HIRSEN: That leads to a question about some other attributes of celebrity that seem to be affecting the culture. For example, there are shows like *Extreme Makeover, The Swan*—

DEVON: My husband's on *Extreme Makeover.*

HIRSEN: I read that. Your husband's a plastic surgeon, right?

DEVON: Right.

HIRSEN: It seems to me that when I go out on the road, I'm spotting—and your husband would know better than I would—but I'm seeing people where it's pretty clear they are having their own little makeovers. But they're having them in Idaho and in Omaha.

DEVON: Oh, completely.

HIRSEN: Do you see a connection there with this celebrity obsession and with people sort of living Hollywood lives all across the country?

DEVON: You know what? I do. I see it maybe in different ways. And there's starting to be a little bit of a backlash about that. It's funny because, going back to my teenage years and looking at those covers of magazines, I didn't know at the time that they were airbrushed. Some people knew, but I didn't. And I didn't know that they would go in and trim a little bit of the arm off and trim a little bit of the hip off with graphics. Later they started doing some stories on that. You started realizing a little bit more what went into those.

I've done those shoots and I know what goes into it. You spend an hour in hair, an hour in makeup, your clothes are pinned perfectly behind you. Any wrinkle you have that accidentally, God forbid, shows up is airbrushed out. So I used to spend a lot of time really trying to look like those magazine covers, and then I had a more realistic expectation after a lot of that became more public.

What we're seeing now, I think, is a little bit of a backlash. If you've noticed some of the tabloids lately, what they're doing now is saying, "They're just like you. These celebrities are not perfect." You've seen the cellulite on the front covers, and they show these huge full-page pictures of all these celebrities getting in and out of cars, bending over at the beach, whatever. They're showing cellulite. So I think that the pendulum is swinging the other direction. It's more not how beautiful and how great they are, but that they're just like you.

HIRSEN: The term *backlash.* I see how that could happen. It reminds me of the reality show with Kirstie Alley.

DEVON: I think that that's probably the ultimate pendulum swinging the other way. We're not seeing twenty-year-olds date each other and give out roses in a ceremony. We're seeing someone who really says that she's battling Hollywood fat.

HIRSEN: Speaking of reality programming, it seems as if there are no boundaries left. Do you have some thoughts on reality programming?

DEVON: I think that the ones that have tended to be the most successful are the ones that we can all relate to in some way, although *Survivor's* pretty extreme. I mean we're not ever going to find ourselves on an island with these people and we group into tribes and have alliances and things like that. But I think it was symbolic in ways, like politics at a workplace.

We've all been where you go up against someone that has

a lot of friends and you're scared. You're politically scared, you're fired, you're whatever. I think it's probably just a great symbolic example of what we all deal with on a day-to-day basis. If you look at *The Apprentice,* which was very successful, I think the reason it was so successful is we all know an Omarosa. We all know what it feels like to be in a board room. I just think that was really real. And those characters, for some reason, really resonated with people.

HIRSEN: It's interesting that you call the participants "characters" because it seems like reality shows are anything but reality. Aren't they highly programmed or scripted?

DEVON: More so than I think even I realize. I just heard recently that there was a reality show. They taped the entire thing. Then they came back and went to a location that looked like the location it was supposed to be in, which it wasn't, and rewrote their testimonials—you know, the part where they pull the person off and they kind of recap what their emotions are. So I think more and more they're becoming scripted television.

HIRSEN: The networks have been engaging in cross promotion, and they've been highly criticized. For example, the *Today* show and *Good Morning America* have had people on as guests who have been kicked off reality programs the night before. There are moments when Katie Couric or Diane Sawyer appear to be journalists and are very serious. Then there are other moments when they're doing lifestyle sections or promoting an entertainment show.

DEVON: Right. You know, the morning shows, to me, have evolved greatly over the last, probably, decade, two decades. I think with good reason, because they're not necessarily positioned as completely serious news programs for the full three hours. I think what they try and do—and I do think they do a good job of this—is a full-service program. They've obviously done a tremendous amount of market research. They start out very hard in the morning. They do the hard interviews. Then they gradually get softer and softer as more and more people are staying at home or you're watching at your desk.

I think, truly, Katie Couric has the hardest job in the business. She has to go from a head of state or Palestinian leader to Omarosa or whatever. That's a tremendous amount of versatility and a tremendous amount of research. And it's a lot on a person to be able to swing that way. I've seen so many people good at one thing or the other. Very few people have the chops to be able to do both and do it well like she does. And Matt [Lauer] does very well also.

HIRSEN: You have your own giant fan base, you know. You're all over the Web. You are a star yourself. Here's the question: the notion of journalists as stars. Barbara Walters will sometimes interview someone who is less famous than she is. Do you think that it affects a journalist's attitude and coverage, in the sense that there are trappings that go along with stardom—the more famous you are the more there is a protective coating around your life—and that may make you lose contact?

DEVON: I always thought of myself as a conduit to the celebrity. And I thought my best job was when I opened up something about that celebrity, and they let something out with me that they hadn't let out before. But if it's me posturing in front of the camera and trying to be the star of the interview, there's no time left for anything to come out about the star. It becomes all about me. And our show is not the Dayna Devon Show, it's *Extra*. And it's about celebrities. [At *Extra*] they have gone to extraordinary lengths to keep it about the celebrity, not about us.

Now there are other shows where there is more personality worked in, and they go to more lengths to bring the personalities out of their hosts. I love having personality. There are times for it. And I've done some great pieces that I'm really proud of that have a lot of personality in them and where I was a little bit more of a focus.

I did a segment called "Dayna TV." I'd go to different sets and I'm in the show. But what I was trying to do was [make it as] if someone from middle America got a role on the *George Lopez Show* or *Charmed* or the *Gilmore Girls* or a Barker's

Beauty on *The Price Is Right.* I was trying to let them see it through my eyes, like how exciting it is, and how fun it is. I was trying to look at it like I was from the Midwest and this is the first set I'd ever been on. I didn't try and go in like I was a star, because I really honestly kind of giggle when I hear that, because it's so foreign to me. I've gone to great lengths to try and not be that, and not go there, because you do lose touch and you do start thinking it's about you.

HIRSEN: You interview people in Hollywood regularly. How do you handle it when you're interviewing a star and trying to get past the veneer we talked about earlier, and you pull back the veneer and political rhetoric comes out?

DEVON: That's a great question, actually, and one I think we're finding our way on. Lately we've noticed that our ratings seem to do really well with a harder lead, and we've done a lot of political stories, which is interesting, because you wouldn't necessarily think of *Extra* as leading with a political story. But because celebrities have used their fame so much more lately to promote a candidate or put their stance out there, i.e., Michael Moore at the Oscars—whether people agree with it or not, they're still doing it. And I think they're doing it more and more and more. We're finding out that our leads are doing better when we lead with politics.

In general, Hollywood is such a liberal and Democratic stronghold, they're routinely talking about the politicians, and it's actually given us some good leads. I mean, Michael Moore, love him or hate him, was a gift for us because it brought up a very serious topic in a way that we could cover it.

We have trouble with serious topics, because how are you going to really cover terrorism in Hollywood? We found unique ways to do it. We interviewed James Woods about how he had reported to the FBI that he'd seen what he thought was the terrorists doing a dry run. And Denis Leary raising money for the firefighters, that kind of thing. We found our way, but it's a difficult path and he [Moore] was a gift to us, actually, because he took Hollywood, and he's very popular in Hollywood, and gave us a softer way at a hard story.

HIRSEN: In bringing up Michael Moore, you know he's been severely criticized for some factual lapses. What sometimes happens with Hollywood celebrities when they get political is that they're not that well informed and they make misstatements. As a journalist, do you think you are supposed to challenge them?

DEVON: I think it essentially comes down to a time issue. I'll give you an example. If you're interviewing a celebrity on the red carpet and they're talking about Michael Moore's film, you get one or two questions before a publicist is tapping you on your arm. You have not only a political question to ask, you have something about the movie that they're going to see, you have something about their next project.

What we're seeing right now is that publicists are ruling Hollywood. They are able to dictate a lot of the content that goes on the show and the questions you get to ask. Or they limit your access. I think we'll see changes in that, but you're not necessarily free to ask a celebrity whatever you want. And you're not necessarily to challenge them. And you don't necessarily have the time to challenge them, either.

HIRSEN: Unlike when a press conference is called and there are members of the AP, UPI, etc., present. It's spontaneous and there are no publicists dictating boundaries.

DEVON: Exactly.

10

LAND OF THE FREE

After the journalistic scandals of the past decade, which were punctuated by the CBS/Dan Rather mess, the often-maligned *National Enquirer* looks pretty darn reliable. In fact, that was the point of a book published in 2005 by an *Enquirer* reporter, Mike Walker. In *Rather Dumb* (a tome on the longtime CBS anchor), Walker maintains that while the mainstream media have long sneered at tabloids like the *Enquirer,* news organizations like CBS could actually learn a thing or two about proper reporting and vetting of stories.

To pursue this idea further, I spoke with Iain Calder, who ran the *Enquirer* for more than three decades.[1] Working as a reporter in England in the 1960s, the Scottish-born Calder got the job of his dreams at the age of twenty-five: London bureau chief of the *Enquirer.* By the age of thirty-six he was the *Enquirer's* president. In his many years at the helm, Calder altered forever the definition of news, the method of getting stories, and the power of the photograph. Whether it was Gary Hart's boat ride, Pete Rose's stay in prison, Elvis Presley's wake, or Tommy Lee's misadventures, it was Iain Calder who ensured that *Enquirer* readers got what they paid for.

Calder and I discussed the fact that the *Enquirer* pays for its stories, something that tends to make conventional journalists bristle. But as discussed in Chapter 7, one could argue that CBS's full-court press on Private Jessica Lynch constituted an attempt to "buy." In that instance, the network took a more subtle tack, though. Instead of offering money, it dangled an enticing package—MTV appearances, affiliate goodies, movie offers, and the like.

Calder says it's nothing new. He remembers an occasion when one of the networks "flew in the lawyers for the particular person—and they took them to dinner. They paid for their airfares. They bought them show tickets. They spent thousands and thousands of dollars on these people and made all kinds of deals. And, of course, they got an exclusive on it."

He also describes how, with regard to the big-name stars and their movie projects, the "PR people say, you can have celebrity actors coming out with a big movie, but to have him we expect you to—and it almost goes unsaid—to say the movie is very good. That is the first thing. And secondly, if we give you him, we have another person next week in another movie—and it's some B player or something—you've got to have that person on. So they make these deals all the time."

Calder reminds me of a familiar pattern that then follows. He says, "When you go and you see it, and it becomes a bomb, and everybody says it's awful—and you know these people really didn't think it was good, but that was the price they were paying. These plugs are worth millions and millions of dollars." Calder points out that at least "what the *Enquirer* does is we say, 'Yeah, we're out front, we'll pay for it.' "

Calder also notes the change in the number of media voices today as compared with the past. "If you go back twenty years, the only news sources in television were your local news and the network newsies, the three of them," he remarks. "If you look into the early '70s, Frank Reynolds and group [at ABC], they had a tiny, tiny audience compared with CBS and NBC. So you really had two and three-quarter networks perhaps." But now, he says, "you have twenty-four-hour-a-day CNN, Fox, and all the other channels. So you need stuff to fill them." And this "gives people huge choices. That is why it makes it more difficult for any one magazine or TV show to be dominant."

We can see the elite media and Hollywood gatekeepers wringing their hands.

BRIGHT LIGHTS ON THE MEDIA HORIZON

At the beginning of this book I conveyed the notion that, having spent so much time examining the mega-merger of the news media and Tinseltown and exploring the effects of the coupling on our culture, I find myself with a sense of enhanced vision. In these pages I've tried to describe just what I see as I look out upon the Hollywood Nation terrain.

In clear view is the image of our insatiable entertainment impulses, expanded fame universe, and increased zeal on the part of the mainstream media and Hollywood libs to overhaul our news, views, and attitudes.

Also in plain sight is the "News Is Big Entertainment and Entertainment Is Big News" phenomenon, with agenda-driven journalists scrambling for unsuspecting viewers and readers and "progressive" prone entertainers inserting their mind-bending messages in movies, TV shows, and the like.

The elite news media tirelessly try to force their views into our heads, fancying themselves as objective conduits of information as they sport their bias on their sleeves. Remember how the sporadically journalistic *Today* show gave Kitty Kelley three days to hawk her credibility-challenged Bush-bashing book, how the ethically wobbly CNN allowed its hosts to simultaneously work for Democrat John Kerry's campaign, and how bullheaded Dan Rather and his enabling CBS News chums spent their time defending bogus documents? All-too-familiar scenes on the Hollywood Nation landscape.

And loads of Tinseltowners seem to think they have artistic license to rewrite history in a way that suits their liberal ideology. In this book I've given examples of how in the 2004 election, filmmakers like Michael Moore became indistinguishable from campaign operatives, how in the same election cycle a series of cinematic efforts were used to try to pull votes to the Dem side, how scores of the same critics who kissed the ring of Michael Moore slammed the door on Mel Gibson's *The Passion of the Christ,* and how the documentary and docudrama are being used as tools of deception.

For anybody but an ivory tower media figure, liberal Hollywood mogul, or card-carrying lefty, things might look bleak.

But on the Hollywood Nation horizon I also see a mounting force that's riding to the rescue like the proverbial cavalry. And it's profoundly altering the information and entertainment climate.

For starters, liberal favoritism is quite effectively being countered by the New Media, which started as a ragtag group of talk radio hosts and websites but is now a force to be reckoned with. While various members of the elite look at the new kid on the block with disdain, they can't hold their pompous pusses in the same expression forever. Well, except for maybe Frank Rich and Eleanor Clift.

Fortunately, the public can find ideological sources that are openly tagged as such. And it can find news sources that strive for a neutral point of view. In a free market, an effort to satisfy each and every appetite will be there.

The elite detractors have also been Chicken Littles when it comes to media ownership. They've been running around in a tizzy forecasting the end of media diversity, because in their acorn-bopped heads they believe the coercive conglomerates are gobbling up media businesses left and right, and that means the free-press sky is falling.

But let's look at the state of the press today. I asked author, analyst, and political consultant Dick Morris about this. "I think in the era of the Internet, there is no such thing as media aggregation," he says. "I mean, on the one hand, they point to the increasing aggregation and conglomeration within television or within radio. But then look at the fact that households using television during prime time is only about half of what it was ten years ago or fifteen years ago."

Morris thinks that the idea of a news monopoly today is ludicrous. "Let's say that a guy owns a TV station and the newspaper in the same city," he says. "That used to be a total monopoly. But now anybody who goes online gets the political news from all over the country or the world. I read as many articles in the *Cleveland Plain Dealer* as in the *Atlanta Constitution* as in the *L.A. Times* as in the *Washington Times,* the *New York Times.* I just go online and I read all those stories, and I'm not being spoon-fed in one market. I don't even notice most of the time what market the stuff I'm reading is from. So I think it's [the idea of monopolizing the news] an anachronistic conclusion."[2]

Which brings us to the following questions: Are the mainstream news media and the Hollywood honchos better or worse than they've been in the past? And are they still viable today? In order to understand where we are news and entertainment–wise, and where we're going, we need to take a look at where we've been.

When I spoke to Lawrence O'Donnell, the Democratic political analyst and Hollywood writer and producer, he pointed out, "A hundred years ago, most people were illiterate and most people consumed nothing. And during the Lincoln presidency, most Americans were not capable of consuming any news at all. They couldn't read."[3] Things have obviously changed quite a bit. It makes sense that our high level of literacy today is a significant part of why we have an information explosion going on.

It's also instructive to compare the media of the recent past to today's. In the 1970s the big-three alphabet networks—CBS, NBC, and ABC—were our only choices, except for an independent station or two and the snooze-inducing PBS. Today, with the help of our remote controls, we can surf through hundreds of channels. They come to us via cable and satellite television, and more and more they're coming to us courtesy of the Internet.

Speaking of Al Gore's discovery, countless resources—including news portals like NewsMax.com, myriad blog spots, and bulletin boards to suit every fancy—are bringing in info from every nook and cranny on the planet. We've got DVDs. We're able to order our favorite flicks electronically. And we've got almost double the amount of radio stations available to us, if you factor in Internet, cable, and satellite radio.

In the old days, starting up a newspaper, radio, or television broadcast business was beyond the financial scope of most people. But now with the blogosphere anyone from the Arleta bowling league to the *Times* editorial board to the former talk show host, Kmart spokesperson, magazine mogul, and Broadway producer Rosie O'Donnell (at the blog called formerlyrosie) can be up and running on the World Wide Web in less than an hour. E-mail and text messaging are also allowing for instant communication to and from anywhere in the world. New forms of wireless digital interactive communication are springing up every other week. And technology is allowing a new breed of filmmaker to transform the face of Hollywood. The future's so bright we gotta wear virtual shades.

The New Media are changing everything and pretty much rocking the status-quo world. In 2004 individual blogs actually covered the conventions of both parties and led the mainstream media in breaking and interpreting important news.

Believe it or not, despite the cheery forecast, some express anxiety over an info *shortage*. I see it as the opposite. Our predicament is that we have more info and entertainment choices and voices than we're even able to process.

Lawrence O'Donnell puts a "glass half-full" spin on this. He says, "Now what our very luxurious worry has become, in the huge success of this society, is the amount of misinformation that is available to people who are educated enough to actually consume it. You've got an extremely successful society when that is your worry."[4]

One thing I find curious is that those who are anxious about a rightward bias are typically the same folks who would like the government to fix things. Inevitably, the repairs that they seek appear satisfactory only if the media are then tilted in their direction. But if the content of the media were artificially skewed by the state, freedom of the press would officially be finished. And that's no Chicken Little prediction. That's a "Congress shall make no law" axiom.

The correct answer to the media quandary is the same one we've been scoring with for over two hundred years—freedom. The more we encourage the establishment of New Media conduits through new technology, the more diversity of thought and the larger the array of choices that are available to us.

In this charmed situation, the burden of determining truth shifts to the court of public opinion. Much like the dueling advocacy in a legal setting, where each side presents its case from a distinct point of view, the information consumers, just like a jury, become fact finders. The New Media provide the "check" to the long-standing sources. The multitude of choices and voices enable us to unearth the truth, and we're able to do so by using our own preferred modes. We're in the digital driver's seat. Finally. So now even when we're hit with something as audacious as a Rather-stained memo or as demeaning as a Michael Moore schlockumentary, we can be confident that the free-wheeling, pajama-wearing thumb typers, bird-dogging radio broadcasters, and cable fact sniffers will be on their tail.

Hollywood itself is changing, too. In fact, a New Hollywood is on the march.

Tinseltown continues to be a place where kudos from critics and peers are generally given to those who incorporate the twisted into their "art." But when Mel Gibson did an end run around the Hollywood elite, it inspired other industry folks to move forward with projects that have politically incorrect ideological themes. In

2004, for the first time ever, two film festivals that featured conservative subject matter were held. One took place in Dallas and was dubbed the American Film Renaissance. Another took place in the heart of Hollywood and was called the Liberty Film Festival. I moderated a panel discussion at the latter, which featured film-maker David Zucker *(Airplane, Naked Gun, Scary Movie),* producer and Michael Moore's former manager Douglas Urbanski *(The Contender),* talk show host and movie critic Michael Medved, and actress Morgan Brittany. The energy of the panelists and audience was palpable. A new day had dawned on the Left Coast.

Walden Media, founded by business tycoon Philip Anschutz, has already rearranged the Hollywood pecking order with its family hit *Because of Winn-Dixie* and its joint venture with Disney to release C. S. Lewis's *The Chronicles of Narnia.* Isolated no more, producers, directors, writers, and actors with conservative, traditionally religious, patriotic, or libertarian sympathies are connecting, communicating, and collaborating. Coming to a theater near you—movies made by the New Hollywood.

The New Media and the New Hollywood run parallel. Both were born of necessity because of the lockstep worldview held by the mainstream media and elite in Hollywood. And facilitating their advancement were the quantum leaps made in digital technology.

So where does it all leave us? In a pretty exciting place, where old boundaries are breaking down and new categories are springing up. The Old Media are squawking. The New Media are forging. The Hollywood libs are chattering. The entertainment rebels are smirking. The pundits are arguing. The frustrated are fretting. And the public is seeking, sampling, discerning, deciding, and indulging.

As for our Hollywood Nation, it's the place we all hail from now. Still the land of the free and the home of the brave. With a lot more glitz.

AFTERWORD FOR THE PAPERBACK EDITION

HOLLYWOOD DISCONNECTED

Hollywood's disconnect with Middle America became intensely apparent as the 78th annual Academy Awards approached in 2006. Judging by the subject matter of ballyhooed films such as *Syriana*, a movie that showed the softer side of terrorism, and *Munich*, which asserted a moral equivalency between terrorist thugs and those who act to prevent terrorism, one may have suspected that the Academy of Motion Picture Arts and Sciences had been secretly taken over by our enemies in the War on Terror.

You may recall that host Chris Rock began the festivities at the 77th Annual Academy Awards by telling the audience to "Sit your **** down." Rock continued with a stand-up act that featured hackneyed Bush jokes and gratuitous political humor. The performance left a lot to be desired in how it represented the United States to the rest of the world. And when clips of legendary TV personality and sterling Academy host Johnny Carson were aired during the telecast as a tribute to the much-loved late-night pioneer, the contrast between the two was striking.

But even that year's disgraceful dismissal of Mel Gibson's *The Passion of the Christ* could not prepare the public for the 2006 Academy Awards.

Actor James Woods once said, "In this politically correct era, the middle-aged heterosexual white guy gets to play one part, he

gets to play the a**hole in this suit." Giving Woods's words a politically correct modern-day twist, I'll say that playing someone
other than a heterosexual these days seems to be the surest and easiest way to get Hollywood kudos, as 2006's awards show would
prove.

Gender blending was on display in *Transamerica*, where Felicity
Huffman, of the ABC show *Desperate Housewives,* was up for Best
Actress for her role as a preoperative transsexual who found out that
years earlier "he" had fathered a child. Gender politics was the
theme of *North Country*, which starred Best Actress nominee
Charlize Theron and told the story of a sexually harassed female
worker. And Best Actor nominee Philip Seymour Hoffman played
the gay title character in *Capote*. The Academy so appreciated Hoffman's tedious nasal droning it awarded him the coveted statuette.

Back in 2001, host of the awards show Steve Martin cracked,
"This show is being watched by roughly a billion people around
the world, and everyone is thinking the exact same thing: That
we're all gay." Martin's gay gag would have been even more suit-
able had he been hosting 2006's 78th Annual Academy Awards.
The flick that would have taken a trophy had there been one for
the most amount of buzz would undoubtedly have been *Brokeback
Mountain*.

Over the years actors like Tom Hanks, Hilary Swank, and
Charlize Theron have scored Oscars by playing gay characters. But
the film that took the trophy for the most preshow buzz in 2006,
Brokeback Mountain, pushes the envelope further than ever before.
Known as the "gay cowboy movie" and carrying the tagline
"Love is a force of nature," the film is an unapologetic cinematic
rendering of same-sex relations.

The setting is Wyoming, 1963. Two cowboys are hired to herd
sheep. When the audience is introduced to the two main characters, Ennis (played by Heath Ledger) and Jack (played by Jake Gyllenhaal), they appear to be red-blooded macho cowpokes. Then
one cold night when a drunken Ennis bunks down with Jack, they
become intimate and fall in love.

After the summer gig ends, the two head to their respective

homes. They each marry but continue to meet annually over a two-decade span for fishing trips on which no fish are ever caught, much to the chagrin of their wives.

Brokeback's premise begs the question: "Why would Hollywood bet on a film that runs counter to the values of the majority of filmgoers, especially when the box office is tanking?"

As Robert Knight, director of Concerned Women for America's Culture and Family Institute, told the Associated Press, "I can't think of a more effective way to annoy and alienate most movie-going Americans than to show two cowboys lusting after each other." Knight characterized it as "a mockery of the western genre embodied by every movie cowboy from John Wayne to Gene Autry to Kevin Costner."

My own theory is that the content of *Brokeback* was not aimed at the general public, it was aimed at the community of mainstream-media film critics. The idea was to create buzz, generate nominations, get awards, maybe an Oscar or two, and then sell tickets.

The PR plan worked. The buzz for the movie was deafening. Roger Ebert told Reuters, "*Brokeback* will become the kind of movie that you hear about at dinner parties that you feel you have to go see."

The marketing of the film reflected this festival-and-awards season. The movie was released initially on only fifteen screens in order to drive up the sales per screen. Locations were picked where such fare would be well received—that is, urban areas with a high population of homosexuals. The scheme worked effectively: the film broke box-office records by obtaining the highest per-screen average for any movie released in 2005.

Brokeback's reception at film festivals and among the critics paid off big-time in the pre-Oscar awards. It was named Best Picture by the Los Angeles Film Critics Association, the Boston Society of Film Critics, and the New York Film Critics Circle. It led in number of nominations from the Broadcast Film Critics Association and received seven nods from the Golden Globes, the biggest pre-Oscar event, including Best Picture–Drama, Best Actor, Best Supporting Actress, and Best Director. This is important because despite the fact that the Golden Globes are chosen by only ninety foreign reporters, some of whom work part-time for overseas news outlets, the awards are traditionally viewed as predictors of the Oscars and may influence Academy voters as a result.

The 2006 Golden Globe Awards proved to be a politically charged affair, with the first award setting the tone for the evening. It went to George Clooney for Best Supporting Actor in a Motion Picture for his performance in *Syriana*. During his acceptance speech, Clooney said, "I want to thank Jack Abramoff [the lobbyist who pleaded guilty to various and sundry campaign funding charges] . . . you know, just because. First one up, get the ball rolling," The jesting liberal added, "Who would name their kid Jack with the last words 'off' at the end of your last name? No wonder that guy is screwed up."

Clooney didn't just joke about Jack Abramoff. He targeted the man's parents. Since when are someone's folks fair game? The joke drew the ire of Jack Abramoff's father, Frank, who didn't find it funny at all. The senior Abramoff wrote a letter to *The Desert Sun* newspaper calling Clooney's barb a "glib and ridiculous" attack.

In an appearance on CNN's *Larry King Live*, King asked Clooney whether he would apologize for the ill-conceived joke. "I make no apologies for that—it was a joke," Clooney told King. "Believe me," the actor added, "the person who's disparaged the Abramoff name is not me." Well, what do we expect? Clooney didn't even apologize after he joked about Charlton Heston being stricken with Alzheimer's.

Continuing the evening's theme, Rachel Weisz took home the Golden Globe for Best Supporting Actress for her performance in *The Constant Gardener*, a liberally distorted conspiracy thriller about villainous pharmaceutical corporations. (She eventually also won the Best Supporting Actress Oscar.)

As expected, *Brokeback Mountain* snagged the biggest awards. The "unconventional" cowboy film won Best Picture–Drama, Best Director for Ang Lee, Best Screenplay, and Best Song. (The song was cowritten by Bernie Taupin and titled "A Love That Will Never Grow Old.")

Adding to the gender-jumbled theme of the evening was Felicity Huffman's Best Actress in a Drama win for her role as a male who seeks to become a female in *Transamerica*. Philip Seymour Hoffman took the award for Best Actor in a Drama for *Capote*. And the Golden Globes shamefully picked the anti-American *Paradise Now* as the Best Foreign Language film.

The Golden Globes reinforced the message that, cinematically speaking, we are not in Kansas anymore. And likewise the Kansas farmhouse is swirling farther and farther away from Hollywood.

As Oscar night approached, a strange thing happened: some voting members started to privately express their displeasure with the hoopla over gay cowboys. Tony Curtis, a legend of film from the Golden Age and Jamie Lee Curtis's father, decided to go public with his feelings. During the Oscar voting period, Curtis told Fox News's Bill McCuddy that he hadn't yet seen *Brokeback Mountain* and had no intention of doing so. He claimed that other Academy members felt similarly. "This picture is not as important as we make it. It's nothing unique. The only thing unique about it is they put it on the screen. And they make 'em cowboys," Curtis said. Curtis reminded folks that his contemporaries wouldn't have cared for the highly acclaimed Best Picture nominee. "Howard Hughes and John Wayne wouldn't like it," Curtis said.

The beneficiary of the quiet backlash against *Brokeback* was the less-discussed movie *Crash*. *Crash* was actually the gem of the Best Picture nominees because of its original and candid approach to the subject of race. But *Brokeback* continued to dominate the film press and had won the most pre-Oscar awards, even sweeping all the major categories in the British version of the Academy Awards, the BAFTAs. The tedious *The Constant Gardener* was another BAFTA fave with ten nominations, but *Brokeback Mountain* won for director, screenplay, best supporting actor, and best movie.

In the end, *Brokeback* won an Oscar for Score, Adapted Screenplay, and Directing, but it was *Crash* that took home the evening's grand prize, Best Picture.

As it turned out, the most outrageous thing about the 2006 Oscars wouldn't be the gay-cowboy theme. It would be the terrorist one.

DESPERATELY SEEKING STATURE

As far as the Academy was concerned, lovable terrorists were a main theme of the 2006 Oscar message. It seemed to have forgotten Jack L. Warner's admonition: "If you want to send a message, use Western Union." The Academy gave five nominations to the morally contorted *Munich* and two nominations to the terrorist-sympathizing *Syriana*.

Syriana expands upon the liberal mantra "It's All About Oil" by creating the impression that pure and noble Arab youths are forced into terrorism by an oppressive and corrupt United States, which in turn is a mere puppet of oil companies in Texas.

Clooney is both executive producer and costar of *Syriana*. (The title refers to a think-tank term involving the transformation of the Middle East into an Americanized region.) Taking a page from the Charlize Theron handbook on how to clinch an Academy Award, Clooney goes for an unbecoming look by putting on the pounds and donning some shabby clothes. The only thing missing is a little gender bending, but he makes up for his heterosexual slipup by engaging in one of Hollywood's favorite pastimes: making films about gallant tyrants, turncoats, and terrorists while simultaneously dissing the United States.

Reminiscent of a 1970s movie with a paranoid scent (something along the lines of *The Parallax View*), the movie feeds the far Left's delusions. The film's tagline is "everything is connected," and woven together are some of the antiwar crowd's looniest conspiracy theories. Although it is loosely based on *See No Evil*, CIA Agent Robert Baer's memoir, *Syriana* presents itself as a fount of fact. It was written and directed by Stephen Gaghan, who also wrote *Traffic*, and it was filmed in the same starkly realistic style.

Using handheld cameras to create an illusion of on-the-spot TV news reporting, an Oliver Stone–like plot is presented in which Arab potentates, predatory oil companies, prevaricating law firms, and unprincipled government agencies secretly band together in an attempt to gain wealth and power. Like *Traffic*, it uses the technique of interweaving multiple plots in an effort to heighten the intrigue. The story lines are numerous and quite complex, with the following subplots taking place:

- Two U.S. oil companies maneuver to merge.
- A Mideast prince sells oil-drilling rights to China.
- An energy analyst (Matt Damon) exploits a tragedy to gain favor with the prince.
- An attorney tries to push through an oil merger on behalf of Big Oil.
- A Pakistani father and son are laid off from their jobs in the prince's oil fields, and the son deals with his termination by becoming a terrorist.
- The prince loses his position as heir to the throne because he ticks off Big Oil and ends up getting knocked off.
- Bob Barnes (George Clooney) is a longtime CIA agent who is close to retirement. After a failed mission, Barnes is given an assignment to whack the noble Arab prince. His mission goes haywire and the CIA turns on him.

Terrorism rears its head toward the end of the movie, but it is portrayed in liberal fashion. The young terrorists use a boat loaded with explosives to crash into an oil tanker. Contrary, of course, to what typically happens when terrorists strike, women and children are spared from harm in the incident.

To fully develop the subplots, the story should have been presented as a miniseries with a small-screen release. As it stands, *Syriana* is simply a two-hour long disjointed left-wing fantasy. Clooney, however, was rewarded for his extreme unsexy makeover with a Best Supporting Actor Oscar.

Clooney actually doubled his chances in the award-chasing season by having another film in the nomination mix. *Good Night, and Good Luck* is Clooney's black-and-white cinematic depiction of the Edward R. Murrow television tug-of-war with Senator Joseph McCarthy.

The drama-laden episode in history—the 1950s anti-Communist investigations of McCarthy—will forever be an absorbing narrative. And Clooney chooses to feature an engaging central character, the legendary journalist Edward R. Murrow. But, as expected, McCarthy is depicted as a shallow, cartoonish, and demonic figure. Just as predictably, the movie ignores all of the new facts produced by the Venona Intercepts and Soviet archives revealing that McCarthy's basic premise that Communists had infiltrated our government was not only right, it was underestimated.

The film starts and ends with a Murrow speech to his peers that warns of the blending of news and entertainment. Yet when it came to the news and entertainment fuse, Murrow was actually one of the pioneers of the showbiz trend with his celebrity interview show *Person to Person*, which was deftly depicted in the movie.

Unlike many of today's media types, Murrow understood that individual bias could have an effect on the reporting of facts. In one instance while on the air, the CBS anchor said, "Everyone is a prisoner of his own experiences. No one can eliminate prejudices—just recognize them." Murrow also said, "A great many people think they are thinking when they are really rearranging their prejudices."

Interestingly, Clooney's own biases seem to manifest themselves in what he chooses to leave *out* of his film. Publicity materials for the movie contain the following slogan: "In A Nation Terrorized by Its Own Government, One Man Dared to Tell the Truth."

Actually, most conservatives recognize the need for restraint on government. They understand the potential for harm that resides in the unfettered state. And, of course, history demonstrates that during the "Red Scare" period, there was good reason to be apprehensive about a lot of things, the investigative excesses of McCarthy being among them. But at that time the fear of Communist leaders and their agents was vital to our nation's survival. And although some people unjustly lost work and their reputations, there were also despots who were busy engineering mass murder and were intent on destroying the United States.

Maybe Clooney avoids facts such as these because including them would have jeopardized his Oscar chances. Hollywood, to put it mildly, is obsessed with the McCarthy era and generally holds fast to a one-sided version. But in reality there were front organizations affiliated with the Soviet Union and operating in the United States. And the Venona documents—the Soviet cables that were intercepted by the Army Signal Intelligence Service and the NSA—confirmed that Communist operatives had infiltrated the highest levels of our government.

If we set aside Clooney's omissions, the film has artistic merit that deserves mention. Shot in black-and-white, it has an appealing stark quality. The crisp 1950s dialogue occurs in dimly lit, smoke-filled rooms. You can almost smell the scotch and cigarettes. The musical sound track is understated, consisting of authentic jazz and featuring vocalist Dianne Reeves. The visuals cleverly toggle from fictional scenes to archival news footage.

David Strathairn plays Murrow. He won a Best Acting award at the Venice Film Festival and was a Best Actor contender at the Oscars, ultimately losing out to Philip Seymour Hoffman. Clooney portrays Murrow's production partner, Fred Friendly. Because Murrow and his fellow CBS journalists constantly smoked on and off the air, many of the scenes are filled with lit cigarettes and accompanying plumes. (Strathairn, a nonsmoker himself, apparently used rolled pipe tobacco on the set because it was not as irritating to his throat and nose and looked great on film.) In what looks like an effort to placate the antismoking lobby, the film includes a real ad for Kent cigarettes that links smoking with intelligence, which elicited audience laughter at the theater I attended.

McCarthy appears in the film exclusively in archival footage, which seems to have been carefully selected to show the senator at his worst. To firmly establish him as the villain, the archival McCarthy responds to Murrow with a series of attacks, accusing Murrow of associating with Communist organizations in the past.

Murrow then points out, in his rebuttal, the lack of any factual criticisms in the senator's statements.

The irony for Clooney is that the tactic of avoiding genuine dialogue by using ad hominem attacks, a ploy that his movie so powerfully demonstrates, is most often used today by his friends on the Left.

Good Night, and Good Luck got the second-highest number of nominations from the Golden Globes, including Best Picture—Drama, Best Screenplay, Best Actor for Strathairn, and Best Director for Clooney. But when it came to the Oscars, the film was thoroughly snubbed and received zip.

Spielberg's *Munich*, on the other hand, was stiffed by the pre-Oscar awards but was nominated for five Oscars including Best Picture. The movie is a long way off from the high-minded certitude of *Schindler's List*. The biggest criticism of the film, however, is based on concerns about its treatment of Israel.

Munich tells the story of the hostage crisis that occurred during the 1972 Olympics (known prior to the tragedy as "The Olympics of Peace and Joy") and a chain of nightmarish events that followed. The world watched in real time as a Palestinian group, which referred to itself as "Black September," kidnapped and murdered two Israeli athletes and subsequently held nine others hostage, all of whom were slaughtered during a botched rescue mission at a nearby airport. It could be that the Munich tragedy was a fateful spark that ignited the terrorism of today.

Spielberg brought to his *Munich* project first-time screenwriter Tony Kushner. Kushner's forte is challenging social mores (*Angels in America*), and the playwright may not have been the best pick to help craft the presentation of a factual story of such import and gravity.

The choice of source material, too, may not have been the wisest selection. The film was based chiefly on a book by George Jonas called *Vengeance*, which has been severely criticized for containing factual inaccuracies.

In the cinematic rendering, an elite group is given a somber assignment: Conduct an "eye for an eye" campaign of revenge and assassinate eleven Palestinians thought to be responsible for the Munich disaster. Avner, the group's leader, is a hero's son who takes on the mantle but loses confidence in the mission over time. In contrast to Avner, Steve, the most zealous member of the group, seems never to question his own sense of justice. Ephraim, Avner's contact with the Israeli government, is firm and unrelenting throughout. The remaining participants are defined largely by their specialties: Robert is a former toy designer turned imprecise bomb maker; Hans is the document forger of the bunch; and Carl is the cleanup man. Avner's source of information about the Palestinian terrorists is the shadowy Louis, who at times seems to act as the filmmaker's messenger, expressing disdain for all governments.

In another apparent effort to be fair to both Israelis and Palestinians, Spielberg forces his characters to state all points of view. Consequently, some of the scenes contain artificial-sounding dialogue, with debates taking place on the finer points of the philosophical legitimacy of their missions. In one scene, unaware of Avner's identity, a young Arab terrorist presents an argument to him for a Palestinian homeland and a justification for terror. The result is a message of moral ambiguity.

Although in the opening credits the words "inspired by real events" appear on the screen, some of the movie's content appears to be nothing of the kind. Spielberg's film fails to show the actual response of Israel to the deadly incidents at Munich. Following the Olympic athletes' murders, Israel commenced a counter-terror project called "Operation Wrath of God," which sought to assassinate key individuals, in part for reprisal and in part to prevent future terrorism. The assignments were not conducted by a single group of recruits, and there was no list of preordained targets. In reality, the Mossad and Israel's prime minister directed the entire operation, and professionals who were sporadically sent on multiple missions carried out the assassinations.

Spielberg told the *Los Angeles Times* that in making *Munich* he wanted "to put empathy in every direction, because the situation is not cut and dried." The filmmaker added, "I was not interested in telling that kind of a tale of vengeance and I didn't want this to be a morality play, the way that *Private Ryan* is a morality play." The director referred to the movie as his "prayer for peace." But the attempt at evenhandedness causes the film to compromise its moral perspective and fall short of its potential.

Munich would be a more laudable film had Spielberg put on a journalist hat and provided a factual accounting. Instead he succumbs to moral confusion and engages in delusional diplomacy, Hollywood-style.

Just looking at the 2006 batch of Oscar nominations, one can easily get the idea that Hollywood is more out of touch with America than it has ever been before. Two films that were passed over for the Best Picture category were *Cinderella Man* and *Walk the Line*. These two movies were traditional stories that took place in a moral universe. *Cinderella Man* actually had a scene where the main character returned a welfare check, while *Walk the Line* told the story of a guy who was a faith-filled man, not the kind of stuff that today's Hollywood can tolerate. At the time of the 2006 Academy Awards, twice as many people had viewed the documentary *March of the Penguins* (which on a bright note ended up winning the Best Documentary Oscar) than had seen any of the five nominees for Best Picture (*Brokeback Mountain, Crash, Capote, Munich,* and *Good Night, and Good Luck*). The combined audience total for all of the Best Picture nominations was less than the number of moviegoers who flocked to see a single flick, *The Chronicles of Narnia: The Lion, the Witch and the Wardrobe* (which ended up winning the trophy for Makeup).

If the overt political content of the films wasn't enough to turn off middle America, one of the Best Song nominees surely did it. It was a tune from the film *Hustle & Flow* by the group Three 6 Mafia. Its title? "It's Hard Out Here for a Pimp." Believe it or not, the song won the Oscar, taking its place alongside past winners "Somewhere Over the Rainbow," "When You Wish Upon a Star," "Love Is a Many-Splendored Thing," "Moon River," "The Shadow of Your Smile," "The Way We Were," "You Light Up My Life," "I Just Called to Say I Love You," and "My Heart Will Go On."

The whole thing had the TV execs biting their fingernails over some potentially pitiful ratings. In the end, their fears were justified. The ratings for the 2006 Oscar telecast fell 8 percent, to the second-lowest level since 1987.

"PROUD TO BE OUT OF TOUCH"

When George Clooney took the stage to accept the first statuette of the evening for Best Supporting Actor in the film *Syriana*, he touched on one of the central theses of this book. He announced to the world that he was "proud to be part of this Academy, proud to be part of this community, proud to be out of touch."

Clooney also claimed that it was Hollywood that talked about social issues before anyone else. "We're the ones who talked about AIDS when it was just being whispered," he said. "And we talked about civil rights when it wasn't really popular. This academy—this group of people—gave Hattie McDaniel an Oscar in 1939 when blacks were still sitting in the backs of theaters."

Unfortunately, in the three-hour show no one remembered to send a Hollywood shout-out to the troops, whose starring roles outshine all of Oscar's gold. The implication was clear. Americans should drop to their knees and give thanks to those who really safeguard their lives and liberties: the filmmakers, actors, and industry folks from the Left Coast.

There was a time when Hollywood had mystique and glamour and was the wellspring of entertainment. It now seems a relic of another era. In its place sits a town where superficial social messages predominate and self-absorption has taken the lead role.

NOTES

CHAPTER 1: HOLLYWOOD NATION

1. Ann Oldenburg, "When Stars Speak, Do We Listen?" *USA Today,* 28 February 2003.
2. Ibid.
3. Ibid.
4. Michael Medved, *Right Turns: Unconventional Lessons from a Controversial Life* (New York: Crown Forum, 2004), 357–59.
5. Interview with Joel Siegel conducted by James Hirsen on 12 June 2004.
6. Interview with Monica Crowley conducted by James Hirsen on 20 May 2004.
7. Cynthia Littleton, "Koppel: Nets Blur News," *Hollywood Reporter,* 21 April 2004.
8. Bruce Horovitz, "The Good, Bad, and Ugly of America's Celeb Obsession," *USA Today,* 19 December 2003.
9. Interview with Joyce Brothers conducted on 14 May 2004.
10. Liz Hoggard, "Celebrity Gossip Is Good for Your Health," *Guardian* (London), 16 May 2004.
11. Interview with Joel Siegel conducted by James Hirsen on 12 June 2004.
12. *Searching for Debra Winger,* Rosanna Arquette, Lions Gate, 2001.
13. James Hirsen, "The Left Coast Report," NewsMax.com, 15 June 2004.
14. Bernard Goldberg, *Arrogance: Rescuing America from the Media Elite* (New York: Warner Books, 2003), 86.
15. "Kidman and Law Aim to End Romance Rumors," *World Entertainment News Network,* 24 November 2003.
16. Interview with Laurie Dhue conducted by James Hirsen on 11 June 2004.
17. *Good Morning America,* ABC, 24 June 2004.

STROLL WITH JOEL

1. Interview with Joel Siegel conducted by James Hirsen on 12 June 2004.

CHAPTER 2: STARS OF PAGE AND SCREEN

1. Kathleen Hall Jamieson and Paul Waldman, *The Press Effect: Politicians, Journalists, and the Stories That Shape the Political World* (New York: Oxford, 2003), 95. Originally from Douglas Cater, *The Fourth Branch of Government* (Boston: Houghton Mifflin, 1959), 7.

2. Ibid. Originally from Timothy Cook, *Governing with the News* (Chicago: University of Chicago Press, 1998), 3.

3. Ibid.

4. See website of Albert Mehrabian, Ph.D., http://www.kaaj.com/psych.

5. C-SPAN, 24 May 2001.

6. Ryan Cane, "Journalism's 'Stars,' " *King's Journalism Review,* vol. 9, October 2003.

7. Ibid.

8. Ibid.

9. Interview with David S. Hirschman on Mediabistro.com, cited by Paul Berton, editor in chief, "Celebrity Journalism Threatens Craft," *London Free Press* (Canada), 8 May 2004.

10. "The Problems of Jack Kelley and *USA Today,*" *USA Today,* 22 April 2004.

11. Don Aucoin, "Despite Recent Ethics Scandals (or Maybe Because of Them), the Entertainment Industry Continues to Find the News Business Irresistibly Amusing," *Boston Globe,* 14 April 2004.

12. Jim Rutenberg, "Panel Names Debate Moderators as It Awaits Bush and Cheney's Pledge to Take Part," *New York Times,* 14 August 2004.

13. "Cable and Internet Loom Large in Fragmented Political News Universe Perceptions of Partisan Bias Seen as Growing, Especially by Democrats," Pew Research Center for the People and the Press, 11 January 2004.

14. Nikki Finke, "Dave the Brave: Stupid President Tricks Can Only Be Seen on Letterman," *LA Weekly,* 30 April–6 May 2004.

15. Lisa de Moraes, "White House Spins the Boy Who Yawned," *Washington Post,* 2 April 2004.

16. Panel discussion, U.S. Comedy Arts Festival, Aspen, Colorado, 6 March 2004.

17. David Bauder, "No-Snooze News," Associated Press, 2 March 2004.

18. Lisa de Moraes, "Seriously: Kerry on Comedy Central," *Washington Post,* 24 August 2004.

19. Ibid.

20. Ibid.

21. Ibid.

22. Ibid.

23. Kathy Kiely, "Another Kind of Big Dig Is Underway," *USA Today,* 27 July 2004.

JUST DHUE IT

1. Interview with Laurie Dhue conducted by James Hirsen on 11 June 2004.

CHAPTER 3: SEXING THINGS UP

1 Robert Philpot, "CBS-11 Makes Eyecatching Moves," *Fort Worth Star-Telegram,* 12 July 2004.

2. Ibid.

3. Ibid.

4. Greg Braxton, "Anchors Take a Sexy Turn," *Los Angeles Times,* 14 April 2004.

5. Ibid.

6. Ibid.

7. *Fox News Watch,* Fox News Channel, 24 January 2004.

8. Richard Huff, "A Hot Time 'Tonight': Sexy Katie Sizzles—Ratings Up," *New York Daily News,* 14 May 2003.

9. Adam Buckman and David K. Li, "Hosts Swap Coasts: Jay, Katie Turn TV Topsy-Turvy," *New York Post,* 13 May 2003.

10. Ibid.

11. Douglas Durden, "Katie's Witty Va-Va-Voom Outshines Jay," *Richmond Times Dispatch,* 14 May 2003.

12. Myrna Blyth, *Spin Sisters: How the Women of the Media Sell Unhappiness and Liberalism to the Women of America* (New York: St. Martin's Press, 2004) 179–180.

13. Interview with Laurie Dhue conducted by James Hirsen on 21 June 2004.

14. Ibid.

15. Interview with Dayna Devon conducted by James Hirsen on 26 July 2004.

16. Ibid.

17. Ibid.

18. *Searching for Debra Winger,* Rosanna Arquette, Lions Gate Films, 2001.

19. Ibid.

20. Ibid.

21. Ibid.

22. Ibid.

23. Interview with Holly Herbert conducted by James Hirsen on 9 July 2004.
24. Interview with Laurie Dhue conducted by James Hirsen on 21 June 2004.
25. Ibid.
26. Ibid.

HOLLY COURT

1. Interview with Holly Herbert conducted by James Hirsen on 9 July 2004.

CHAPTER 4: INFO MANIA

1. Thomas Fensch, *Television News Anchors: An Anthology of Profiles of the Major Figures and Issues in United States Network Reporting* (The Woodlands, Tex.: New Century Books, 2001), 3, 16.
2. Interview with Laura Schlessinger conducted by James Hirsen on 6 June 2004.
3. CNN, *Larry King Live,* 15 May 2001.
4. C-SPAN, 24 May 2001.
5. CBS, *The Late Late Show with Tom Snyder,* 8 February 1995.
6. Pew Research Center for the People and the Press, "Striking the Balance: Audience Interests, Business Pressures, and Journalists' Values," March 1999: 79.
7. Pew Research Center for the People and the Press, "News Audiences Increasingly Politicized," 8 June 2004.
8. Ibid.
9. Michael Savage, *The Enemy Within: Saving America from the Liberal Assault on Our Schools, Faith, and Military* (Nashville, Tenn.: WND Books, 2003), 99.
10. Bernard Goldberg, *Arrogance: Rescuing America from the Media Elite* (New York: Warner Books, 2003), 5.
11. Ibid., 4–5.
12. Bernard Goldberg, *Bias: A CBS Insider Exposes How the Media Distort the News* (Washington, D.C.: Regnery Publishing, 2002), 57.
13. Ann Coulter, *Slander: Liberal Lies About the American Right* (New York: Crown Publishing, 2004), 15.
14. Ibid., 56.
15. Ibid., 203.
16. Interview with Ann Coulter conducted by James Hirsen on 14 June 2004.
17. William McGowan, *Coloring the News: How Crusading for Diversity Has Corrupted American Journalism* (San Francisco: Encounter Books, 2001), 10–11.
18. Ibid., 11.

19. Ibid., 26–27.

20. L. Brent Bozell III, *Weapons of Mass Distortion: The Coming Meltdown of the Liberal Media* (New York: Crown Forum, 2004).

21. Eric Alterman, *What Liberal Media: The Truth About Bias and the News* (New York: Basic Books, 2003), 21.

22. Ibid., 20.

23. Ibid., 2. Originally from the *Washington Post,* 20 August 1992.

24. Ibid. Originally from David Domke, Mark D. Watts, Dhavan C. Shah, and David P. Fan, "The Politics of Conservative Elites and the 'Liberal Media' Argument," *Journal of Communication,* Autumn 1999, 46.

25. Ibid.

26. Pat Buchanan, "Is Liberal Media Bias a Myth?" Townhall.com, 16 June 2003 as quoted in Bozell, *Weapons of Mass Distortion,* 7.

27. Ibid.

28. Ibid., 2–3. Originally from the *New Yorker,* 22 May 1995.

29. Ibid., 28.

30. Ibid., 30.

31. Ibid., 28.

32. Bernard Goldberg, *Arrogance: Rescuing America from the Media Elite* (New York: Warner Books, Inc., 2003), 81.

33. *Inside Washington,* WUSA-TV, Washington, D.C., 10 July 2004.

34. CNN, *Reliable Sources,* 17 October 2004.

35. Lisa de Moraes, "UPN Announces Its Amish Show Is Ready to Bow," *Washington Post,* 9 July 2004.

36. Ken Auletta, "Big Bird Flies Right: How Republicans Learned to Love PBS," *New Yorker,* 7 June 2004.

37. Glenn Garvin, "PBS, Once Called Too 'Liberal,' Fights Conservative Label," *Miami Herald,* 10 July 2004.

38. Tim Goodman, "PBS Watches Its Mouth Rather Than Pay Big Fines. Now It's Up to the Other Networks to Fight the FCC," *San Francisco Chronicle,* 12 July 2004.

39. Howard Kurtz, "Media Backtalk," *Washington Post,* 4 March 2002.

40. Timothy Noah, "Gödel, Escher, Brock," *Slate,* 27 Wednesday 2001.

41. Timothy Noah, "David Brock, Liar: A Lifelong Habit Proves Hard to Break," *Slate,* 27 March 2002.

42. Byron York, "David Brock Is Buzzing Again," *National Review,* 14 June 2004.

43. "Heinz Kerry Bankrolling GOP Convention Ruckus," NewsMax.com, 18 July 2004.

44. David Brock, *The Republican Noise Machine: Right-Wing Media and How It Corrupts Democracy* (New York: Crown Publishing, 2004), 2–3.

45. Ibid., 359–60.
46. Ibid., 72–73.

O'REILLY FACTORS IN

1. Interview with Bill O'Reilly conducted by James Hirsen on 8 September 2004.

CHAPTER 5: THE GAME CHANGES

1. Harry Jaffe, "CNN—Crossing the Line with Carville and Begala?" *Washingtonian,* 10 September 2004.
2. Interview with Bill O'Reilly conducted by James Hirsen on 8 September 2004.
3. Mark Memmott, "Coulter Column Canceled After Editing Dispute," *USA Today,* 27 July 2004.
4. Lisa de Moraes, "In a Tuesday Night Showdown, Fox News Channel Outdraws the Big Three," *Washington Post,* 2 September 2004.
5. Bill Carter, "Faced with Poor Ratings, Networks Soul Search," *New York Times,* 3 September 2004.
6. Ibid.
7. Mark Memmott, "Fox Newspeople Say Allegations of Bias Unfounded," *USA Today,* 1 September 2004.
8. Ibid.
9. Ibid.
10. Caroline Wilbert, "GOP Week a Winner for Fox," Cox News Service, 3 September 2004.

CRIER CONFAB

1. Interview with Catherine Crier conducted by James Hirsen on 8 July 2004.

CHAPTER 6: ENTER STAGE LEFT

1. The Center for Responsive Politics, www.opensecrets.com.
2. Mark Z. Barabak and Rachel Abramowitz, "Hollywood Auditions Candidates," *Los Angeles Times,* 11 February 2003.
3. Anne-Marie O'Connor, "Stars Have Kerry in Their Eyes," *Los Angeles Times,* 28 February 2004.
4. "527s in 2004 Shatter Previous Records for Political Fundraising," Center for Public Integrity, available at www.publicintegrity.org/527/report.aspx?aid=435&sid=300.
5. *Rated R: Republicans in Hollywood,* Jesse Moss, AMC, 2004.

NOONAN TIME

1. Interview with Peggy Noonan conducted by James Hirsen on 18 September 2004.

CHAPTER 7: TINSELTOWN TAMPERING

1. Interview with Lawrence O'Donnell conducted by James Hirsen on 5 August 2004.
2. Jim Rutenberg, "To Interview Former P.O.W., CBS Offers Stardom," *New York Times,* 16 June 2003.
3. Peter Y. Sussman, "Rescuing Private Lynch—and Rescuing Journalism: The Pressure for a Compelling Story Can Eclipse the Actual News," *The Quill,* 1 November 2003.
4. *The Reagans,* Robert Allan Ackerman, Lions Gate Films, 2003.

MORRIS MUSINGS

1. Interview with Dick Morris conducted by James Hirsen on 3 June 2004.

CHAPTER 8: MEDIA MINDBEND

1. Interview with Dr. Kelton Rhoads conducted by James Hirsen on 10 August 2004.
2. Rob Borsellino, "Moore Film Takes Emotions on Wild Ride," *Des Moines Register,* 28 June 2004.
3. Bill Adair, "The Accidental Activist," *St. Petersburg Times,* 19 July 2004.
4. "The Lie That Killed My Son," *Guardian* (London), 8 July 2004.

MILLER SPEAK

1. Interview with Dennis Miller conducted by James Hirsen on 21 January 2004.

DAYNA *EXTRA*

1. Interview with Dayna Devon conducted by James Hirsen on 26 July 2004.

CHAPTER 10: LAND OF THE FREE

1. Interview with Iain Calder conducted by James Hirsen on 30 August 2004.
2. Interview with Dick Morris conducted by James Hirsen on 3 June 2004.
3. Interview with Lawrence O'Donnell conducted by James Hirsen on 5 August 2004.
4. Ibid.

ACKNOWLEDGMENTS

Special thanks to Chris Ruddy; Sandy Frazier; my journalist, artist, and expert friends who took the time to sit for interviews and share their wisdom; Mel, Steve, and my mates at Icon; Steve Ross, Jed Donahue, and the sage pros at Crown Forum; Joyce Holway; Ann Corkery; and my many friends in the news and entertainment biz who are in and out of the conservative closet. Thanks also to L. Brent Bozell III and the Media Research Center, as well as Accuracy in Media, for their pioneering (and ongoing) work as media watchdogs.

INDEX

ABC News, 14

Abramoff, Jack, 244

Academy Awards, 224–225, 241–242, 245–247, 248, 252–253

Actors, 1–7. *See also* Celebrities

Actresses, age of, 74

Ailes, Roger, 146

Air America radio network, 108–111

Alexander, 173–174

All the President's Men (film), 37

Alterman, Eric, 85, 93–101, 105, 106

America Coming Together (ACT), 144

Anchors (TV news), 31, 56–76

Anderson, Martin, 168

Angle, Jim, 127–128

Anschutz, Philip, 240

Anti-Defamation League, 219

Anti-Semitism, 92, 218, 219. *See also* Jews

Appearance. *See* Sex appeal

Arita, Maria, 59, 60, 61

Arquette, Rosanna, film by, 73

Arrogance (Goldberg), 85, 86

Auletta, Ken, 102

Baer, Robert, 246

Baker, James, 97

Baker, Nicholson, 150

Barberie, Jillian, 63–64

Barnes, Ben, 132

Barnes, Fred, 106

Bart, Peter, 207, 217

Beattie, Geoffrey, 8

Begala, Paul, 43, 123

Bernstein, Carl, 37

Bias, 15–16, 83–89, 99, 128–129

Bias (Goldberg), 85, 86, 87
Black people, diversity and, 92
Blair, Jayson, 33–34
Blinded by the Right (Brock), 103, 104
Blunt, Roy, 45
Blyth, Myrna, 70
Boccardi, Louis, 136
Bond, Rich, 96
Booth, Alicia, 60–61
Bosley, Catherine, 65–67
Bowling for Columbine, 189, 190
Boxer, Barbara, 88
Boyd, Gerald, 34
Bozell, L. Brent III, 93
Brady, David, 87–88
Brock, David, 85, 103–108
Brokaw, Tom, 29, 37–38, 85, 93
Brokeback Mountain, 242–243, 244–246, 252
Brothers, Joyce, 8
Brown, Janet H., 37, 38
Brownback, Sam, 88
Buchanan, Pat, 96–97, 98
Buell, Susie Tompkins, 104
Burkett, Bill, 134
Bush, George W., 122–123, 130, 145
Butler, Peter, 30

Calder, Iain, 233–234
Calley, John, 150
Cameron, Carl, 146
Campaign ads, attacking Bush, 145
Cannon, Lou, 168
Capote, 242, 245, 252
Carlson, Tucker, 43, 102
Carville, James, 123
Castrillón Hoyos, Darío, 222
Cater, Douglas, 26–27

Catholic Church, 220–222
Caviezel, Jim, 213–214, 215
CBS News, 130–136, 163–164
Celebrities, 25–50. *See also* Actors
    Air America and, 108
    frustration of, 10–11
    influence of, 1–7
    journalists as, 12–14
    Republican, 151
Celebrity Justice, Herbert, Holly, and, 77–81
Chancellor, John, 99
Chappelle, Dave, 17
Christianity. *See Passion of the Christ, The*
Chronicles of Narnia, The, 252
Cinderella Man, 252
Clark, Dick, Moore, Michael, and, 189
Clarke, Richard, 129, 149–150
Clinton, Bill, 28, 130, 201–202
Clinton, Hillary, 105
Clooney, George, 242, 244, 246–250, 253
CNBC, 49
CNN, 40–41
Commission on Presidential Debates (CPD, 2004), 37–38
Communication, 27–29, 238
Conason, Joe, 85, 106
Concerned Women for America's Culture and Family Institute, 243
Condon, Bill, 171
Conservative magazines, agenda of, 106–107
Conservatives, 16, 42, 87–88
Conspiracy theory, liberal media and, 95–101
Constant Gardner, The, 244, 245
Convert communicator, 198

Cooper, Anderson, 6
Cosmetic procedures, 11
Coulter, Ann, 89–90, 98
Couric, Katie, 13–14, 24, 68–70, 90
Coursen, Gary, 66
Craig, Larry, 88
Crash, 245
Crier, Catherine, 138–141
Critics, 19–24, 177–178, 193–196
Cronkite, Walter, 56–57, 84
Crossfire, 43–44, 123
Crotty, Tyler, 40–41
Crowley, Monica, 5
C-SPAN, 30–31
Cultural bias, 99
Curtis, Tony, 245
Cuomo, Mario, 192–193

Daily Show, The, 14 , 43–44. *See also* Stewart, Jon
    guests on, 44–45, 46–47, 48–49
Daschle, Tom, 125
Davis, Judy, 165–166, 168
Day After Tomorrow, The, 169–171
Dean, Howard, 89
DeLuca, Mike, 151
Demme, Jonathan, 147–148
Democratic Party, 48–49, 142–153, 192
Dempsey, Diana, 30
Deniro, Jon, 66
Devon, Dayna, 72, 226–232
Dhue, Laurie, 13, 51–55, 71, 75
Dickens, Reed, 41
Discourse, types of, 196–197
Distraction, 199–200
Diversity, PC approval of, 91–92
Docudramas, 4–5, 160–164, 164–169

Documentaries, 4
    as journalism, 21–22
    techniques in fictional setups, 179–180
Doerr, Tom, 60
Dole, Bob, 97
Dubose, Lou, 106
Dunphy, Jerry, 33

Eastwood, Clint, 16–17
Ebert, Roger, 243
Edwards, John, 42–43, 99
Ehrlich, Kendel, 9–10
Ehrlich, Robert, 9
Election information, sources of, 38–39
Emmerich, Roland, 170
Entertainment industry, 7–12, 158–180, 235–240
Estrich, Susan, 106

"Facts," corrupting, 187–202
Fahrenheit 9/11, 124, 190, 193–196, 196–201
Falsehood, vs. reality, 17
Female anchors, 75
Female journalists, 59–76
Ferrell, Will, 144
Fiction, documentary techniques in, 179–180
Fifth Estate, 50
Financing, 100–101, 101, 142–153
Fineman, Ron, 63
Finke, Nikki, 39, 42
Fishman, Hal, 63
Fontova, Humberto, 149
Fourth Estate, news media as, 50
Fox News, 126–128, 145–147, 245
Franken, Al, 85, 109

Fredriksen, Paula, 209
Freedom, diversity, choices, and, 239
Friedman, Jon, 129
Frontline, 29

Gabler, Neal, 66–67
Gaghan, Stephen, 246
Gibson, Charles, 37
Gibson, Mel, 193–196, 206–225, 241
Gigot, Paul, 98
Glass, Stephen, 34
Global warming, 169–171
Goldberg, Bernard, 85, 86
Goldberg, Whoopi, 11, 74–75
Good Night, and Good Luck, 247–250
Gore, Al, 171
Gould, Howard, 61
Gramm, Phil, 88
Greenwald, Robert, 145–146, 147
Grove, Martin, 36
Gyllenhaal, Jake, 242

Hannity, Sean, 100
Hardball, 192–193
Harkin, Tom, 88, 89
Helms, Jesse, 89
Herbert, Holly, 75, 77–81
Hertzberg, Hendrik, 103
Hewitt, Don, 128–129
Hodges, Bobby, 133
Hoffman, Philip Seymour, 242, 245
Hollywood, 142–153, 239–240
Hori, Shannon, 59–60
Houran, James, 7
Huffman, Felicity, 242, 245
Hunter, Holly, 74
Hunter, Stephen, 177–178
Hunting of the President, The, 201–202
Hustle & Flow, 252

Ideology, of news sources, 236–237
Information, sources of, 237–239
Inhofe, James, 89
Internet, 35, 100, 104–105
Interviews
    with Crier, Catherine, 138–141
    with Devon, Dayna, 226–232
    with Dhue, Laurie, 51–55
    with Herbert, Holly, 77–81
    with Miller, Dennis, 203–205
    with Morris, Dick, 181–186
    with Noonan, Peggy, 154–157
    with O'Reilly, Bill, 112–120
    with Siegel, Joel, 19–24
Isaacson, Walter, 71
Ivins, Molly, 106

James, Linda, 131
Jamieson, Kathleen Hall, 26–27
Jennings, Peter, 83, 85, 87, 93, 109
Jesus Christ. *See Passion of the Christ,
    The*
Jews. *See also* Anti-Semitism
    Kabbalah and, 153
John Paul II, *Passion of the Christ,
    The,* and, 220–222
Journalism, 6–7
    Coulter on, 90
    documentary as, 21–22
    neutrality in, 90
    TV, 30
Journalists
    as celebrities, 12–14, 23–24
    fame of, 26, 36–37
    Goldberg on, 86
    liberal bias of, 96–101

Kabbalah, celebrities following, 153
Kagan, Daryn, 40–41

Karlin, Ben, 47
Kelley, Jack, 36
Kelley, Kitty, 122
Kellner, Jamie, 70–71
Kelly, Brian, 123
Kelly, Michael, 106
Kennedy, John F., 9
Kennedy, Ted, 88, 89
Kerrey, Bob, 45–46
Kerry, John, 46–47, 99–100, 123,
    144
Kilborn, Craig, 43
Kill Bill, critics on, 177–178
Killian, Jerry B., 130, 131, 132, 133,
    134
King, Larry, 68, 93, 122–123, 244
Kingdom of Heaven, 174–176
Kinsey, 171–173
Klein, Jonathan, 136
Knox, Marian Carr, 134
Koch, Ed, 106
Koppel, Ted, 6, 48, 49, 109
Kristol, Bill, 97–98
Kurtz, Howard, 48, 104, 160
Kyl, John, 88
Kyoto Protocol, 170

Labeling, of liberals and
    conservatives, 87–88
Lamb, Brian, 29
Larry King Live, 244
Lauzen, Martha, 62
Lebowitz, Fran, 25
Ledger, Heath, 242
Lee, Ang, 244
"Left Coast Report, The" (Hirsen),
    107
Left-liberal publications, 106–107
Left wing, 32–33, 87. See also
    Liberal(s)

Legal system, celebrities and, 78–79
Leno, Jay, 39, 42, 68–69, 111
Letterman, David, 39–41
Lewinsky, Monica, 28
Liberal(s)
    Alterman on meaning of, 98–99
    media coverage of, 87–88
    media distortion by, 85
    venues for getting out messages,
        111
    in Writer's Guild of America, 160
Liberal media, 89–90, 121–122. See
    also Media
Liberty Film Festival, 240
Limbaugh, Rush, 100
Lipscomb, Lila, 198–199, 200
Lynch, Jessica, 163–164

Ma, Jonathan, 87–88
Male news anchors, 56–59
Marlane, Judith, 63, 64
Marshall, Garry, 23
Martin, Steve, 242
Mary Tyler Moore Show, The, 31, 33
Matley, Marcel, 131, 133
McAuliffe, Terry, 130, 192
McCain, John, 126
McCain-Feingold law, 143
McCain-Lieberman Climate
    Stewardship Act, 171
McCarthy, Senator Joseph, 248–250
McCaslin, John, 143
McCuddy, Bill, 245
McGowan, William, 85, 91
Media. See also Liberal media
    changing landscape of, 136–137
    current state of, 236–240
    liberal distortion of, 85
    news-entertainment industry
        merger and, 235–240

Passion of the Christ, The, and, 222–223
political leanings of, 89–90
religion in, 179
trust in, 84
Media bias, 15–16, 83–89, 99, 121–122, 158–180
Media figures, 26–27
Media Matters for America, 105, 107–108
Medved, Michael, 3, 222
Mehrabian, Albert, 28
Miller, Dennis, 49–50, 203–205
Million Dollar Baby (movie), 16–17
Minorities, PC sensitivity and, 91–92
Mitchell, Pat, 101
Moonves, Leslie, 165
Moore, Michael, 4, 21, 106, 124–126, 189–196, 201–202. *See also Fahrenheit 9/11*
Moraes, Lisa de, 102
Morgenstern, Maia, 214–215
Morris, Dick, 181–186, 237
Moseley Braun, Carol, 89
MoveOn.org, 144, 145, 147
Moynihan, Daniel Patrick, 99
MultiCultural Radio Broadcasting, 110
Munich, 241, 246, 250–252
Murrow, Edward R., 82, 83, 105, 248–253

Narrative, as discourse, 196–197
Nation (magazine), 93–94
National Enquirer, 233–234
National Guard story, regarding Bush, George W., 130–136
Navarro-Valls, Joaquin, 221
Nazis, propaganda of, 188

Networks, 86, 97, 237–238. *See also* Air America radio network
New Hollywood, 239–240
"New Journalism," 33
New Media, 236, 240
New Republic, 98
News. *See also* Journalism; Journalists
celebrities and, 29
as entertainment, 6
National Enquirer and, 233–234
sources of, 237–238
News, business of, 5
News media. *See also* Media
buying of stories by, 234
critiques of, 93
current state of, 236–240
entertainment synergy with, 163, 235–240
ideology of, 236–237
star opinions in, 2
Newsweek, 99
New York Times, 33–34, 88, 98, 100
Nickles, Don, 88
Nightline, 48. *See also* Koppel, Ted
Noah, Timothy, 104
Nonverbal communication, 27–29
Noonan, Peggy, 124, 154–157
North Country, 242
Novak, Bob, 98
Noxon, Christopher, 208

Objectivity, 82–83, 86, 105. *See also* Bias
O'Donnell, Lawrence, 159–160, 237–238
Olbermann, Keith, 57–58, 146
O'Neill, John, 123
O'Neill, Paul, 129
Online publications. *See* Internet
Opinions, movie shaping of, 4

O'Reilly, Bill, 112–120, 127, 208,
    225
O'Reilly Factor, The, 208
Outfoxed, 126

Pacing, as propaganda tool, 199
Palasat, Greg, 85
Paradise Now, 245
Parallax View, The, 245
Passion of the Christ, The, 206–225,
    241
  vs. *Fahrenheit 9/11,* 193–196
PBS, 101–103
PC attitudes, 91–92, 178–179
Penenberg, Adam, 35
Phillips, Kyra, 40
Plastic surgery, 71–73, 75–76
Polemic, as discourse, 196–197
Political advertising, 144–145
Politics and politicians, 37–50, 89–90
Pope, *Passion of the Christ, The,* and,
    220–222
Press Effect, The (Jamieson and
    Waldman), 26–27
Priming, 201
Propaganda, 187–202
Public Broadcasting Service. *See* PBS
Purpuro, Larry, 143
Putnam, George, 31–32, 33,
    168–169

Racism, 92
Radio, 100, 108–111
Raines, Howell, 34
Rather, Dan, 33, 83, 85, 93, 127,
    130
Ratings, 161–162, 179
Ratner, Ellen, 106
Reagan, Ronald, 97, 164–169

Reality shows, 11
Redford, Robert, 148–149
Religion, 152, 153, 179
Reporters. *See* Journalism;
    Journalists
Republican National Convention,
    126–128
Republican Noise Machine, The
    (Brock), 105
Reverse blacklist, 150–151
Reviews. *See* Critics
Rhoads, Kelton, 196–201
Rich, Frank, 103, 219, 221, 225
Rieder, Rem, 123
Riefenstahl, Leni, 188
Right wing, 42, 97–98
Roberts, Julia, 23
Rock, Chris, 241
Rooney, Andy, 134–135
Russert, Tim, 29, 99

Saban, Haim, 143
Sanchez, Lauren, 64–65
Sarbanes, Paul, 88–89
Savage, Michael, 84–85, 100
Sawyer, Diane, 13, 14, 65–66
Scandals, journalistic, 233
Schieffer, Bob, 37
Schlesinger, Laura, 83
Schneider, Bill, 107, 108
Schur, Paul, 127
Schwarzenegger, Arnold, 39
Scott, Ridley, 174–176
Searching for Debra Winger, 73–74
See No Evil, 246
Sena, Suzanne, 59
Sex appeal
  of female journalists, 59–76
  of male news anchors, 56–59
Sexuality, in movies, 172–174

Shales, Tom, 87
Shattered Glass (film), 34–35
Sherman, Len, 149
Shine, Bill, 128
Siegel, Joel, 4, 9, 19–24
Simpson, Don, 73
60 Minutes, 128–129, 130
Slander (Coulter), 89
Slate magazine, 104
Smart, Elizabeth, 164
Smith, Shepard, 127
Smith, Ted III, 87
Snow, Tony, 98, 211
Soros, George, 144
Spears, Britney, 9–10
Spencer, John, 159
Spielberg, Steven, 250–252
"Spin," O'Reilly on, 112–120
Spin Sisters (Blyth), 70
Stanley, Alessandra, 167–168
Staudt, Walter B. ("Buck"), 131, 133
Stephanopoulos, George, 14, 98
Stewart, Jon, 39, 43–44, 45, 46–47
Stone, Oliver, 5, 173–174, 246
Streisand, Barbra, 166–167
Sullivan, Andrew, 106
Superstar, 25
Surgical alterations, 11
Syriana, 241, 244, 246–247, 253

Talese, Gay, 33
Tales from the Left Coast (Hirsen), 1,
    3, 150–151
Talk shows, 38–50
Tarantino, Quentin, 177
Taupin, Bernie, 244
Tay, Sharon, 62–63
Television, 5–6
Theron, Charlize, 242
Thomas, Evan, 99–100

Thompson, Andrea, 71
Thornburgh, Richard, 135
Tomasky, Michael, 103
Transamerica, 242, 245
Transport, involvement in story as,
    197
TV anchors. *See* Anchors

Ullman, Tracey, 74
Urban legends, in *Fahrenheit 9/11,*
    190
USA Today, 36

Valenti, Jack, 222
Values, movie shaping of, 4
Van Susteren, Greta, 70, 71–73, 79
Venice Film Festival, 147–148,
    178–179
Vieira, Meredith, 6
View, The, 6, 13

Walden Media, 240
Waldman, Paul, 2, 26–27
Walk the Line, 252
Wallace, Chris, 127
Wallop, Malcolm, 88
Walsh, Mark, 110
Walter, Richard, 1, 3
Walters, Barbara, 12–13, 24
Warhol, Andy, 25
Washington Post, 88–89, 99
Watchdog group, conservative media
    and, 104–105, 107–108
Weapons of Mass Distortion (Bozell),
    93
Weisz, Rachel, 244
West, Betsy, 163
West Wing, The, 159–160

We Were Soldiers, 212

What Liberal Media?(Alterman), 94, 105

Will, Emily, 131

Williams, Brian, 58–59

Winer, Noah T., 147

Winger, Debra, 73–74

Witherbee, Jay, 30

Women
  female anchors, 75
  sex appeal of female journalists, 59–76

Woods, James, 241–242

Woodward, Bob, 37, 129

Workman, Chuck, 25

Zahn, Paula, 70–71

Zahn, Steve, 35

Zanuck, Darryl, 23

ABOUT THE AUTHOR

James Hirsen is a commentator, news analyst, law professor, and author of the *New York Times* bestseller *Tales from the Left Coast: True Stories of Hollywood Stars and Their Outrageous Politics*. He has appeared on *The O'Reilly Factor, Scarborough Country, People in the News, Fox & Friends, Hardball with Chris Matthews, Inside Politics with Judy Woodruff, Dennis Miller, Politically Incorrect,* BBC Television, and numerous other television venues. His ideas have been quoted in major publications, including the *Washington Times, Weekly Standard, New York Times, San Francisco Chronicle,* and *London Times.*

Hirsen is a pundit for NewsMax.com and creator of the popular weekly column "The Left Coast Report," where he takes a humorous poke at the politics of Hollywood.

He is a law professor at Trinity Law School and teaches mass media at Biola University, both of which are located in Southern California. Before setting his sights on the legal, communications, and publishing worlds, he worked as a professional musician, and for a number of years was keyboardist for one of the most legendary groups of all times, the Temptations.

He makes his home on the Left Coast.

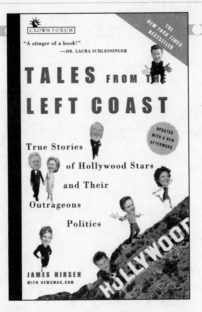